Interpreting Justice

Routledge Advances in Translation Studies

1. **Applying Luhmann to Translation Studies**
   Translation in Society
   Sergey Tyulenev

2. **Interpreting Justice: Ethics, Politics and Language**
   Moira Inghilleri

Interpreting Justice

Ethics, Politics, and Language

Moira Inghilleri

Routledge
Taylor & Francis Group
NEW YORK LONDON

First published 2012
by Routledge
711 Third Avenue, New York, NY 10017

Simultaneously published in the UK
by Routledge
2 Park Square, Milton Park, Abingdon, Oxon OX14 4RN

Routledge is an imprint of the Taylor & Francis Group, an informa business

First issued in paperback 2012

Typeset in Sabon by IBT Global.

Library of Congress Cataloging-in-Publication Data
A catalog record has been requested for this book.

ISBN: 978-0-415-89723-5 (hbk)
ISBN: 978-0-415-82169-8 (pbk)
ISBN: 978-0-203-14796-2 (ebk)

For my sons, Louis and Pablo

Contents

Preface

This book has its origins in my interest in the enduring issue of incommensurability in language and culture. The complex issue of the relationship between language, culture, and thought often settles around the theme of incommensurability, which can be a matter of the capacity for understanding evident between minds as much as between cultures, and always mediated by some communicative form. The products and processes of translation can symbolize the key to the often submerged but occasionally glimpsed 'holy grail' of mutual understanding so commonly lost in the face of human diversity, at the same time they can represent its ultimate impossibility. My own intellectual trajectory with respect to this question has taken a somewhat circuitous route. Though my original field of research was, broadly speaking, sociolinguistics, sociological and philosophical methods of analysis have guided my thinking the most. Since being introduced to the field of translation and interpreting about a decade ago, these methods have continued to inform my research. Within this field, incommensurability has been examined mainly with regard to the translation of written texts, especially through the interrogation of the notion of equivalence. This issue has not been accorded the same attention with regard to the translation of the spoken word. Perhaps this is due to the face to face immediacy of spoken interpreted encounters which has encouraged more attention to the cognitive demands of the interpreter's task. Paradoxically, within the field, the problem of the unacknowledged visibility of the translator of written texts has received more critical attention than the questionable insistence on the invisibility of the highly visible interpreter of spoken utterances. This book addresses this deficiency through an examination of the status of interpreters' visibility in institutional contexts where interpreters are spatially and temporally co-present with others in situations of considerable moral, ethical, and political significance. In these situations, I argue, the challenge for interpreters involves an instantly demanded ethical and political response.

In the book, relationships amongst the relevant actors, communicative acts, and institutional settings are interpreted implicitly through a Bourdieusian approach, though unlike this approach more generally, I am concerned to represent both the communicative and social practices that emerge from underlying structures and the agents who perform them. For many sociolinguists, this must also include micro-analysis of the discursive strategies which these agents carry out. This is not my aim, however. What interests me more is what motivates and compels communicating agents' responses to one another. For insights regarding these processes, I rely on philosophical discourses on inter-subjective understanding amongst similar or diverse others. The book thus attempts to characterize the social and moral spaces in which the translation of the spoken word occurs in ways that reflect the realities of the trans-nationally constituted, locally and globally informed environments in which interpreters work.

Chapter 1 presents a perspective on language, culture, and thought that is informed by insights from linguistic anthropology and linguistic philosophy, reading these via a pragmatist mode of inquiry. The pragmatist perspective introduced in this chapter serves as the foundation for the central arguments of the book: that all endeavors toward mutual understanding between different perspectives involve cooperative human action in interaction with the environment; and that this is a dialectical process involving fragmentation and incoherence as much as increasing coherence and integration.

Chapter 2 examines the ethical nature of all communicative encounters. I explore the value and potential limitations of neo-Kantian and non-Kantian approaches to ethical communication, with special reference to discourse ethics and its implicit influence on interpreter codes of ethics, particularly as evidenced in the principles of impartiality and neutrality. The chapter reiterates the view that languages are not divided from one another as incompatible systems, particularly where this view suggests the need for a master vocabulary or system of meta-rules that would permit the commensuration of all discourse. It concludes that the justification for different beliefs articulated in communication is not achieved through metaphysical guarantees, but through the very fissures, contradictions, and innovations that it is the task of translation to reveal, not to obscure.

Chapter 3 introduces the contrasting concepts of 'role' morality, which claims objectivity through a discourse of professionalism, and 'ordinary' morality, which is perceived as subjective, whether individually or culturally based. In this chapter, I link these concepts to the interpreting profession where individual ethical responses to an interpreting situation are negatively associated with partiality and are, therefore, considered violations of professional codes. I then examine debates over legal ethics, particularly with regard to lawyers' neutral partisanship toward their clients to demonstrate some distinctive and instructive parallels between the legal practitioners and interpreters. In both professions, I argue that from a sociological perspective, the notion of role morality ensures the maintenance of structural hierarchies of power and knowledge, and from a philosophical standpoint, it encourages moral unaccountability.

Chapters 4 and 5 present further empirical support for the theoretical arguments presented in the previous chapters. Chapter 4 focuses on the function of interpreting and interpreters in the asylum system, taking as its starting point the question of hospitality and the irresolvable tension involved in the ethical demand to grant safe haven to outside others, and the hard realities of national sovereignty and global politics. Based on in-depth interviews I conducted from 2002 to 2007 with the relevant players in the asylum adjudication process—judges, lawyers, applicants, and their interpreters—the chapter considers the different alliances that were formed amongst these individuals and the extent to which these partnerships were aimed at contributing to the overall presence of a justice-seeking ethics in the asylum system. Chapter 5 examines the motivations behind the decisions taken by Iraqis and other Arabic speakers to serve as interpreters and translators for the U.S. military in the Iraq war, taking into account the justifications for the invasion and occupation based on the principles of Just War theory. I also consider the range of motivating factors, as reported in media accounts, which were involved in these decisions, including: personal histories, economic factors, politics, and patriotism. As in the previous chapter, I consider the different types of alliances that emerged between interpreters and military personnel—particularly in the face of the often complex friend-enemy distinction that war creates—and the ethical demand these generated for both. Both chapters highlight the tensions between the relevant actors, their communicative objectives, and the institutional—juridical, political, and military—settings in which their actions are embedded.

Chapter 6 circles back to the question of the interpreter's visibility and its central role in a reinvigorated ethics of interpreting. This chapter considers the historical lack of perceived ties between the translation of written and spoken language despite the ethical issues common to both. I suggest that though part of the reason for this may lie with the linguistic orientation of much interpreting research, it is also true that translation scholars have not perceived any theoretical common ground between spoken texts and fictional or nonfictional works. I conclude that, despite important differences in the ethical relationships that interpreters and translators develop due to the distinct environments in which they work, there are sufficient overlaps to suggest the possibility of greater collaboration in research and practice and, especially, a more productive dialogue between the two domains in the areas of language, ethics, and politics.

Acknowledgments

The research and writing of this book was made possible by a three-year Fellowship from the Economic and Social Research Council (ESRC) RES-063–0-27–0165 and three previous research grants (RES-000–23–1293, RES 000–22–0521, and RES 000–22–3772) which funded an ethnographic study of interpreters in the U.K. asylum system from 2002 to 2007. I am sincerely grateful for the continuous support of the ESRC and for their acknowledgment of the significance of translation and interpreting as important contributors to the causes of justice and human rights.

I extend my deepest appreciation to Mona Baker, Joan Colin, Theo Hermans, Marilyn Martin-Jones, Ian Mason, and Christina Schäffner for their support and efforts on behalf of my research.

I would also like to express my appreciation to the lawyers, judges, and asylum applicants who gave of their time to participate in the research.

My conversations with the many interpreters who spoke candidly about their experiences working in stressful and sometimes emotionally difficult situations were a starting point for many of the issues I explore in the book. The same is true for the interpreter trainers and coordinators I interviewed. They may or may not agree with some or all of its conclusions. I would particularly like to thank Ruswel Piñeiro for serving as a liaison with the courts. And to Dragana Jakovljevic who graciously allowed me to observe in her classroom, and who after many enlightening conversations became a valued friend, I acknowledge my utmost thanks.

Finally, my greatest thanks are to my husband, Roger Hewitt, whose unwavering emotional, intellectual, and domestic support, provided in vast quantities throughout its different stages, helped to make this book possible.

A modified version of chapter 5 appeared in *The Translator*, 16 (2), 2010.

1 The Significance of Language in Translation

Acts of translating heighten our awareness of the fact that different languages and cultures need not imply the impossibility of achieving a unity of ideas or of purpose, however partial and impermanent. There are, however, radically different views about how, or indeed if, language achieves this unifying function and about the fundamental nature of language itself: its epistemological and ontological status. Is it a medium, a tool, a set of rules for our engagement with the material world, or reality itself? Translation scholarship, with regard to the written word, has considered this question through intellectual traditions such as German Romanticism, hermeneutics and structuralism, postmodernism and postcolonialism. This range of influences reflects the close relationship between translation studies, literary theory, and the written word. Interpreting scholarship has considered the same question with regard to the spoken word mainly through the lens of structural linguistics, and has incorporated many of its assumptions and orthodoxies about language—namely that signs have determinate forms, that each form has a determinate meaning and capacity for linear, contrastive combination with other signs, and that knowledge of this 'system of signs' or *langue* is shared amongst its speakers. Saussure emphasized the primary function of language as one of reference to a pre-given world; a correspondence view that assumes a pre-linguistic consciousness, a 'truth' about the world to which language corresponds.

These ideas are particularly evident in the fundamental emphasis in interpreting research and training in the interplay between rules pertaining to linguistic or cultural competence and principles underlying codes of practice. Much of interpreting theory and practice operates on the assumption of an ideal sender-receiver, context—and culture-neutral model of communication, in which thoughts are transferred from a speaker to a hearer and back again. On this assumption, the interpreter is the channel which ensures that the concept being transferred from one speaker to another becomes the 'same' concept in both linguistic systems. Variations on this, while allowing interpreters a degree of interpretation of utterances based on contextual and cultural knowledge, ultimately remain loyal to the pre-eminent status of *langue*. This view can be directly traced to the evaluation inherent in

Saussure's initial distinction between *langue* and *parole*, later reproduced in Chomsky, where *parole*/performance is seen as largely irrelevant to the proper workings of the language system. Even in situations where cultural mediation is accepted as a legitimate part of interpreter practice, the communicative competence deemed necessary is usually conceived of as a set of prescriptive, pragmatic rules, similar in kind to rules of grammar. Consequently, breakdowns in interpreted communication are usually attributed to one or more of the participants' inability to use language appropriately—to choose a word, syntactic form, or utterance—based on rules of *linguistic* competence, i.e., lexico-grammatical knowledge, or rules of *communicative* competence, i.e., cultural or contextual knowledge (see Berk-Seligson 1990; Hale 2004). The assumption is that where rules of competency are mastered, and the appropriate choice selected, more successful translation, greater equivalence, can be achieved.

This chapter critically examines some of the key ideas from structural linguistics, sociolinguistics, and linguistic anthropology that have influenced many of the principles guiding interpreting theory and practice.[1] I will argue for an additional, alternative point of view regarding the relationship between language, meaning, and the world which draws ideas from a number of different but related perspectives, with a particular emphasis on relevant work in linguistic anthropology and philosophy. My aim is to shift the focus of attention in interpreting contexts, and in translation activity more generally, from language as a mediating device or a barrier to communication to language as a tool which, along with an assortment of other tools, helps individuals achieve their communicative objectives in a given context. My central point is that interpreted interactions are not constituted by the presence of *langue*, but by the occasions of utterances. Interpreters must therefore be permitted *visibility*, openly facilitating negotiations over meaning and maximizing the possibility that the communicative objectives of all participants are met. This, I suggest, has significant consequences for how the interpreting task, and most importantly, the interpreter's impartiality is conceived.

TO FOLLOW A RULE

Interactional sociolinguistics and linguistic anthropology shifted the emphasis from *langue*, the context-independent, synchronic logic of systems, to *parole*, where speakers make choices in real time and real situations (see the collection of influential papers in Gumperz and Hymes 1972; Giglioli 1972). Dell Hymes distinguished between linguistic competence and communicative competence in order to address the split introduced by Saussure and Chomsky between competence and performance by offering an account of the role of context and culture in relation to *langue* (Hymes 1972). Hymes' view derived from the cognitive anthropologist,

Ward Goodenough, who defined culture as whatever an individual needed to know in order to function as a member of a group (Goodenough 1964). Culture itself was perceived to exist in the minds of each individual member of a society, as a set of rules or organizing principles for generating behavior appropriate to his/her culture. Thus, 'appropriate' linguistic or cultural responses to a given situation were seen as displays of knowledge of the mental models or rules which 'competent' native speakers possessed for perceiving and interpreting their own cultures. Communicative competence assumed a knowing subject who was able to use language appropriate to a given situation. It presented a view of competence that included not just the natural acquisition of the rules of grammar, but the rules for its use in a variety of cultural contexts.

The term communicative competence, however, although it purported to write culture and context into communication, helped to sustain the view that sentence meaning or *langue* (in Chomsky's terms, competence) provided a fundamental and context-neutral basis for communication; while *parole* (for Chomsky, performance) acted as an extra-linguistic environment from where information was drawn to assist communication in situations of uncertainty or ambiguity. This conceptualization of communication thus reinforced the dualist epistemology inherent in Saussurean accounts of language and validated the synthetic/analytic dichotomy central to structuralist models.

Communicative Competence: Mastery of Rules or Language Game?

Since Wittgenstein, critiques of systems- or rule-governed models of language have centered on their inability to account for the flexible and innovatory nature of communication and for their limitations in explaining the dialogic or dialectical nature of communicative practices. In an insightful critique of Saussure, the linguist Roy Harris has argued that *langue* was Saussure's attempt to resolve the apparent contradiction between the uniqueness of our individual linguistic histories and the apparent facility with which we communicate with other members of the same linguistic community (Harris 1987: 196–237). Like Chomsky's universal grammar, Saussure wished to guarantee a basic systematicity between sign and reference amongst speakers of a language—and between speakers of different languages. Harris argues instead for a 'principle of cotemporality' with respect to the sign that acknowledges temporal parity not between signifiers and signifieds, but between linguistic and non-linguistic events in human experience (Harris 1981).

The anthropologist, Johannes Fabian, has similarly suggested that speech events are inextricably involved in temporality and can therefore never meet the criterion of synchronic coexistence essential to the structuralist conception of a code (1979: 9):

> This also means that such temporal units are not conceivable in terms of contrasts or oppositions only, they must also be seen dialectically, i.e., as results of processes in terms of which contradictions are being worked out. It is not difficult to think of contradictions as starting points and basic determinants of communication. I and others, speakers and audiences, speaking and silence, verbal and non-verbal, form and content, inclusiveness and exclusiveness, of communication and so forth.

Contradiction then, and not correspondence, can be thought of as a potential 'starting point and basic determinant of communication'. More recently, Fabian has returned to this issue, identifying such speech events as instances of 'ethnographic objectivity' (Fabian 2001: 11–32) during which the content of knowledge is transformed inter-subjectively through "confrontation that becomes productive through communication" (*ibid.*: 25). According to this view, it is not systematicity between sign and reference that is the source of individual or inter-subjective understanding. Subjectivities and collective understandings are created in and through the use of language, not the rules of a language or cultural rules of appropriateness. It is in the act of communicating with others that a shared world is apprehended: there are no prior determinants, no prior truths. As Harris illustrates in the following example (Harris 1998: 38):

> Keeping in step, for example, as in a parade, might be regarded as subject to rules, but the only rules that govern keeping in step require the parties involved to synchronize the movement of their feet—the rules define what constitutes keeping in step—they do not generate programmes that if followed mechanically by the participants will achieve the required synchronization. For that, each party must adjust from moment to moment to the perceived movements of the others. A's keeping in step with B is dependent upon B's keeping up with A. No system of rules can in principle generate all and only the correct moves for either A or B to carry out separately because the necessary adjustments required for unpredictable contextual factors cannot be foreseen. In this context, the potential behavior of A and the potential behavior of B present two relevant but quite unpredictable sets of contextual factors.

In this dialogic account, a mastery of the rules of marching, i.e., what constitutes keeping in step, can no more guarantee the successful synchronization of the marchers than the mastery of the rules of a language can guarantee successful communication. The fact that marchers do manage to keep in step in a consistent and predictable fashion is not down to the rules of marching but to their shared understandings of the task, an understanding that develops through hard work, practice, and sometimes getting it wrong. In interpreted events, 'keeping in step' may be even more unpredictable, given that the moves take place amongst speakers who are members of different linguistic or cultural communities, who do not necessarily share the same understandings of communicative behavior, and whose restricted contact with one another may mean they never will. This may particularly be the case in situations defined by some form of conflict amongst participants, where the individuals or groups who require an interpreter tend to be viewed as excludable outsiders rather than persons with whom the other participants seek to develop a mutually inclusive set of understandings regarding communication and the nature and aims of a particular task.

Communicative Competence and the Ethnographic Encounter

It is important to note that Hymes' notion of communicative competence was initially introduced in order to support the claim that individuals from different linguistic and cultural backgrounds, though not competent in the same way (each adhered to different rules of appropriate communicative behavior), were nevertheless equally competent. That is, it backed a difference and not a deficit view of linguistic, cultural, and cognitive behavior. 'Communicative competence' thus operated as a politically expedient or "strategically essentialist" (Spivak 1988) embrace of cultural and linguistic relativism. The focus on 'inter-cultural communication' (Gumperz 1982) that emerged in this period supported a similar agenda; it also appealed to a number of explicit and implicit assumptions of relativism: that linguistic differences reflect cultural differences; that individual and cultural worldviews are potentially incommensurable; and that therefore, where language variation occurs the potential for incommunicability exists. The suggestion, that instances of failures to communicate between speakers from divergent linguistic backgrounds, is due to misreadings or intentional uses of culturally specific communicative strategies supports these assumptions.

Such conclusions, however, can end up supporting an inherent essentialist rather than a strategic essentialist view of culture(s) that simultaneously downplays variation within different groups. Such a view suggests that individuals are often, if not always, trapped in their cultures through language and vice versa. Moreover, it can create the assumption that individuals are not capable of interactively 'reading' their own and others' cultures through a process of negotiation of social and cultural conventions into mutually oriented or orienting communication. While this may sometimes be the case, in the inter-cultural communication models, cultural differences become a taken-for-granted fact rather than a potentially salient factor in interaction.

In a critical assessment of communicative competence, written some thirty years ago when the notion had only recently emerged in sociolinguistics, Fabian provides an insightful analysis of two uses of the concept that continue to contribute to essentialist views regarding inter-cultural communication: first, a reliance on binary terms like appropriate/inappropriate or successful/unsuccessful, and second, an emphasis on pre-given, rule-governed linguistic or cultural competencies rather than dialectically and interactively created ones. In an effort to challenge these tendencies, Fabian points to types of speech events in which paradoxes arise. He cites as examples from ethnographic fieldwork occasions where in the course of an exchange, information and intentions can turn from initial norms of 'appropriateness' to 'inappropriateness' in relation to code, participants, and/or setting, or where some state of 'inappropriateness' is transformed into a state of 'appropriateness'. In either case, change is brought about not by an abandonment of the right or wrong communicative rules or codes of practice, but by some form of explicit or implicit challenge to these, their applicability or validity within the space of the interaction. Such changes, Fabian suggests, are themselves crucial moments in the constitution of the speech event for they demonstrate the ethnographic significance of communicative interaction itself (Fabian 1979: 25):

> Ethnographically, however, the results of either scenario can indicate/establish the boundaries of communication in the movement and the degree of ideological closure against outsiders. Both are instances of creative communication (ethnographically speaking) even though or because it is constituted by a negative dialectic. On the level of actual communicative events, maintenance of a 'wrong', of a slightly wrong code might have to be considered as creating intentional if not conscious contradiction with prevailing norms.

Fabian refers to these moments of contradiction where violations of 'communicative competence' arise as 'time outs' or temporal intrusions, a speech event embedded in a speech event (*ibid.*). His point is that though they emerge out of apparent violations of appropriateness they paradoxically create appropriateness for the larger ethnographic moment.

Interpreting activity can be experienced as a kind of 'time out', a temporal intrusion into the workings of one or more normative linguistic and cultural systems that have been determined in advance of the situation of use. As suggested above, a dominant assumption with regard to interpreted interactions is that interpreters must operate between two essentializing mediums to 'recover' appropriate linguistic and cultural forms of competence between two distinctive worldviews. Interpreters must simultaneously embody and mitigate the effects of what is perceived as an intrusive communicative violation; they are expected to move efficiently and effectively between different instantiations of *langue* in order to resolve semantic uncertainties. The underlying belief is that semantic and pragmatic certainties are there to be found in the distinctive systems rather than created in and through the interactional specifics of the particular interpreted communicative event. This view of interpreting activity, however, denies the interpreted event its ethnographic significance. It ignores the vital role that language and translation play, not in recovering, but in indicating, establishing, and challenging the boundaries of communication.

The continuing influence of this model of communicative competence is evident in role play activity used in interpreter training to prepare community interpreters to play an advocacy role in cases of cultural misunderstanding or where discriminatory practices may be involved. The conflict scenarios designed to train interpreters to negotiate misunderstanding between some other professional and the individual or family in need of an interpreter are for training purposes represented as a consequence of linguistic or cultural differences which it is the role of the interpreter to perceive and help the parties overcome. The role plays usually attempt to reproduce 'worst case scenarios' with respect to the identity/social function dualism. The result is a strong tendency toward cultural and linguistic essentialism and an emphasis on the incommensurability between members of the host country, on the one hand, and clients and their interpreters, on the other. The intended purpose is to train interpreters to serve most effectively as advocates through clarifications or repair of misunderstandings due to clashes of culture or language while maintaining impartiality. In practice, however, the paradox between cultural brokering and neutrality is often strengthened rather than diminished. Interpreters are expected to key into some 'essential' social and cultural nature of the interlocutors' respective communities despite the complex nature of such ties and, simultaneously, are obliged to occupy an effectively neutral space between different cultural and linguistic communities. Moreover, what frequently occurs is that role plays that are set up to illustrate conflicts due to discriminatory practices are interpreted in the same way as ones that would be better characterized as instances of communication constituted by the 'negative dialectic' which Fabian refers to above. In the latter cases, these involve interactional moves which may produce 'inappropriate' or 'unsuccessful' responses in any of the participants, but that can nevertheless create the possibility for critical and innovative communication.

The adherence to rule-governed linguistic and cultural competency models in interpreting theory and codes of conduct misconstrues language as a medium and supports the view that it is different languages, in the sense of *langue*, that act as barriers between peoples and cultures. It also encourages a view of interlocutors as overly culturally determined. The role of the interpreter becomes that of a mediator between different linguistic or cultural systems, ignoring the other equally legitimate behavioral components—individual beliefs and motivations, prior conversations, positional power—that permit or constrain mutual understanding amongst communicative partners. As a consequence, the dialectically and interactively created 'conversation' that comprises actual interpreted events—involving linguistic and non-linguistic behavior—has remained undertheorized with regard to both interpreting research and practice.

BEYOND OBJECTIVISM AND RELATIVISM

A range of instructive alternatives for considering the role of language and culture in creating or constraining exchanges between communicative partners can be found in contemporary philosophical debates which attempt to account for the fact that what we think of as the 'meaning' of an utterance is not given in language via some form of direct correspondence, but is an outcome of the relationship between utterances in specific contexts where 'language' is but one of many tools used by participants to communicate. This observation raises relevant questions regarding the contingent, historicized nature of linguistic practices; how communication is achieved without an appeal to stable shared rules; the origin of any consensus that may arise in habitual patterns of communicative action; and the role of social and political hierarchies and authority in forms and contexts of communication. A consideration of these issues in interpreting contexts can shed light on interpreted communication in ways which challenge the underlying assumptions of existing interpreter codes of practice and allow us to envision alternative ways of understanding communication more generally.

The World Brought Into Being

Eighteenth-century rationalist and empiricist accounts of knowledge mostly did not challenge the Cartesian distinction between the 'inner' minds of individual human subjects and the 'outer' phenomenal world of sense data. Both rationalists and empiricists shared the view of language as a medium for intervening between the self and reality, a means to ensure their contact. Kant attempted to unify these points by asserting that the basis of all human knowledge was certainly received from the outside world, as the empiricists had claimed, but that human beings themselves organized this data through the imposition of a priori forms and categories. The world of experience, the phenomenal world of appearance was the outcome of innate, conceptual categories that established the necessary conditions of possible experience. Importantly, however, though Kant attempted to synthesize sensory data and understanding, the 'world' remained essentially the phenomenal world only, as it had been for the empiricists. Because for Kant all our thoughts are only about things as they appear in the mind, in order to answer the question of how we come to know things as they are he posited the existence of a noumenal world, the world of things-in-themselves, but this was a world that humans could never directly know. The world was accessible to them only through innate categories of the mind, and the perceptions which these engendered unveiled a reality that was necessarily separate and distinct from the world of things-in-themselves. So although Kant explored foundations of human knowledge that were neither solely innate nor experiential, he underemphasized the role of an active, creative, and unconstrained perceiving mind.[2]

It was not until the twentieth century that philosophers began to view how humans relate to the world through language in radically new ways. Wittgenstein's *Philosophical Investigations* introduced the notion of meaning as given in or by use: the idea that what we think of as meaning is a matter of words being used as part of broader purposeful human activity, rather than a matter of a special mental act of grasping of an abstract/sensory entity of some kind. For Wittgenstein, attributions of meaning and understanding were possible only between human beings within social practices. He wrote (1953/1963: 53):

> But can't the meaning of a word that I understand fit the sense of a sentence that I understand? Or the meaning of one word fit the meaning of another?—Of course, if the meaning is the use we make of the word, it makes no sense to speak of such 'fitting'. But we understand the meaning of a word when we hear or say it; we grasp it in a flash, and what we grasp in this way is surely something different from the 'use' which is extended in time!

Wittgenstein raises questions here about two related phenomena—what he refers to as words and meanings 'fitting' one another and meaning being grasped in a 'flash'. The idea of words and meanings 'fitting' one another recalls the feeling we intuit when we produce a word or utterance which strikes us as right. This is the phenomenon of seeing that a word has the meaning required by a particular situation: those moments when we feel that a word, the meaning of a word, fits a particular context or when we see that one expression can be substituted for another in a certain sentence without changing the significance of the sentence.

The idea of grasping meaning in a 'flash' is the phenomenon we experience at the moment of reception of an utterance when we have the feeling of things making sense, a confidence that we have come to understand a certain expression. This experience can happen when one is trying to understand a particular term or someone is trying to explain its meaning and an example or analogy is used, at which point something clicks and we feel confident that we can go on and use and understand the term correctly, that we have grasped the meaning.

For Wittgenstein, from these feelings of flash and fit, it does not necessarily follow that a meaning has been represented in the mind through language. He viewed these experiences more as cues for understanding—ultimately whether one's choice of meaning works is a matter of whether the proposed use of the word works. What is experienced in such moments is not language serving as a mediating element between our minds and the world. This leads to the mistaken assumption that language somehow fits the world, that it functions as a unity of sorts, a third thing that stands in some determinate relation with two other unities, our individual selves and some objective reality. This assumption, as Richard Rorty has suggested, has led to the erroneous view that a language is like the pieces of a giant jigsaw puzzle (representing the world) with all languages capable of being united with all other languages in one grand super language. This assumption makes sense only, according to Rorty, "once we accept the view that there are non-linguistic things called 'facts' and 'meanings' which it is the task of language to represent" (Rorty 1989: 13), a view which Rorty and others reject.

A Pragmatist Perspective on Language

The perspective on language presented above shares something in common with a pragmatist model of philosophical inquiry. The relationship with pragmatism is indirect in the case of Wittgenstein (see Putnam 1995; Goodman 1998), while Rorty explicitly identifies with the pragmatist tradition. Though pragmatism has meant different things to different people, what is relevant to the present discussion is its focus on the human agent as actively engaged with the world and its understanding of the relationship between language, thought, and meaning.

William James and Charles S. Peirce, whose work established the earliest principles of pragmatism, understood our beliefs about the world as rules of action rather than attempts to represent reality. For James, different and conflicting forms of inquiry—e.g., common sense, scientific, philosophical—provided evidence for the idea that our beliefs were not insights into the nature of things; they were routes of inquiry and investigation, all equally 'true', in the sense that they were instrumentally good for different purposes, "mental modes of adaptation to reality" (James 1975/1907: 94), subject to both modification and justification. In the pragmatic tradition, the justification of beliefs is not given in the form of metaphysical guarantees but through cooperative human interaction and the active intervention of the environment.[3] As the pragmatist philosopher Hilary Putman explains, quoting James (Putnam 1995: 71–72, original italics),

> The problem of subjectivity and intersubjectivity was in the minds of pragmatists from the beginning—not as a metaphysical worry about whether we have access to a world at all, but as real problems in human life. They insisted that when one human being in isolation tries to interpret even the best maxims for himself and does not allow others to criticize the way in which he or she interprets those maxims, or the way in which he or she applies them, then the kind of "certainty" that results

> is *in practice* tainted with subjectivity. Even the notion of 'truth" makes no sense in "moral solitude" for "truth presupposes a standard eternal to the thinker".

Central to the pragmatist tradition and to Wittgenstein's view of language as a 'form of life' is the idea that words acquire meaning in interaction with others, not in isolation or by being paired with experiences or things; for both, the meaning of words is determined by use. For Wittgenstein, language games are also ways of acting based on habits, instincts, and emotions. In his case against the possibility of a private language, Wittgenstein argues that it is impossible for speakers to know whether they are using the words of their language 'correctly' or the 'same' with reference to a sensation or an object or an experience, for no language can refer to a sphere of private things. Pragmatists like Rorty and Putnam share this understanding and the implication underlying it: that the impulse to 'view the world from Nowhere' or from a 'God's eye view' is untenable (Rorty 1989; Putnam 1981). They reject the notion of rationality as fixed by a set of immutable rules and a priori principles, preferring to view rationality as revisable and contextual, grounded in public norms and practices.[4]

The influential language philosopher Donald Davidson has similarly argued against adhering to this distinction between determinate realities and a set of words or concepts which may or may not be adequate to them. For Davidson, all attempts to describe the 'truth' of utterances through notions of conceptual schemes fall back on the same erroneous assumption that languages organize or fit something like an objective 'reality' or sensory experience (Davidson 1984: 183–198). According to Davidson, there is no such task for language to perform. Our intuitive predictions about others' beliefs are not a product of linguistic or cultural competence in the way this is understood in structural linguistics or sociolinguistics. Davidson argues against the assumption of stable shared rules for linguistic or cultural understanding. Instead, he suggests that speakers proceed on intuitive predictions of meaning based on their immediate context and previous habits of linguistic understanding. In interpreting others—within their own or into other languages—speakers assume a connection between the contents of their own thoughts and those of their interlocutors. They attribute rational causality to how those thoughts got there in the first place. Although Davidson would agree that what we call a 'natural language' is an existing pattern embodying a set of distinctive conventions, he would not agree that it is by virtue of these existing patterns that a hearer/interpreter is able to understand the meaning of what another speaker says. For him, there is nothing for a language to be, only the occasions of utterances.

Davidson wishes to replace a correspondence view of truth, language, and reality with the view that when we communicate we have only our 'passing theories' to rely on—a set of guesses about our interlocutors' total behavior, theories which must constantly be adjusted to new circumstances with the same or new interlocutors (D. Davidson 1986). This suggests that what two people need if they are to communicate with one another is the ability to converge on their passing theories from utterance to utterance. Where communication succeeds, an individual's passing theory about what to do next, including what utterances to use and their expectations about what each other will do or say under the circumstances, more or less coincide (*ibid*.: 446):

> A passing theory is really like a theory at least in this, that it is derived by wit, luck, and wisdom from a private vocabulary and grammar, knowledge of the ways people get their point across, and rules of thumb for figuring out what deviations from the dictionary are most likely. . . . In linguistic communication nothing corresponds to a linguistic competence as often described. There is therefore no such thing [as a language, as usually conceived by linguists and philosophers] to be learned, mastered, or born with. We must give up the idea of a clearly defined shared structure which language-users acquire and then apply to cases.

Our own passing theories allow us to interpret other speakers' sentences as 'holding true'. They allow us to anticipate that speakers will mean what they say, and on the occasion of an utterance, to decide what was meant. With speakers whose beliefs or values prove unfamiliar or different from our own, we try to accommodate the views they hold based on a 'principle of charity'. In constructing a viable theory of beliefs and adversarial meanings 'held true' by our conversational partners, "there is a presumption in favor of truth of a belief that coheres with a significant mass of belief" including our own (D. Davidson 1990: 121). This is the common ground on which we make whatever sense we can of one another in a particular context. This three-way conceptual inter-dependence between knowledge of oneself, knowledge of others, and knowledge of the world is the 'other orientedness' of communication. It is this, our very inter-subjectivity, that constitutes 'objective meaning'. For Davidson, this implies a rejection of cultural relativism, of the idea of incommensurable systems of belief (see also, Hollis and Lukes 1982; Rorty 1991c) on the grounds that to possess attitudes and be capable of speech is already to be capable of interpreting others and to be open to interpretation by them. As Davidson remarks (1984: 196–197),

> What matters is this: if all we know is what sentences a speaker holds true, and we cannot assume that his language is our own, then we cannot take even a first step towards interpretation without knowing or assuming a great deal about the speaker's beliefs. Since knowledge of beliefs comes only with the ability to interpret words, the only possibility at the start is to assume general agreement on beliefs [. . .] this

> method is not designed to eliminate disagreement, nor can it; its purpose is to make meaningful disagreement possible, and this depends entirely on a foundation—some foundation—in agreement.

The 'foundation' Davidson has in mind is the 'other orientedness' of communication which, for Davidson, constitutes 'objective meaning'. This view shares something in common with Fabian's notion of 'ethnographic objectivity' which views the ethnographic encounter as an action-driven processual theory of knowledge. Both views understand 'objective' knowledge to be achieved in communication through confrontations of beliefs and attitudes. They consider communication with others—reacting and responding to others—as central to the concept of an objective world. Both also reject the idea that meaning is convention- or culture-bound in favor of the view that the 'truth' of an utterance is relative to the circumstances of its use. Importantly, in both these perspectives, dialogue, in the sense of meaningful agreement or disagreement, is viewed as emerging from a cognitive capacity for mutual understanding, rather than as the means to achieve it. For Davidson, we can't have any ideas to reach agreement or disagreement over until we share a picture of a world.[5]

Interpreter codes of practice which view the interpreter's job as one of resolving questions of semantic uncertainty frequently appeal, sometimes simultaneously, to relativist arguments about language and culture and to objectivist accounts of meaning. Relativist arguments, following notions of communicative competence, construct the interpreter as a cultural mediator whose role it is to identify and explain difference in order to overcome it. Objectivist arguments support a universalist account of language and cognition and the accompanying belief that there is meaning 'out there' to recover through the medium of language. The consequence of embracing either of these perspectives is to perceive the interpreter's role as one of seeking to establish the sameness of a world beyond language. But this view of the interpreter role only serves to reinforce a view of language as a 'unity' intervening between the self and some non-linguistic reality, culturally or universally given, which it is the task of language to represent (see Rorty 1989: 3–22). The alternative view proposed here, that there is nothing for language to be, only the occasions of its utterances, shifts the focus of attention to language as a tool which along with other tools helps interlocutors to achieve their communicative objectives in a given context. As Putnam suggests (1981: 116),

> One can understand the assertion that a translation fails to capture exactly the sense or reference of the original as an admission that a better translation scheme might be found; but it makes only an illusion of sense to say that all possible translation schemes fail to capture the 'real' sense or reference. Synonymy exists only as a relation, or better, as a family of relations, each of them somewhat vague, which we employ to equate

> different expressions for the purposes of the interpretation. The idea that there is some such thing as 'real' synonymy apart from all workable practices of mutual interpretation, has been discarded as a myth.

In interpreted interactions, the search for 'workable practices of mutual interpretation' includes factors such as: what is at stake for individual participants in an interpreted event; what are the professional, ethical, political, social, or personal risks involved in the interaction; is there a potential for conflicting views over what may be reasonably meant or understood by an utterance in the particular situation; and what ethical, political, or social factors may lie behind a claim that one participant's understanding of an utterance is reasonable or that another's should be challenged.

Passing Theories and the Relative Status of Interpreters

In an instructive discussion of the interpreting in the O. J. Simpson trial, Anthony Pym (Pym 1999) references Davidson's notion of 'passing theories' in his analysis of the various theories about language and interpreting that were offered by the trial judge and the prosecution and defense lawyers, amongst others. Pym notes how these theories served as active constraints on discourse as the behaviors they 'described, justified or condemned' moved the discourse in the courtroom some ways more easily than others (*ibid.*: 275). In the context of the trial, certain articulated beliefs about a particular interpreted exchange (regarding the interpreter, choice of word, cultural factors, etc.) circulated in the courtroom, influencing the flow of discourse both within and outside the trial itself. Pym points to potential problems with allowing discourse such latitude. He suggests that granting equal time to effective and ineffective hypotheses can simply add to a "directionless diversity" (*ibid.*: 281). Pym concludes:

> The problem of the Simpson trial, with its plethora of theories, was that it made far too many constraints visible, pushing issues well beyond any criterion of importance. Oppositional passing theories were allowed to prevail over stronger consensus-building approaches.

That the plethora of theories in this case were framed in essentially oppositional/monologic rather than consensual/dialogic terms is not surprising given the adversarial legal system in which they were expressed. But for Pym, the bigger issue is how different theories can work more effectively to create consensus concerning semantic or pragmatic matters in interpreted interactions. He proposes that "default trust" should prevail in the decisions of interpreters themselves (and presumably the theories that underlie them) and that outside interventions should be permitted to help solve a specific problem only, not to propose entirely new sets of principles. While this proposal appears oriented to grant interactional authority to the interpreter role, at the same time Pym suggests that interpreters themselves should not be encouraged to comment on a specific problem that arises in their interpreting, fearing that this would pose an unnecessary and potentially harmful challenge to the existing theory of professionalism that proposes: "interpreters do one thing ('verbatim translation') and lawyers do another ('interpretation')." Instead he argues, "If there are to be comments on the problems of cross-lingual rendering, it seems they should ideally come from a further profession, that of experts and scholars, whose theories need not directly challenge those of lawyers, since the latter can 'interpret' them as well" (*ibid.*: 280).

This view seems to contradict the default trust Pym wishes to invest in interpreters. Moreover, it assumes that professional demarcations like the one above are objective and that the presumed distinction between 'verbatim translation' and 'interpretation' is a valid one. It is unclear why more legitimacy should be granted to "experts and scholars" than to interpreters' attempts to resolve 'problems of cross-lingual rendering', and it is also unclear why lawyers would be better able to 'interpret' the former's passing theories than they would those of the interpreters involved. This adds a clear social dimension to the idea of a passing theory; one that establishes an unequal distribution of both knowledge and authority within the communicative space regarding what does or does not constitute an effective theory. The idea that explicit commentaries by interpreters on 'problems of cross-lingual rendering' are problematic for lawyers is a view that has also been expressed by Susan Berk-Seligson (1990: 195–196) who is cited in Pym's article. Based on evidence from mock trial settings which were designed to examine the effects of interpreters in bilingual courtrooms, she emphasizes the problems for attorneys when interpreters bring themselves and their task into view:

> Both Hispanic mock jurors and the entire sample as a whole consider an attorney to be less competent when the interpreter stops him repeatedly in order to clarify some point in reference to her impending interpretation, or to request that he repeat a portion of his question for her. Such interruptions often can justifiably be interpreted by the listener as an indirect criticism of the attorney by the interpreter. When an interpreter states that the attorney's question is so long that it exceeds the limits of her retention, she is in effect complaining to him that he is not sensitive to her professional needs. It is to imply that he should know better. When she asks permission to change the grammatical form of the question, she is indirectly criticizing the lawyer for not being sensitive to the linguistic needs of the witness. Apparently mock jurors, particularly Hispanic mock jurors, judging by their evaluations of the attorney who is interrupted, sympathize with the veiled criticism made by the interpreter. For Hispanic listeners an attorney who repeatedly is interrupted by an interpreter is perceived as not only less competent, but also less intelligent.

At first glance, Berk-Seligson appears to be commenting here about the negative effects of interpreter interventions on the mock jurors' views of the attorneys. In the same passage, however, she interjects her own belief in the justifiability of their interpretations. It is not at all clear why the mock jurors or Berk-Seligson perceive the interpreter's requests for clarification, shorter sentences, or changes in tense negatively as 'veiled criticisms' of the attorney's intelligence or his lack of sensitivity to the needs of either the interpreter or the witness rather than as positive interventions designed to better ensure that mutual understanding occurs amongst all participants in the trial. This is the presumed objective of both the interpreter and attorney, and the witnesses and jurors as well. This is not to say that all interpreters perform their tasks equally competently or tactfully, but this can also be said of attorneys and other professionals. The real issue, however, is not about competence, but about the relative status being allocated here to interpreters and lawyers. Although Pym wishes to demonstrate in his article how 'passing theories' consistently serve as active constraints on discourse not "in terms of specific people, norms or institutions" (1999: 175), what he reveals in the end is precisely how they are actively constrained by these very terms with his recognition of "a significant degree of power-play underlying the various levels of theorization, most prominently in the silencing of interpreters' theories" (*ibid.*: 280). Pym ultimately has to acknowledge, though not without some degree of ambivalence, what I wish to argue in this book: that the interpreter's part in the situated evaluation of what an utterance is intended to communicate is very like that of their conversational partners. All proceed on intuitive predictions of meaning based on the current context and previous habits of linguistic understanding. The decisions taken by any one of the interactants—for example, about whether to attempt to disambiguate the use of an utterance, whether to privilege only the verbal aspects of an interaction or to in some way explicitly or implicitly recognize or reveal their wider purposes, whether to accommodate or fail to recognize another's view of the world, whether or not to attribute rational causality to utterances—will be influenced by previous contexts, institutional demands, political or economic motivation, and, in situations of heightened or violent conflict, the decision to recognize or not another's human rights. Where interpreters differ from their conversational partners, however, is in their right to have their 'passing theories' recognized and ratified without constraint.

ACKNOWLEDGING UNCERTAINTY

While professional codes of practice may offer some protection to interpreters, may help guide their decisions, these codes erroneously assume that the principle demand on interpreters is a linguistic or sociolinguistic one. Across a range of interpreting contexts, and particularly in situations defined by conflict—whether an asylum application hearing or the heightened conflict of a war zone—the decisions interpreters make and must make extend far beyond their linguistic abilities. They force them to confront the boundaries of their knowledge, their beliefs, their prior experiences, and their ethical practice both professionally and personally. It is precisely at these moments where professional codes stressing impartiality and loyalty confront questions of justice and individual conscience. And it is precisely at these moments where notions of objectivity and inter-subjectivity become one and the same. Attempts to resolve semantic uncertainties by any one of the participants involved in a communicative exchange, interpreted or not, involve decisions not discoveries about the meaning of a spoken utterance. Particular accounts of these sorts of decision processes in interpreted encounters are presented below in the form of personal reports taken from interviews I conducted with interpreters and asylum judges working in the U.K. asylum system and the published written accounts of two military interpreters working in Iraq and Guantánamo.[6] Their comments offer important insights into what is at stake in interpreted events that go beyond the linguistic and cultural issues typically foregrounded in codes of practice.

Communicative Objectives, Situated Knowledge, and Utterance Meaning

In the first example, the interview segment begins with me asking an interpreter to articulate her approach to interpreting for a lawyer and a client during an interview about an asylum application claim. In the course of the interview, the interpreter illustrates her approach to interpreting by describing an intervention she made in the course of an appeal hearing in the course of a summation to the judge made by a Home Office representative, the government agency responsible for immigration and border control, designed to discredit an Iranian appellant's case for asylum (Interpreter interview, 2004):

M: What would you do if you were speaking to a solicitor who perhaps wasn't very experienced say with Iran or, having any Iranian clients, for example and what if something came up that you knew to be potentially confusing in the way that the person

INT: I would intervene of course I would give them the background of that, yes.

M: Right, and now what would constitute your feeling that you ought to intervene, I mean would it be a meaning of a word or would it be if they were discussing a political situation

INT: Yes

M: Either way

INT: Yes

M: If you felt the solicitor needed your

INT: Yes, I would give the solicitor some more information about, just about the political matters, if it's about the cultural, especially cultural matters, yes . . . I was sitting monitoring one hearing about nine months ago when the Home Office representative was pointing out to the judge that this man is saying he never left the country [Iran] but he says that he's been in Azerbaijan. And the judge was listening, the interpreter didn't say anything, I just checked with my barrister and made eye contact, and the barrister asked permission to talk to his interpreter and it was given and I told the barrister, look Azerbaijan is in Russia, fine, but one part of Azerbaijan is in Iran, that part of Azerbaijan in Russia belonged to Iran once, that's why it's called Azerbaijan, it still has the name, but the Azerbaijan our client is talking about is the part which is in Iran, so we just left it there, as the barrister wanted it to be left, or our client would lose credibility. So they have to be very aware of the situation, that interpreter didn't get the point. I'm sure he knew that Azerbaijan was in Iran, definitely, because he was a doctor, but he didn't notice that point, these are the crucial points that we have to pick up quickly, don't let it go, and explain about them later. This is the last chance the client has sitting there in front of an independent judge.

The suggestion that an applicant is lying about any aspect of his or her case is a common strategy used by the government to discredit an entire claim. As such, the Home Office representative has represented Iran and Azerbaijan as two different countries in order to render the appellant's utterance as contradictory. The interpreter's intervention demonstrates her awareness of this strategy and of the importance of re-establishing this client's credibility in the face of the government's attempt to identify his statements as contradictory. She provides the appellant's barrister/lawyer an account of the historical and political geography of the region of Iran under scrutiny—describing Azerbaijan as 'in Iran' in order to interpret the appellant's utterance that he never left Iran but had been in Azerbaijan as 'holding true' based on their assumed shared knowledge. The official interpreter in the proceedings has not intervened to make this point, although in the interview the interpreter appears certain that he too would share this knowledge, implying that his position as a doctor would make this so. Though it is not clear why the official interpreter does not intervene, the interpreter suggests that it is the lack of awareness on his part of the strategic move being undertaken by the government and the importance of the point of clarifying this issue for the official record.

Despite the interpreter's expressed belief in the common knowledge of the region held by the three Iranians involved—the appellant and both interpreters—the appellant's lawyer recognizes that the complex and contested history, politics, and geography of the territories currently known as Iran, Azerbaijan, or Russia cannot be materially established in the present by the court's criteria of indisputable and relevant fact. All that can happen is that the interpreter's information can be formally recorded as offered to the court to contradict the claim by the Home Office. The 'truth' of each position exists not in relation to an immediately evident material reality, but as competing forms of coherence, or language games, presented simultaneously as part of the record of the court's proceedings. The government official may have been willfully interpreting the appellant in such a way as to convince the judge to make a negative decision in order to win his case. It is also possible that neither of the interpreters present may be 'interpreting' the appellant in the way in which he intends, despite the certainty the interpreter expresses in the interview. Attempts in the context of the asylum system to link inconsistency of utterances to credibility are a strategic move in a legal and political game, but they do not reflect 'facts' and an objective reality which an interpreter should hope to or be expected to resolve.

In the next example, the interpreter, himself a torture victim, discusses interpreting for some Kurdish applicants who claim to have undergone torture (Interpreter interview, 2004):

> I have witnessed liars get granted asylum and genuine refugees be refused. I have been tortured so I know what torture is. When I hear people say they have been tortured for 5 to 10 minutes with electric shock I know they are lying as it only takes 1 or 2 minutes to make an impact. I know what the pain of torture feels like. When you are hung in chains, for example, you sweat, lots of people never mention this, I think they are lying.

For this interpreter, torture means his experience of torture. He assumes continuity between his experience and those of other people who claim to have been tortured. Where this continuity does not appear in a claimant's utterances, he assumes they are lying. His own experience of torture has come to represent an 'objective truth' for him; he never suggests the possibility that torture may vary or that thresholds of pain or physical responses to pain may vary. But having said this, this interpreter simultaneously recognizes an alternative set of intentions which asylum applicants' utterances regarding can also reflect—not about what torture is or is not, but what the claim to have been tortured means in this context. Both the 'liars' and 'genuine refugees' share a similar communicative objective, one which he himself has already met—to establish a recognized valid claim for persecution in order to strengthen their chances of being granted asylum. About the alleged liars, he tells me, "[Y]ou gotta do what you gotta do", and utterances claiming torture, according to this interpreter, serve these applicants' communicative objectives. The fact that genuine refugees lie to achieve certain objectives, however, is recognized within the refugee system. As Dawes reports, citing Larry, a legal officer working for UNHCR (Dawes, 2007: 83),

> Even those who truly merit refugee status will lie if they believe another story will be more likely to succeed, if they believe they will harm somebody by telling the truth, or if they wish to hide how they managed to enter the country. "Human nature being what it is, when someone lies to us we think they're a liar", Larry comments. "You have to put that aside. Someone can lie and still be a refugee". Legal officers, Larry explains, have several strategies for cross-checking facts and gauging consistency of stories during interviews, and he emphasized that they work carefully to determine which lies are irrelevant and which are material to the final decision. It is slow work.

In a similar vein, although the interpreter interviewed appeals to his set of 'facts' about torture to brand certain applicants as liars, he implicitly recognizes a separate reality created by the particular context—that liars and genuine refugees may indeed be one and the same thing.

In the next example, the focus shifts to interpreters in the asylum system who can themselves come to embody the national or ethnic conflicts on which a claim is based. Utterances are 'interpreted' by any or all participants within a larger symbolic economy of legal rights and political positioning, and trust amongst conversational partners can be easily undermined. The segment below is taken from an interview conducted between myself and an asylum judge. The judge is discussing the dilemma she faces when she senses or sees what she takes to be a sign of conflict between interpreters and appellants, in this case, Eastern European interpreters and Roma Gypsies (Immigration Judge, 2004).

A: Well, there have been instances in the past where I have had Eastern European interpreters, with perhaps a Roma gypsy, and I can immediately see that the predator that they [the Roma] face in their own country is sitting right next to them, because they [the Interpreters] are sitting three feet away, whereas normally you would expect the distance to be a normal sort of chair, perhaps eighteen inches, that sort of thing

M: Yes, and does that, I mean apart from the kind of unpleasantness of that in the space that they're occupying, does that concern you that then it would be affecting the interpreter's ability or willingness or in some ways distort the interpreter's role?

A: Yes, well, I'm conscious of that, and I think in those circumstances it's important to keep the questions straightforward and simple, but it's very easy when you're speaking English to, or any language I guess, to make a very convoluted question. And if you've got to the point where I felt that it was affecting, although

> your question is how would I know it was affecting, then I would just stop and adjourn and give them another interpreter. But I have, in the appeals system we have written statements, we have what they've said in the past, so provided nothing, if something totally different came out, and I thought the interpreter was misinterpreting, I would stop immediately.

In her comments, the judge likens the interpreter relation to the applicant to a predator, a predator in this case menacing its prey from a notable distance. For this judge, the body language of the actual interpreter and her experiences with previous interpreters from Eastern Europe indicate the possibility that the interpreter's view of the world does not necessarily accommodate the appellant's view regarding the persecution of Roma Gypsies or of this Roma Gypsy in Eastern Europe. In cases such as these, the judge claims to consciously adjust her language, to keep her questions 'straightforward and simple' to make both the questions and subsequent responses less vulnerable to the potential manipulation of the appellant's utterances she anticipates by the interpreter. She also registers the possibility of consulting previous statements on record (which are produced from previously interpreted oral testimony) and, if all else fails, to cease communicating with this particular interpreter altogether.

It is interesting that in this case the judge is prepared to use inconsistencies between past accounts and present spoken utterances to challenge the interpreter's credibility, not the appellant's. She implicitly recognizes that any participant's utterance in an interpreted event, including the interpreter's, can operate strategically to achieve communicative objectives. She acknowledges that she cannot operate with absolute certainty about the correspondence between utterances and facts about the world but must rely on extra-linguistic factors as well, including body language, her prior experience of similar instances, and her authority to adjourn the hearing and start the process all over again.

Interpreting the Enemy

A similar tension is evident in the written accounts of two U.S. military linguists: Kayla Williams' *Love My Rifle More than You* (Williams 2005) based on her time in Iraq from 2002 to 2003 and Eric Saar's *Inside the Wire* (Saar and Novak 2005) based on his six months in Guantánamo in that same period. Both accounts reveal a set of tensions: for Williams in her relationship to the Iraqis she was sent to liberate; and for Saar in his relationship to the detainees.

In her book, Williams recalls the orders given to her 'peacekeeping' unit when the threat level is placed at high. When confronting a 'guy on the side of the road with a cell phone' they are instructed to point their weapons at him and if he won't get off the phone, to opt to shoot him in the event he is revealing their position to the insurgents. Williams, who believes she is "better equipped than most soldiers to see these civilians as people" because she speaks Arabic and has Arab friends, describes the point at which she and her unit choose certainty over self-doubt and decide to "assume the worst about everyone" (Williams 2005: 238):

> In truth, every incident that happens is a completely discrete incident, but it's almost impossible to live this way. Basically we all reach a point where we have to assume that everyone is friendly (and respond accordingly), or assume that everyone is a potential enemy (and treat them as such). It simply becomes too overwhelming to play that line at every single moment. To look at each person and make that choice over and over and over again. To ask yourself: Will I give this person food? Or will I point my gun at this person? So we make one choice: We come to assume the worst about everyone. And we stick with it.

Like the judge in the previous example, Williams and her unit rely on prior experiences to interpret a certain behavior in a certain way, even though in her case it may mean shooting an innocent person. Her unit's decision 'to assume the worst about everyone' requires that they must stop judging each person each time in order to make the right choice. Similar to the judge, Williams and her unit make a decision about who is the predator and who the prey in a context where trust has broken down. Unlike the courtroom, however, in the uncertainty of war, there is little time to think about whether one's judgment is correct, and there is no way to postpone a life or death confrontation and start all over again.

During the same period, Saar operated in a dual capacity at Guantánamo Bay as a translator and in military intelligence operations. His book offers an 'insider' account of the treatment of detainees in the camp and of the illicit tactics used by military intelligence during interrogations. Part 'confessional' and part exposé, Saar reveals an ongoing tension between his patriotism concerning the 'war on terror' on the one hand, and on the other, his moral uncertainty regarding the treatment of many of the prisoners during interrogations in which he participates in his capacity as interpreter.

Saar recalls a particular conversation with one of the detainees, Wael, a university-educated Saudi living in Afghanistan who had been captured by the Northern Alliance during a raid on his village outside Kandahar along with "every Arab man in the area" (Saar and Novak 2005: 80). Wael has requested an interpreter in order to claim his innocence and appeal for help, and Saar consents to listen to him after Wael accepts that Saar can do nothing for him in his role as a linguist (and not his interrogator). In response to Saar's question about how he ended up in Afghanistan, Wael explains that he went there in the late 1990s looking for work, got a job in an orphanage, met a woman, got married, had three children, and ended up working for a farmer. He then tells Saar about his arrest and torture by the Northern Alliance and subsequent detention and interrogation by the Americans. The following exchange, which takes place in Arabic, is described in the book, followed by Saar's commentary:

S: Wael, I know you wanted to tell me your story, but there is really nothing I can do.

W: Basam, I miss my children. They have no idea why their father is gone. How do I explain this to them?

S: What do you want me to say, Wael?

W: I just wanted you to know. I want anyone who will listen to know. I believe that you cannot help me. I just want you to know. Don't believe all the lies they are feeding you, Basam. Not every detainee is a terrorist. Just ask some of the men who haven't seen their interrogators in months.

As Wael speaks, a number of different worlds converge for Saar, as evidenced in the following passage (*ibid.*: 81–82):

> I had noticed that many of the detainees never seemed to go to interrogations, and I wondered why this was the case. We linguists had heard many similar stories of detainees being seized by the Northern Alliance, an ad hoc confederation of anti-Taliban militia and warlords with whom the United States had formed a loose and strictly expedient partnership in the war in Afghanistan. Recent press reports had indicated that the United States was paying bounties for terror suspects, and American officials had made reference to this happening as well. It was a troubling piece of information. We all knew people who would turn in their own grandmother for the right sum, and five thousand dollars went a long way in a place like Afghanistan.

Both Wael and Saar enter into the conversation to achieve a particular end. Wael's objective is to voice his innocence and to try to gain support for his wish to be released. He lets Saar know who he is, where he comes from, and that neither he, nor every detainee, is a terrorist. As one of the linguists assigned to Guantánamo, Saar has experienced frustration at being assigned the job of translating day-to-day communication with the detainees, instead of working on intelligence analysis and interrogations. But he has also become increasingly doubtful, as have some others in his unit, about the involvement of many of the detainees in terrorism. The conversation with Wael creates an opportunity for Saar to learn for himself whether the stories and press reports about bounties and the Northern Alliance as well as his own observations about detainees and interrogations have any bearing. Though the book does not provide any information about whether speaking to Saar directly helped Wael achieve his ultimate objective, Saar reports leaving the conversation with some of his former beliefs disturbed, if not altered (*ibid.*: 82):

> Later that night, after dinner in front of the TV, Wael's story nagged at me. I wasn't necessarily convinced it was true, although he sounded believable. But the very possibility that he could be right, the notion that I could be contributing to this man's wrongful detention, bugged me. Ahmad had mentioned his doubt that all the detainees at the camp were really terrorists on my very first day inside, but until that conversation with Wael, I'd been able to put the issue very effectively out of my head.

Saar relies on a number of factors to decide whether Wael's story was true: the accounts about the Guantánamo detainees he had heard from others; his own observations in the camp; and the statements from Wael that sounded believable to Saar, including, perhaps, his concern for his children, his connection to his family. Given the wider context in which this occurred, however, though it may have led Saar's beliefs to converge with Wael's at the time, and over time, it did not necessarily secure Wael his release.[7] Saar was a member of the military and was thus complicit in the war and in Wael's detention. However, his position as a military linguist is not untypical of interpreters more generally. In interpreted interactions, interpreters act on and in the world as communicating social agents, whether they are perceived or see themselves as helpless or useful conduits, cultural mediators, language brokers, cultural experts, or social workers. They participate through language in contexts which foster ambiguity, contradiction, misunderstanding, and different forms of violence and betrayal which are resolvable only in relation to the communicative objectives which give rise to them in the first place, not through an appeal to an objective reality outside the boundaries of the encounter itself. In contexts in which these objectives are tied to social, political, economic, or militarist agendas, interpreters face additional challenges to their professional roles and ethical codes of practice.

OBJECTIVITY AND SUBJECTIVITY REVISITED

Acknowledging semantic uncertainty as an aspect of all communication and all interpreted interactions does not imply that confrontations of beliefs and attitudes in communicative encounters must lead to misunderstanding or reinforce differences. All confrontation is productive communication in that it defines over and over again, from one communicative context to another, how we understand, perceive, and experience the world. There is, however, no way to stand outside of our beliefs to check their validity, or to check whether our beliefs coincide with the beliefs of others.

In dialogic encounters, the relevant interlocutors enlist their own interpretive theories to understand the role that any utterance produced plays in its producer's (and interpreter's) relation to the world. It is through these interpretive theories that interlocutors come to an understanding about the reasons, i.e., the content of the beliefs, behind a particular utterance, including the specific context in which it is presently embedded (as in the interpreter's understanding of the use of the word torture by the asylum applicant). An interlocutor's interpretive theory is not evidence of a conceptual scheme or of communicative competence, however; it is an outcome of the triangulation between speakers, hearers, and an 'object' or environment which represents the "simplest interpersonal situation" (D. Davidson 2001: 129). Importantly, it is not until people start communicating that they perceive a relationship between their thoughts. This does not mean that they will mean the same thing by the same words, only that they interpret what each other will say or do based on expectations formed at the time as well as on prior experiences that assist them in their present understanding. There is no guarantee that interlocutors will accurately predict the effects of their words or control their effects, though it is the case that where individuals interact with one another verbally in ways that are effective enough, often enough, for all concerned, then more or less congruent patterns of verbal production and uptake can emerge.

2 Ethical Communication

For interpreters and their interlocutors—those for whom and with whom they speak—codes of ethics and codes of practice serve as non-binding contractual agreements that aim to ensure the truth and accuracy of all interpreted utterances. Given that it is frequently only the interpreter who understands all of the languages used in an interaction, these codes also serve to reassure the other participants that interpreters have an obligation to speak their words in the way they intended. The existence of codes that guarantee an interpreter will not add, alter, or omit any aspect of an utterance reinforces the notion of inter- and intra-lingual systematicity between signs and referents: that aside from the occasional need for cultural clarification of a word or an utterance meaning, semantic and pragmatic equivalence is a realizable end, and one that is achievable without the need for engaged interpretation or negotiation of meaning.

The previous chapter argued that many of the prevailing perceptions about language and communication that inform interpreting theory and practice do not adequately reflect the actual tasks involved in all forms of communication. This chapter questions the extent to which existing codes of ethics, and the principles they subscribe to, permit interpreters to honor their professional obligations and, at the same time, to act socially and ethically responsibly. I explore the sources in deontological, or duty-based, ethics for the principles of neutrality and impartiality that inform these codes and consider whether they serve as adequate guides for the decisions interpreters are sometimes compelled to make. I also consider alternative perspectives on ethics which move beyond questions of duty and impartiality and help to chart new ground for an ethics of interpreting which acknowledges semantic uncertainty and moral certainty as legitimate guides for interpreter practice.

ETHICS AND THE INTERPRETED ENCOUNTER

Codes of ethics and codes of practice are commonly taken to be perceived by all the parties in an interpreted interaction as serving both a practical and an ethical purpose. From a language perspective, such codes are seen to limit the potential for misunderstanding and guarantee that interpretations are true and accurate. From an ethical perspective, they are deemed to provide the necessary ground rules for ethical conduct primarily through the maintenance of 'neutrality' and the 'faithful' reproduction of original utterances—the adherence to truth. Codes are assumed to help interpreters avoid certain practices such as: omitting potentially incriminating information; manipulating testimony or questioning in favor of one party or another; or offering meta-textual information to any one party which might provide an unfair advantage with respect to their communicative objectives. The obligation of interpreters to aspire to objective or impartial positions, it is assumed, encourages them to interpret utterances not based on their own or another party's self-interest, but on rational, objective criteria established by and in language itself.

The Limits of Duty

Codes of ethics are not legally binding contractual agreements. Interpreters comply with codes of ethics not from fear of prosecution but from a sense of duty and professional obligation. A deontological approach to ethics—that is, ethics perceived as a set of objective rules or duties that decide ethical behavior irrespective of their consequences—is stressed in both interpreter training and practice where the emphasis on duties and obligations is tied to principles of fidelity and neutrality. The assumed link between duty and neutrality is what permits interpreters to claim, and their interlocutors to demand, that the interpreters should 'just translate' even where abuses of power or instances of injustice are in evidence, or when faced with questions of personal conscience.[1]

Justification for this link is partly rooted in a deontological approach to ethics associated with Kant which relates duty to rational principles and the establishment of compulsory moral rules of ethical behavior. To be truly ethical, according to this approach, our perceived duty toward others must be rooted in rational and universal principles, such as the maxim that all human beings deserve the right to freedom and control over their lives. These principles must be intended to serve, without contradiction, as a universal maxim for all. The deontological view imagines a process in which a rational individual puts him or herself in the position of another and reaches a moral judgment that would hold for or be applicable to all across time and space. And importantly, individuals behave morally responsibly when acting out of a sense of duty to these principles rather than responding to personal emotions or a concern for the consequences of their behavior, legal or otherwise. In interpreted interactions, interpreters' compliance with the principle of impartiality is viewed as crucial to their fulfillment of this ethical obligation.

The following extracts, taken from interviews I conducted with interpreters in the U.K., illustrate some potential benefits of impartiality to the parties involved. The first involves a Roma Gypsy from Poland seeking to apply for asylum. In this example, a Polish interpreter describes her interaction with a Roma Gypsy and a lawyer in the U.K. She expresses her dismay at having to repeat the client's words verbatim, because the applicant was swearing a lot and because in her view he (and others like him) was lying. The interpreter bases her decision to be "the voice of this person and nothing else" on her duty as an interpreter, despite her apparent disapproval of the style and content of the Roma asylum seeker's utterances:[2]

> You just see the person, you just hear when they start saying things and you just, oh my god, you know, but you can't do anything, you can't do anything. Then you are interpreting, you were interpreting and they were swearing, yes they were swearing, I was swearing to the solicitor, and I was saying exactly what they were saying. So there's a lot of things and it's like you just want to say, 'oh my god, what are you doing, just stop', but you can't, you are the voice of this person and nothing else. (Interpreter #3)

In the second example a Lebanese interpreter describes the testimony of a Lebanese Palestinian asylum seeker who she felt "pretty sure" was giving his lawyer intentionally false information about the Lebanese or Palestinian government's issuance of IDs for travel. Although she believed the "solicitor didn't have a clue what the client was talking about", she also felt she "couldn't get involved really". This interpreter does not mention her duty; instead, she relates her decision to remain impartial to her desire to protect the Palestinian asylum seeker out of feelings of sympathy based on his circumstances and their shared culture. As she states,

> You have to be blind. Sometimes you have to, maybe to protect your own culture and you don't realize, maybe it's something in your blood, you don't know. You know what I mean? I mean, maybe I knew, well not maybe, I was pretty sure he wasn't telling the truth, but maybe I ignored it because of my culture I felt sorry for him, maybe the circumstances, maybe something. (Interpreter #4)

This statement suggests that interpreters sometimes do draw on personal feelings or concern for consequences and not duty alone as a professional motivation to act impartially and ethically in some circumstances. Although from a strict deontological ethical perspective only the first interpreter would be deemed to have behaved ethically as her decision to remain impartial was related to duty alone, from the perspective of existing codes of interpreting practice, both interpreters would be perceived to have behaved ethically as they both remained impartial, regardless of whether they responded to duty or feelings.

There are many other situations in which interpreters experience conflict and uncertainty over what constitutes their primary duty and what counts as ethical behavior. In such instances, they must determine, sometimes in seconds, whether their obligation should be to their profession, to the person or institution paying their fee, to a member of their own culture, religion, gender, or ethnic group, or to a particular country or set of principles. Any one of these factors may make an interpreter decide that it is ethically permissible to break with professional codes of practice. This raises several crucial and relevant questions: what would motivate an interpreter's decision to break with the 'duty to remain impartial' in actual practice, and under what circumstances might such a decision become professionally, i.e. ethically, acceptable; are there circumstances in the course of professional duties where it would be professionally acceptable for feelings or consequences to motivate interpreters to act partially but behave ethically; are there circumstances in the course of professional duties where it would be professionally acceptable for feelings or consequences to motivate interpreters to act impartially but behave unethically; and what would constitute examples of ethical or unethical practice if these notions were detached from the notion of impartiality as defined in existing codes of practice?

Breaking with Duty

Although the primary duty of interpreters to remain impartial is intended to protect the rights of all parties in an interpreted interaction, there are circumstances when interpreters must weigh the rights of one individual against another to ensure that the communicative objectives of all participants are given equal or adequate space within the interaction. Interpreters' decisions to break with their professional codes of ethics in these circumstances are usually not arbitrary or irresponsible attempts to undermine their interlocutors' rights or the setting aside of professional duties. They are attempts to balance one ethical obligation against another, moments of genuine ethical insight, not violations of duty. Interpreter behavior that is typically characterized as an example of inappropriate 'partiality' might be better understood as similar in kind to the action of a mediator, not in the sense of a bridge or liaison between two parties as this role is commonly understood in interpreting, but as one who carefully considers the (self) interests of all parties concerned before deciding how to intervene to ensure that all interests are represented fairly. Although codes of ethics which restrict the interpreter role to the 'faithful' reproduction of original utterances do not necessarily prevent this form of mediation role from occurring, particularly where the right to be heard is unequally distributed or enforced within an interaction, they deny interpreters the professional license to negotiate openly with their interlocutors over participatory rights where relevant. In the end, by refusing to admit or acknowledge in interpreted interaction the types of interactional negotiations that naturally occur in the process of interpreting any utterance, codes of ethics often force ethically minded interpreters to communicate 'under the radar' rather than in open dialogue with their interlocutors.

In the following example, an interpreter describes her decision to communicate in this way in order to balance one ethical obligation against another. According to the interpreter, who worked regularly for the U.K. Home Office, in the session referred to below the interviewing officer was particularly impatient as she was in a hurry to leave for the day to pick up her child from school. The officer became increasingly frustrated with what the interpreter herself acknowledges were the asylum applicant's "rather convoluted" responses to her questions and instructed the applicant through the interpreter to "be more concise and stick to the point". The interpreter was concerned that this would cause the applicant to omit important details about his experiences which might ultimately lead to a denial of his application and so decided to deliver what she refers to below as "creative interpreting" (Rycroft 2003: 38; and see *ibid.*: 2005: 237–238):

> In order to compensate for the officer's unfairness I believed it was appropriate to deliver what I call 'creative interpreting'. The officer showed impatience with [X's] long answers and told him a few times to be more concise and stick to the point otherwise we would be there forever. I judged for myself that she was unfairly hurrying him up by appealing to a non-existent reciprocity of perspectives as the best use of interview time. So I interpreted, every time, that he needed to be more concise and stick to the point of the question but to make sure to say everything that happened to him that would assist a decision in his case. Here I broke the canons of interpreting in his interest, because I knew something that he did not, i.e., that by her behavior the officer was depriving him of the only opportunity to make his case fully.

It is important to note that in interviews of this kind, asylum applicants do not necessarily have legal counsel present, or may not have received any legal advice from a legal representative prior to their interview. It may also be the only record of their claim. The interpreter's advice that the applicant should provide as many details as he could was based on both her knowledge of this fact and her awareness of the wider legal framework in which his statement would be evaluated. In the event itself, the interpreter's decision to interpret faithfully what the officer said but to add the advice to "say everything that happened" was grounded in her wish to compensate for what she judged to be unfair behavior on the part of the government official. Although she has not altered or added anything to either the official's or the applicant's utterances, the interpreter herself believes she has broken her professional code by not remaining impartial despite the circumstances surrounding her decision.

The next example is from an interpreter with fourteen years of experience working at a charity dedicated to providing assistance to refugees and asylum applicants who have been victims of torture. In this interview excerpt, the interpreter admits that he does sometimes "offer an opinion" or "make a suggestion" in order to fulfill what he identifies as his primary duty—to help therapists help torture victims make progress during therapeutic sessions. He cites his exposure to a range of therapeutic techniques as the justification for breaking with official codes of practice. Since a number of the therapists who work at the charity are volunteers with little or no prior professional contact with torture victims, the interpreter believes that it is "not out of order" to share with these practitioners the strategies that he has observed work most effectively:

> I have been known to offer an opinion to other practitioners outside the one I mentioned who empowers the interpreter. You know, because sometimes we're the only people who work with them all, you know, we work with, every week with ten different people, you know, and you're getting a lot of insight, you know, whose style works, you know, whose phraseology works, and many of the blockages you meet you've seen being dealt with in different ways, and you've seen dropping out. So surely it's not out of order to make a suggestion. (Interpreter #5)

Despite the considerable experience of this interpreter, he still feels the need to justify his decision to make a suggestion or opinion to those practitioners who have not explicitly 'empowered' him, that is, given him permission to do so. The popular image of interpreters as neutral participants means that many professionals with whom they work do not acknowledge their ability to make independent and specialist contributions toward the achievement of communicative objectives. The extent to which interpreters are recognized in this way depends in large part on the specific contexts in which they work. In the previous example above of the Home Office, the presence of an independent and informed interpreter can be perceived as a hindrance to the workings of a bureaucratic system designed to set limits on applicants' participatory rights. In the second example of the charity, the potential exists for the development of trusting partnerships between interpreters and their interlocutors, despite the existence of codes of ethics that would deny them these rights, although interpreters remain vulnerable to others' decisions to grant or refuse them communicative rights in a therapeutic session.

These interpreters' commentaries on their practice suggest that it is not solely or even primarily in the interpretation of linguistic forms that interpreters exhibit particular forms of ethical or unethical behavior; it is in their often subtle reactions and responses to the perceived wider communicative objectives of a particular interaction. Ethical and unethical behavior is accomplished through the decisions interpreters make both within a particular interaction, e.g., in their choice of body language or intonation or their decisions to offer advice, provide information or remain silent, and outside the space of the interaction, e.g., in their choice to turn whistle-blower or witness due to the perceived unjust or unethical behavior of others. Interpreters who appear even slightly incredulous or hostile or who physically distance themselves from an interlocutor can inadvertently signal doubt about the credibility of an asylum seeker, a witness, a prisoner, etc. Though such responses might be seen as expressions of partiality, none formally violate codes of ethics. And although the maintenance of silence is generally looked upon as ethical in that it demonstrates impartiality, in a context where an interpreter has incriminating information about an interlocutor, for example, to say nothing might equally be construed as unethical if to say nothing supports an institution's attempt to violate individual human or legal rights or helps an individual to deceive a legal representative or manipulate a legal or political system.

THE QUESTION OF ETHICS

Codes of ethics are believed to serve as reasonable starting points for professional interpreting practice, offering a view of interlocutors as potential equals operating under social and interactional rules as they ought to be. However, in situations where conflicts exist or may emerge with respect to the communicative objectives of participating interlocutors, questions of ethical judgment extend beyond the ideals of linguistic objectivity and interpreter neutrality. Communication in heightened conflict situations is frequently characterized by the willful misrecognition of others, whether in the persons of asylum applicants, refugees, detained prisoners, innocent civilians, or interpreters themselves. For certain individuals working with interpreters under these conditions, e.g., journalists, military personnel, government officials, the importance of linguistic accuracy can actually become less important than their trust in an interpreter's loyalty or in their interpreter's ability to gather information accurately, provide contacts, arrange interviews, and 'interpret' a situation on the ground correctly. Extra-linguistic knowledge obtained from interpreters which clarifies significant or subtle confusions over linguistic, cultural, or historical practices can also help health professionals or legal representatives better advocate for their patient or client.

Interpreters require ethical models—and codes of ethics—that can help them to create the conditions for mutually effective dialogue amongst conversational partners across a range of contexts. Interpreting codes of ethics that stress compliance with principles of impartiality leave interpreters on their own to resolve the clashes that occur in the moral and social spaces of human interactions. They do not adequately acknowledge the dialectically and interactively created 'conversations' that constitute interpreted events, involving both linguistic and non-linguistic behavior. They also fail to recognize interpreters as active players in dialogic communication and the significance of the social and political relationships that obtain amongst all parties involved in the dialogue.

There is an increasing awareness that a further evaluation and reconsideration of the codes of ethics which currently guide interpreter training and practice are needed. An important step in undertaking this exercise must be to extend understandings of what actually might constitute ethical behavior in interpreted communicative contexts beyond those currently in place; that is, beyond questions of duty and impartiality. Neo-Kantian and non-Kantian approaches to ethics provide a number of relevant insights regarding the complexities involved in conceiving of and constructing ethical behavior in human interactions more generally. Many of these approaches move beyond the individualist deontological perspective of Kantian ethics, recognizing that ethical relationships—and ethical subjectivity itself—are inherently inter-subjective events. They differ significantly from one another however on the status given to the role of impartiality (and universality) in ethical relationships and the implications for questions of moral responsibility. Given the centrality of this issue for interpreters and interpreting codes of practice, a number of these different views are explored in detail below. I wish to consider whether or to what extent these approaches might provide a platform for a broader and more comprehensive ethics of interpreting than is currently available.

Neo-Kantian Discourse Ethics: Universality, Reciprocity, and Recognition

Scholarly work in what is referred to as 'discourse ethics' offers a number of relevant insights into the relationship between ethical and communicative behavior (see, for example, Apel 1977; Habermas 1990; McCarthy 1991; Benhabib 1992; Honneth 1995). Habermas and others drawing on the earlier work of the Frankfurt school have in different ways attempted to reconstruct Kantian ethics by shifting the frame of reference away from the isolated moral consciousness of the individual toward a more inter-subjective approach to ethical subjectivity. Scholars working in this tradition ground discourse ethics in participant-based, political-moral action aimed at the self-realization and self-determination that defines human autonomy. They take as their starting point not the individual struggle for autonomy found in Kantian ethics but the establishment of relations of mutual recognition as the means to both personal and political autonomy. Habermas' discourse ethics shifts the emphasis "from what each can will without contradiction to be a general law, to what all can will in agreement to be a universal law" (Habermas 1990: 67). Following Habermas, discourse-based approaches to ethics have attempted to articulate normative principles underlying the inter-subjective nature of ethical relationships. But they have also criticized political theorists like John Rawls for maintaining that to achieve consensus amongst individuals who hold different worldviews, participants must operate behind a 'veil of ignorance'; that is, they must leave their own and others' 'comprehensive doctrines' or 'background cultures' outside the frame of deliberation (Rawls 1995).

Habermas' work on discourse ethics serves as a starting point for much of this work which while varied shares his wish to identify the moral, ethical, and discursive conditions necessary for personal and political autonomy, conditions which socially and historically define and are defined by our encounters with others. Habermas views the relationship between the individual subject and a wider, universal community (consisting of "all possible alter-egos") as an inter-dependent and complementary one (Habermas 1992: xvii). He criticizes Kant for failing to recognize that rational and universal ethical principles cannot be decided by individuals monologically, arguing instead that universally realizable moral judgments are formed and discovered dialogically in unconstrained communication. Habermas thus replaces the priority of a solitary private consciousness with that of communicative relations (McCarthy 1978: 162) through a philosophy that seeks to promote cultural unity and avoid the fragmentation associated with the postmodern condition.

Habermas bases his universal pragmatics on the belief that all communication possesses formal universal features. He maintains that "the supposition of a common objective world is built into the pragmatics of every single linguistic usage" (Habermas 1992: 138). His argument that the "expectation of future resolutions" is presupposed in the general structures of possible communication is founded on the notion of the primacy of reason underlying all communicative action oriented toward understanding. Through communicative reason, Habermas believes, individuals and cultures can transcend the authority and domination that are "inculcated as rules for interpreting the world and of action" in the grammars of language games (Habermas 1977: 358). In contrast to Chomsky who draws a distinction between linguistic competence and performance, and for whom generative grammar refers only to the linguistic competence of the ideal speaker-listener, Habermas claims that actual linguistic performance or 'communicative competence' also contains a universal core (McCarthy 1978: 274–275). According to Habermas, all dialogue presupposes normative rules; as we dialogue, we employ reason. Every speech act anticipates or presupposes the argumentative procedure of providing and evaluating reasons in support of the universal validity claims of comprehensibility, truth, truthfulness, and rightness. All human beings possess the cognitive potential to engage in the discursive justification of validity claims, and this suggests the possibility of a universalist ethical standpoint.

Habermas is clear that 'undistorted communication'—the discursive realization of a common objective world—rarely if ever occurs. He is critically aware of the ideological nature of language and its potential role as a medium of domination that serves to legitimate the interests of the status quo. He has nonetheless remained committed to the belief in rational argumentation as the means to challenge state and institutional power through public political procedure and debate aimed at creating mutually effective dialogue amongst individuals and groups who do not necessarily share similar histories, values, or beliefs. For Habermas, the presupposition of an idealizing concept of truth or validity is what makes dialogue possible, especially across rival conceptions (Habermas 1992: 138):

> Even in the most difficult process of reaching understanding, all parties appeal to the common reference point of a possible consensus, even if this reference point is projected in each case from within their own contexts. For, although they may be interpreted in various ways and applied according to different criteria, concepts like truth, rationality, or justification play the same grammatical role in every linguistic community.

Though Habermas' ideas have evolved over decades of writing and public debate, certain criticisms have persisted over time. Some of his earliest writings in particular have been criticized for betraying a cultural-historical and ethnocentric bias in his assumption that claims to validity and truth can be taken as universally binding principles rather than the idiosyncratic beliefs and values of Western culture alone. His claim that all human beings possess a similar cognitive capacity to engage in the discursive justification of universal validity claims has been read as betraying an anti-particularist stance that takes distinguishing biological, social, or religious factors amongst human groups to be morally irrelevant. He has also been criticized for emphasizing procedural theories of justice over substantive ones. Many of these criticisms have been taken up and developed into alternative theorizations of discourse ethics.

Seyla Benhabib: Concrete Universalism

While defending Habermas' universalist model of rational argumentation, Seyla Benhabib argues that discourse ethics must not be focused on public procedural justice alone, but must be considered as the means by which social relationships are sustained in "ordinary moral conversations" structured around the Hegelian notion of reciprocal recognition (Benhabib 1992: 52–53). She suggests that such conversations originate in our earliest communicative actions where we learn to engage in moral conversations of justification with proximate others, a capacity which expands over time and space and can come to include all of humanity (*ibid.*):

> In the final analysis, universalizability requires us to practice the reversibility of standpoints by extending this to the viewpoint of humanity.

> Such a capacity is essential to being a good partner in moral conversation, and it is furthered by the practice of moral conversation. [. . .]. Discourse ethics projects such moral conversations, in which reciprocal recognition is exercised, into a utopian community of mankind. But the ability and the willingness of individuals begins with the admonition of the parent to the child, "What if others threw sand in your face or pushed you into the pool, how would you feel then?"

Benhabib takes up the point less developed in Habermas that validity claims must be considered in light of the concrete historical traditions and practices of particular individuals and cultures, in her terms, 'concrete others', allowing all members of society to participate in social life without disadvantage. She argues for the possibility of a more "historically self-conscious universalism" (*ibid.*: 30), a 'concrete universalism' that preserves the principle of universality but remains sensitive to the individual, social, and historical contexts within which people engage in moral decisions. Benhabib envisions a type of transnational dialogue, accomplished through what she calls 'democratic iterations', borrowing the notion of iteration from Derrida for whom it suggests the state of indeterminacy of meaning, his view that in the repetition of a linguistic utterance the 'performative force' of the utterance breaks from prior established contexts of socially established meanings. Benhabib takes up this idea, arguing that diverse linguistic, cultural, or religious practices, for example, can and must be taken up in the context of a complex cultural dialogue in which both particular group identities as well as the inter-dependence of all participants is acknowledged (Benhabib 2004: 179).

With the notion of a democratic iteration, Benhabib wishes to acknowledge the possibility of a context-independent universalist moral language that can coexist with the complexities of and potential overlaps in the moral, ethical, and evaluative discursive frameworks within which different cultural/national groups conduct their lives (Benhabib 2002: 40–42). Democratic iterations demonstrate the capacity of the force of an utterance to assume new contexts and new meanings. Although Benhabib maintains her trust in a 'universalist moral language' to challenge existing forms of legitimacy, she acknowledges that whether an individual or group is judged worthy of equal treatment and respect as a conversational partner—their right to recognition—will ultimately determine the type and extent of their participation in public deliberations (*ibid.*: 56).

Axel Honneth: The Moral-Psychological Conditions for Reciprocal Recognition

This last point is the central focus for Axel Honneth in his examination of the normative expectations of individuals or groups in society concerning their recognition rights. Rather than locate the emancipatory, transcending potential of society in the presuppositions of language as Habermas does, or in the expansive force of utterances within more inclusive state institutions or civic organizations as Benhabib does, Honneth locates this potential in individuals' anticipation of reciprocal recognition in their public and private encounters with others, quite apart from the expression of a single utterance. According to Honneth, this expectation of recognition involves the guarantee of three basic principles: self-trust (the right to basic self-confidence), self-respect (a sense of authorship over one's life), and self-esteem (the right to live in a semantic-symbolic environment that enables a rich self-interpretation), each of which is necessary for all members of society to achieve individual autonomy (Honneth 1995; Honneth and Anderson 2005). Honneth is less focused on the moral-political conditions necessary to guarantee participatory rights and more concerned to elaborate the moral-psychological conditions vital for personal identity formation. In situations where these conditions are not met, whether over a prolonged period of time or as a result of specific instances of injustice, individuals come to feel disrespected, humiliated or in more extreme cases such as torture, to "view their own feelings with suspicion, and to distrust their own desires" (Honneth and Anderson 2005: 134):

> The importance of mutual recognition is often clearest in the breach. Consider, for example, practices and institutions that express attitudes of denigration and humiliation. They threaten individuals' own self-esteem by making it much harder (and, in limit cases, even impossible) to think of oneself as worthwhile. The resulting feelings of shame and worthlessness threaten one's sense that there is a point to one's undertakings. And without that sense of one's aspirations being worth pursuing, one's agency is hampered [. . .] And so even if one's effort to maintain self-esteem in the face of denigrating treatment is successful, the question of justice is whether the burden is fair.

Honneth places the responsibility for the impact of withheld recognition on the historically institutionalized principles of recognition operating within a given society. He links the feelings of social injustice experienced by individuals at the psychological level to public discourses and the normative principles of recognition underlying them which "determine the linguistic horizon of socio-moral thoughts and feelings in a particular society" (Fraser and Honneth 2003: 249–250). This 'moral grammar' influences the extent to which individuals feel in possession of "the universal dignity of persons" and serves as a crucial marker of social justice and injustice in the deliberative contexts of a society. As his colleague and translator Joel Anderson explains, according to Honneth (1995: xiv):

> To have self respect, then, is to have a sense of oneself as a person, that is, a 'morally responsible' agent or, more precisely, as someone capable

> of participating in the sort of public deliberation that Habermas terms 'discursive will formation'.

Both Honneth and Anderson, however, contend that public contexts which aim to create "real or fictitious conditions of impartiality" through a Rawlsian veil of ignorance risk masking the reality of human inter-subjectivity (Honneth and Anderson 2005: 139). They argue that all parties in social interactions should be aware or made aware of each other's inter-subjective vulnerability so that each will be judged worthy of equal treatment and respect, even under procedural constraints aimed at generating impartiality (*ibid.*: 140). All individuals, they suggest, learn to perceive of themselves as 'recognized' through processes of inclusion mediated not only by language, but by gestures and through different media. These are the collective means through which individuals achieve a sense of their public 'visibility'. Where these expectations are unfulfilled, individuals are left feeling insecure and invisible—withheld recognition thus becomes a crucial factor in the struggle for social justice.

Although Honneth's focus on the role of withheld recognition in micro- and macro-semantic environments reveals an important psycho-social dimension of discursive encounters, it treats reciprocal recognition as a transcendent quality of human inter-subjectivity, something to be reclaimed dialogically rather than viewed as always contingent on the social and political relationships within which it is constructed and negotiated. Such claims ultimately minimize the role of the particular, bracketing out interactionally salient unequal powers and resources in order to focus on the ideal discursive conditions under which the 'universal dignity of persons' can be achieved for individuals in institutional contexts that are not set up exclusively for this purpose. Instead, what frequently occurs in many public deliberative contexts is that the particulars of the encounter—the socially, politically, and historically motivated beliefs and practices of interlocutors—undergo processes of elimination, assimilation, or distortion, or are given minimal significance in the dialogue.

Discourse Ethics, Impartiality, and Social Justice

Discourse ethics has made a significant political and philosophical contribution toward understanding the link between social and communicative practices. It presents a notion of ethical subjectivity that recognizes its inherent inter-subjectivity, links the ethical beyond the question of duty, and demonstrates how communicative reason and reciprocal recognition can work together to achieve expanded worldviews or consensus amongst many different individuals and groups. It is also committed to a continual re-examination of the principles of recognition and reciprocity that underlie deliberative contexts in which frameworks for social justice are formulated. The attempt of discourse ethics to merge communication, ethics, and politics also sheds valuable light on the complex nature of the communicative contexts in which interpreters work. But while the elaborations of the notion of communicative reason by Benhabib, Honneth, and others better accommodate pluralism, particularism, and the psychological impact of withheld recognition on political participation and access to justice, their commitment to the moral and political intuition of impartiality and universality undermines these efforts. They assume that from the outset all conversational partners share a common communicative framework from which universally realizable moral judgments can be made and through which individual differences and agendas can be accurately interpreted and reconciled dialogically. However, as they readily acknowledge, in many situations, particularly those where questions of social status, political power, and fundamental beliefs are or become salient factors in the dialogue, universally realizable judgments may not be a shared aim.

Principles like truth, rationality, and justification cannot play the same grammatical role in every linguistic community because verbal transactions are always constrained by the nature of the social and political relationships amongst the participants involved. It may not be strategically beneficial for participants in one linguistic community to engage in a process in which their particular beliefs and practices are enlarged or subsumed into a universalizing discourse—whether they begin from positions of power or from social, political, or interactional disadvantage. In many juridical-political domains, the social and interactional value of particular utterances—and any rational or justificatory principles that are perceived to underlie them—is decided by the more powerful conversational partners and the institutions they embody whose 'particular' worldviews are strategically or unconsciously misrecognized and misrepresented as 'universal' and impartial. Even a more concrete universalism is not necessarily in the interests of interactionally disadvantaged others where it means conforming to models of rationality and autonomy that distort or exploit their own particular agendas.

Ultimately both discourse ethics (explicitly) and interpreter ethics (implicitly) count on the presuppositions of discourse as the means to achieve, and even guarantee, ethical ends. They share a view of impartiality and rationality as the means to guarantee equality—a justification that remains unjustified in many of the public deliberative contexts in which interpreters work, where equal participatory rights are not a given and distorted communication remains the norm. Like discourse ethics, interpreting codes of ethics assume that the communicative, moral, and ethical tasks of interpreters can be accomplished simultaneously through the re-iteration of utterances in presumed democratic institutions. They assume a pluralistic democratic public sphere that is open to both expanding the semantic-symbolic environment and eroding the disjunction between 'law as power' and 'law as meaning' (Benhabib 2008: 49). However, in the public deliberative contexts in which interpreters work—where fundamental inequalities can exist with regard to recognition rights—the justification of impartiality often contributes to the legitimization of the moral, ethical, or evaluative discursive frameworks of powerful public institutions at the expense of less powerful voices. Even in institutions explicitly committed to giving a voice to the less powerful, the norm of interpreter impartiality can serve a prohibitive function in the fulfillment of this agenda. In the case of torture victims, for example, who Honneth rightly suggests come to view their own feelings with suspicion and to distrust their own instincts and desires, the standpoint of interpreter impartiality can, in some cases, be detrimental to the goal of helping to restore to post-trauma victims their inter-subjective security and visibility in the space of an interaction. Legal professionals in private practice or mental health professionals representing charitable institutions, bowing to the norm of interpreter neutrality, can be reluctant to accept the interventions of experienced interpreters or interpreters with personal experience of torture, despite the potential value of their input.

Paradoxically, in both interpreter and institutional codes, the 'duty' of impartiality is often represented as ensuring 'objectivity' in such contexts and as a warrant for the general acceptability of the 'just' outcomes that emerge. This is the same rationale used in support of impartiality in interpreter codes of ethics. Impartiality is believed to work simultaneously to ensure the possibility of semantic and pragmatic equivalence between utterances, to guarantee mutual understanding or agreement between interlocutors, and to position interpreters as neutral participants in deliberative contexts. In reality, however, impartiality taken together with neutrality can work in interpreted exchanges to limit the type of open confrontations envisioned by discourse ethics over how each participant understands, perceives, and experiences the deliberations taking place. Grounding interpreters' ethical and moral choices in universal, rationally accessible principles is inimical to the inherent ambiguity and contingency which characterize interpreted communication. Under certain circumstances it denies interpreters, and their interlocutors, the ability to give expression to what Zygmunt Bauman has described as the inescapable burden of individual conscience and our moral proximity to others (Bauman 1993: 53, original italics):

> Pointing my finger away from myself—'this is what people do, this is how things are'—does not save me from sleepless nights and days full of self-deprecation. 'I have done my duty' may perhaps get the judges off my back but won't disband the jury of what I, for not being able to point my finger at anybody, call 'conscience'. '*The duty of us all*' which I *know*, does not seem to be the same thing as *my responsibility* which I *feel*.

It is precisely at these moments of 'conscience' that the principles underlying current codes of ethics become particularly significant. These principles assume that the interpreter role can, in all cases, be detached from interpreters' personal responses to the injustices or ignorance of others, and that interpreter decisions are arrived at independent both of their relationship to social and institutional contexts and to their interlocutors, and of history. These assumptions are validated by the received wisdom that the view of interpreters as impartial actors is precisely what allows their interlocutors to trust them with their utterances and to trust in their utterances as well. They are also predicated on the belief that interpreters' ethical practices are rooted in and can be guaranteed by the objectivity of language itself. But principles like impartiality and neutrality do not guarantee the production and identification of objectively good and ethical judgments. As Barbara Hernstein Smith argues (1997: 22),

> [. . .] the idea of objectively good judgments, as distinct from judgments that are good under certain (perhaps quite broad ranges of) conditions and from the perspective of certain (perhaps highly relevant sets of) people, appears fundamentally untenable. It follows that no matter what principles we erect or invoke, whether epistemological, ethical or procedural, "the best judgments" will still always be contingent in their production and operation, and also only contingently and contestably identifiable as "the best".

The decisions interpreters make—their best judgments—in response to the promptings of moral and ethical responsibility are influenced by any number of contingent factors including: the nature of their relationship to the individuals, communities, or institutions involved; whether they have or can acquire some professional authority or autonomy in the specific context; and their own prior experiences, values, and beliefs. These factors cannot be bracketed out from the task of interpreting; they are central to interpreters' abilities to make their best professional judgments in a particular context and for a specific group of interlocutors. One broad approach that attempts to take these factors into account is communitarian ethics which relates questions of justice, not to universal principles, but to community-based values, traditions, and histories.

COMMUNITARIAN ETHICS: CULTURAL COMMUNITIES, SOCIAL CONNECTIONS, AND EXPANDING SOLIDARITIES

The term communitarian has been used to describe approaches to ethics that are critical of articulations of morality that rely on (or exclusively on) universalist and impartialist theories of communicative reason or justice. This view of ethics is presented in works that display as many differences as similarities (see Sandel 1982; Walzer 1983; MacIntyre 1988; Taylor 1989). It is not my intention here nor would it be possible to engage with the extensive range of ideas and phenomena they address. The ideas considered below, which informed debates during the 1980s on the 'context of justice' that remain relevant in the present, have been selected for their specific insights into the ethical complexities and challenges interpreters face in attempting to secure just outcomes for particular individuals or groups in particular settings. They suggest possible answers to the question raised at the beginning of this chapter regarding what might constitute an example of ethical or unethical practice if ethical subjectivity were detached from the notion of impartiality as defined in existing interpreting codes of practice.

Communitarians share a similar starting point as Habermas and discourse ethics in exploring the question of how to establish relations of mutual recognition amongst the members of increasingly fragmented modern liberal societies. They dispute the idea that the modern state of liberal society—in which individuals do not share or have access to a single moral culture within which they can learn how they ought to live—requires the prioritization of procedural justice over substantive conceptions of the good. This, they argue, creates an overreliance on the state to resolve conflict and facilitates a vision of society made up of isolated strangers rather than ones in which individuals feel bound together in cultural and political communities. They believe instead that, despite the isolation and differentiation associated with the increasing forms of mobility occurring in modern liberal societies, communal identity continues to be constitutive of an individual's identity; it remains a central force for constructing the self and its attachments to others. Communitarians are also critical of liberal theorists like John Rawls for maintaining that to achieve consensus amongst individuals who hold different worldviews, members of a society must operate behind a 'veil of ignorance'. They do not view individual or collective prejudices as inherently negative, as bars to mutual recognition, but as serving as the conditions for understanding amongst members of the same or different communities.[3] Unlike Habermas and others, communitarians do not see the dissolution or transformation of prior held beliefs coming from an appeal to universal validity or rationality. Principles like truth and justice are not taken to be transcendental concepts, but as terms whose meanings are acquired, contested, and transformed through their articulation in intra- and inter-cultural relationships and their embodiment in social and cultural practices. They are critical of the idea that universal ideals and principles precede the relations of reciprocal trust and justice that are established by persons in the context of communities.

Partiality, Loyalty, and Commensurability

A vital aim of communitarian approaches has been to detach ethical subjectivity from notions of impartiality and universal concepts of justice and to attach it to notions of culture, community, and solidarity, creating a socially constructed and culturally situated inter-subjective approach to ethics that challenges the Kantian distinction between reason and sentiment, in which justice is viewed as rational and objective and sentiment is associated with personal attachments. Rather than view communal actions and identities as secondary to justice, or as inferior forms of morality because they cannot be grounded in impartiality, they are considered as morally significant precisely because they reference the particular over the universal. The 'moral facts' that operate authoritatively in a given community are, in this view, socially constructed and contingent: the product of time, accident, external force, political compromise, fallible and particularist intentions (Taylor 1985: 19). They emerge from the cultural understandings and identities of the members of a particular political community, who at any one time may confirm, contest, or transform received opinion (*ibid.*: 27).

From within the communitarian perspective, Charles Taylor specifically discusses the role of language and communication, highlighting how individual and communal identities are formed in dialogical relations with others within structures of interlocution (1989: 36):

> I am a self only in relation to certain interlocutors: in one way in relation to those conversation partners which are essential to my achieving self-definition; in another in relation to those who are now crucial to my continuing grasp of self-understanding—and of course, these classes may overlap. A self only exists within what I call "webs of interlocution".

According to Taylor, to address someone, to open a conversation, establishes a "public space" (1985: 290) between interlocutors where attributions of meaning and understanding become possible. This space constitutes and is constituted by the individual, social, and historical contexts within which people engage in moral decisions. For Taylor, Michael Walzer, and other communitarians, the moral world and the social world are "more or less" coherent. As Walzer suggests, our "categories, relationships, commitments and aspirations are all shaped by, expressed in terms of, the existing morality" (1985: 20), though, importantly, morality can potentially subvert existing social and economic conditions: "the capacity for criticism always extends beyond the 'needs' of the social structure and its dominant groups" (*ibid.*). Against universalist approaches that seek to discover or invent moralities, Walzer argues that the experience of moral argument is best understood in the interpretive mode. For, he claims, "discovery and invention are efforts at escape, in the hope of finding some external or universal standards with which to judge moral existence" (*ibid.*). Furthermore, he suggests, "the moralities we discover or invent always turn out, and always will turn out, remarkably similar to the morality we already have" (*ibid.*: 19).

The communitarian perspective suggests that as moral discourse is always situated within individual, social, and historical contexts, the issue of the right thing to do is always about the right thing for us to do, according to whatever substantive conceptions of the good presently inform a community. This view challenges the 'view from nowhere' approach to ethical and moral judgment. However, it has also been criticized for internal inconsistencies—e.g., its accounts of justice cannot adequately address global issues; it has difficulty making sense of ethical discourse amongst interlocutors who do not share the same sensibilities and categories; and it is not sensitive enough to ethical pluralism. These have been addressed in different ways by communitarians. Walzer is committed to the view that political communities have the right to shape their own lives and that to be successful they require a sense of their own identity—a sharing of sensibilities and intuitions (Walzer 1983: 62). This grants them the right to protect their collective identity through balanced control over inclusion and exclusion (*ibid.*):

> Admission and exclusion are at the core of communal independence. They suggest the deepest meaning of self-determination. Without them, there could be no communities of character, historically ongoing associations of men and women with some special commitment to one another and some special sense of their common life.

Alasdair MacIntyre grounds his notion of community in the Aristotelian tradition of the virtues which emphasizes the means, or moral goods, by which humans attain sought after ends, their overarching purpose or telos. MacIntyre locates the moral and social goods of a community within its traditions and narratives which both serve as the justification for its actions and continuously affirm its identity. In order for humans to acquire independent judgment in modern society, he argues, they must reclaim as a primary virtue their dependency on others and recognize their own and others' vulnerability (1999: 150):

> To engage in this dialogue of question and answer, so that we make ourselves accountable to others and treat ourselves as accountable to them, we have to become able to assume the other's point of view, so that the concerns to which we respond in giving our account are the ones that are, in fact, genuinely theirs. If we are successful in so doing, we become able to speak with the other's voice and, if the conversation between us is sufficiently extended through time and is wide ranging enough in its subject matter, we will be able to speak with the voice of the other systematically, that is, to assert, to question and to prescribe in the light of the other's conception of our common good.

MacIntyre is doubtful that the nation state and its institutions can create the conditions for the acquisition of such virtues; community level organizations are his preferred sites for the realization of a never finally specifiable human telos that binds all communities together toward a common good, sites he views as inherently political: "To treat someone else as someone for whom we have a regard because of what, one way or another, they contribute to our shared education in becoming rational givers and receivers is to accord them political recognition" (*ibid.*: 141). Thus, it can be seen that Walzer's commitment to community poses limits on how far community can be extended to outside others without the sacrifice of communitarian principles, while MacIntyre's reliance on ideal and quasi-divine notions of political community—a site where different ethical worlds coincide perfectly—oversteps obstinate issues of diversity.

Both discourse ethics and communitarian perspectives recognize the significance of communication and political community to broaden our thinking with a view to increase understanding and reduce misunderstanding between ourselves and different others. Both perspectives acknowledge that linguistic and cultural meanings are not static in time or place. They differ significantly, however, over the question of impartiality. As I argued in the previous chapter, in communicative contexts where mutual recognition and understanding are at stake, there is no place for positions of impartiality or incommensurability; inter-subjective verifiability is possible only through the ethnographic encounter itself. Following Davidson, meaningful agreement or disagreement emerges from the activation of our cognitive capacity for mutual understanding in specific instances of communication, after which point it enters the realm of political discourse and constraint. With regard to interpreted encounters, although interpreters' actions cannot be linked to outcomes in a direct causal chain within public procedures where reciprocal trust and understanding are presumed, interpreters can feel directly responsible for outcomes. These instances make visible the ethical chain that links personal responsibility, political responsibility, and questions of justice.

CHARTING NEW GROUND FOR AN ETHICS OF INTERPRETING

In the following example, the reasons given by an interpreter experienced in working with torture victims for his intervention in a particular interaction, involving the torture victim, a therapist, and the interpreter himself, might easily be construed by some as unethical because of his duty to maintain neutrality. However, based on a combination of his professional experience, his knowledge of this torture victim (or maybe torture victims in general), or perhaps his visceral reaction to another's trauma, he responded based on what he 'felt it right to say' and on what was "a very important interpretation to make" to the therapist under the circumstances:

> I felt it right to say as I was interpreting, you know, "We're losing him! We're losing him!" A bit dramatically put, you know, but it's like the fact is he's [the torture victim] completely phased out, you know,

> I think it's important to, it's a very important interpretation to make, you know, "Hey he is not here at all, you know, we've got to bring him back". (Interpreter #5)

The decision to break with the duty to remain impartial is an important means available to interpreters to respond to the particular issues of justice that emerge in interpreted encounters. In the course of fulfilling their professional role, individual interpreters decide to act partially based on their membership in multiple communities which entail many dissimilar and potentially contradictory roles that are not easily integrated within one identity. Their sense of responsibility toward their interlocutors—whether a member of the public or another professional—can be influenced by feelings of professional or other forms of solidarity that may induce intense sympathy, moral responsibility, or hostility. These factors are traditionally viewed as irrational and without justification in interpreting activity, yet, they are the very things that inform and come to constitute a socially constructed ethics. There are no guarantees in these instances that interpreters will have evaluated accurately what is at stake in the interaction, just as there is no certainty that their judgments will produce a positive outcome for the victim, but this does not necessarily make their behavior 'unethical'. Fallibility is a part of and must be written into our understandings of the socially constructed moral spaces that interpreters inhabit.

The stage monologue *Witness*, written originally in Swedish and based on real events concerning a female interpreter who translates the stories of survivors of the war in the former Yugoslavia, addresses these issues directly. In the monologue, the interpreter—whose father was from the former Yugoslavia—recounts her struggles to maintain an emotional and psychological distance from the survivors of rape, torture, and imprisonment whom she translates for in their therapy sessions. As the play unfolds, the audience discovers that the interpreter became involved personally, including sexually, with one of the survivors, a male ex-prisoner of war, in clear violation of her professional code of ethics. In the following excerpt, she recalls the letter she wrote to him after witnessing him struggling to relate his experiences to the therapist, Göran, whom she perceives has become indifferent to his clients' stories (Parkert 1995: 42):

> 'Dear friend.' No, wait a minute, that's not what I wrote. 'Hi,' I wrote.
>
> 'Hi, I know that you need help and I don't know if I can help you. Your story moved me deeply and I got the impression that you know what it is that you need help with here in Sweden. Is that right? Is there anything I can do for you? Don't be afraid to ask me. Your fellow citizen.

Her break with duty is revealed when, after the client collapses at a refugee center, the police are called and take him to a psychiatric ward from where he calls her, and then Göran. As the play ends, the interpreter searches for justification for her actions (*ibid.*: 51):

> I was only trying to help. To DO something. And the moral is: Don't help out unless it's ethically correct? Is that what you want me to say? That my actions were wrong and selfish? Basically we're all as anonymous as the night and the dark.

The interpreter is traumatized by what she hears in the disturbing narratives she interprets, but as the monologue unfolds, it also becomes clear that she is traumatized by her inability to occupy a moral or social space both that feels legitimate to her personally and that is legitimated by her professional role. She struggles to find an identity from which to help, to do something that "comes from within" as she says (*ibid.*: 17):

> I've been interpreting for Göran for nearly three years. It's a long time to be someone else's voice and ears. It's hardly surprising you begin to wish you could act independently. Say something for yourself that comes from within.

This conflict is evident in her recall of the letter to the client, where she corrects her memory of using 'dear friend' as the term of address and replaces it with the less personal "hi", just as she concludes the letter with the apparently public 'fellow citizen'. However, the playwright sustains an ambiguity around fellow citizen insofar as there is not actual fellowship in their citizenship, yet at the same time the interpreter yearns to express the fellowship of suffering which she feels with him. This interpretation is reinforced earlier on in the text where the interpreter describes the point at which her own painful and tangled experience meshes with that of her client: "We talked a lot about what it's like when you no longer feel yourself, and about what the war has done to humanity" (*ibid.*: 43).

With respect to Göran there is a related ambiguity. Her critical perceptions of the interactions between Göran and his clients exist side by side with a certain admiration for the authoritative ease with which he can fleetingly inhabit these morally complex spaces: "I really admire Göran. He sort of has everything in its place" (*ibid* : 27). He has the power to decide on the direction of the interaction and to affect that through his utterances. She on the other hand has a voice which cannot speak.

As the monologue comes to an end, the interpreter describes seeing the client with one of the female survivors speaking about their ordeals during the war and enjoying a kiss. She comes to believe that her fellowship of suffering cannot be as spontaneously apprehended by him as that of another survivor: "He listened to her as someone who really understands and can listen. I was never able to listen to him that way" (*ibid.*: 50). Ultimately, she has lost confidence in both her voice and ears to sufficiently service the situated ethical responses to individuals with whom she feels in fellowship. Her obligation to maintain a neutral and impersonal moral starting point has proved impossible to uphold; and her role as interpreter does not provide her with any capacity to be a moral co-participant. The code of ethics which instructs her "that you mustn't become involved with the participants or bring them into your private life" (*ibid.*: 40) constructs an illusory boundary between the preservation of 'anonymity' and the exercise of moral subjectivity. The expectation of neutrality requires her to perform the impossible, to remain outside of any web of interlocution and to transcend the inherent situatedness of her identities, her loyalties, and her sentiments.

Interpreters must be permitted to exercise their agency to voice their concerns, to make what they deem to be the right ethical choice in the moment, even if their professional duty suggests otherwise. To be forced to inhabit a role without the ability to act on what they feel, as professionals, to be right at the time dooms interpreters to the kind of subservience portrayed in Kazuo Ishiguro's novel *The Remains of the Day* by the butler, Stevens, who in order to uphold the professional servant's ideal of dignity never allows himself to be "off duty"—as his character states in the novel (1989: 169):

> Any butler who aspires at all to a "dignity in keeping with his position" . . . should never allow himself to be "off duty" in the presence of others . . . A butler of any quality must be seen to inhabit his role, utterly and fully; he cannot be seen casting it aside one moment simply to do it again the next time as though it were nothing more than a pantomime costume.

Through the character of the butler, Ishiguro addresses the moral dilemmas of professionalism where inhabiting a role "utterly and fully" can lead to choices that cause the occupier of the role to experience confusion and regret. Stevens considers his employer, Lord Darlington, to be a good man and as such he is willing to remain loyal to him at all costs. On one occasion, for example, instead of attending to his father who lies dying in the upstairs bedroom, he stoically serves Darlington's dinner guests. At another point at his employer's request, Stevens dutifully fires two loyal servants because they are Jewish. When Darlington is later revealed to have served as an unwitting pawn of Hitler and eventually dies in disgrace, Stevens, who has always believed that his "professional prestige lay most significantly in the moral worth of his employer"(*ibid.*: 114), expresses his misgivings for his own lack of autonomy (*ibid.*: 243–244):

> Lord Darlington wasn't a bad man. He wasn't a bad man at all. And at least he had the privilege of being able to say at the end of his life that he made his own mistakes. His lordship was a courageous man.

> He chose a path in life, it proved to be a misguided one, but there, he chose it, he can say that at least. As for myself, I cannot even claim that. You see I trusted . . . All those years I served him, I trusted I was doing something worthwhile. I can't even say I made my own mistakes. Really—one has to ask oneself—what dignity is there in that?

Interpreters are often similarly dependent for their own personal dignity on the moral behavior of other individuals or the institutions in which they work. In the interaction with the torture victim referred to above, had the interpreter not intervened or not been given license to intervene for fear of violating an interpreter or institutional code, the suppression of the interpreter's voice may have contributed to the continued silence of the torture victim.

The ability of interpreters to act ethically and morally responsibly is also often hindered by the fact that in most interpreting situations the status of interpreters' knowledge remains contingent on the willingness of more powerful interlocutors to grant it social, political, legal, and interactional legitimacy. In interpreting contexts where an interpreter does not perceive a public deliberative procedure to be operating in the interest of justice, he or she may experience professional conflict and moral uncertainty. In these situations, existing codes of ethics offer little guidance for morally responsible action. This suggests that alternative ethical models are required which view conflict, uncertainty, and injustice as an inevitable condition of discourse rather than a temporary state of affairs that can be resolved in rational, discursive activity through communicative reason. Interpreters need an expanded view of the appropriate means for exercising professional ethical responsibility that doesn't require 'pointing my finger away from myself' or walking away.

Interpreters are acutely aware of the limitations of communicative reason, of the difficulty, and sometimes the impossibility, of making the meaning of one individual's utterances clear enough to another in a given context, especially in the face of opposing communicative objectives and imbalances of social or discursive power. They observe how and when the 'meaning of utterances' and 'meaning beyond utterances' merge in dialogue. They witness—and can themselves be party to—the rejection or acceptance of an utterance based on its merits, or because of a prejudice based in an individual's race, gender, religion, or ethnicity. In any conversation the potential for misunderstanding or misrecognition is a difficulty which interlocutors normally try to overcome. In interpreted interactions, it is an interpreter's greatest challenge.

Interpreter codes of ethics champion the impartial interpretation of utterances because it presumes to offer the same rights to all parties, regardless of their relational status or power within the interaction. It also allows interpreters who act impartially to remain morally blameless, without responsibility for the outcome of the interaction, regardless of whether it results in an individual being wrongly imprisoned or set free, deported or granted asylum, tortured or even killed. But when domination-free communication is not only not guaranteed but is positively constrained by legal and political institutions or between nations at war, the idea that impartiality guarantees the equal rights of interlocutors has a hollow ring. The idea that public procedures exist or can be established for the discursive justification of validity claims takes a long view of communication rights—a view which does not necessarily serve speakers who are discursively and procedurally marginalized in the here and now. More importantly, it is an implausible and untenable view given the contingency of language. No understanding of a given situation is proved right or true based solely on an appeal to discursive or moral rationality, whether the matter involves an individual's claim of political persecution in an asylum hearing or a nation's or group's claim that the war they wage is just. What makes a claim warranted is not its appeal to reason detached from social, economic, political, or cultural conditions, but its acceptance by a sufficient number of relevant others who have the power to determine that the claim is reasonable, and the influence to make others believe it too.

Interpreted interactions are different from other interactions in that they involve additional layers of complexity which may or may not be present in interactions where no interpreter is present. First, the very presence of an interpreter can be indicative of an imbalance of power between interlocutors, between an interlocutor and an institution, or both. Second, the interlocutors in an interpreted interaction may have had few or no prior opportunities to interact directly with one another's beliefs and values, making the linguistic, ethical, and cognitive demands far greater than in conversations amongst interlocutors with prior experience of one another. Third, given a lack of direct prior experience of one another, interlocutors may hold prejudices that negatively influence the degree of charity granted to one another's views. These views may be strengthened or weakened depending on the institutional context.

The triadic relationship between knowledge of oneself, knowledge of others, and knowledge of the world which, for Davidson, constitutes 'objective meaning' is not the end point; it is the starting point for tackling questions of social and interactional solidarity or inequality. The form of inter-subjectivity to which this triangulation process gives rise does not rely on a correspondence between linguistic systems or on the presuppositions of discourse; it relies on the acts of observation and interpretation that help interlocutors to ascertain which beliefs and values people 'hold true' with respect to the world cause them to produce the utterances they do. Though these observations and interpretations emerge in an immediate context, they are guided by intuitive predictions of meaning based on both prior habits and passing expectations of linguistic understanding. This 'simplest interpersonal situation', however, makes a complex cognitive, linguistic, and ethical demand on interlocutors, given the extent to which they must rely on the willingness of one other to act charitably in accommodating others' views, particularly ones which may betray expectations.

In interactions where interlocutors manage to work out misunderstandings or issues of misrecognition with little difficulty, interpreters can continue to act with the kind of minimal intervention prescribed in existing codes of practice. At most this might involve clarifying the meaning of a cultural term or concept, for example. However, in situations where the 'principle of charity' appears to be exhausted, interpreters are, and should be recognized as, an additional and invaluable resource to reinstate the process of inter-subjective understanding; they can help expand their interlocutors' capacity to think. Professional experienced interpreters who practice forms of 'creative interpreting' are attempting to do just this, sanctioned or not by the individuals or institutions in which they work. Interlocutors with the least powerful voices in an interaction depend on interpreters to be reliable agents for the retelling of their stories. Likewise, many professionals acknowledge and welcome interpreters as an invaluable resource in their own work. Operating within the triangular configuration of relations, interpreters occupy a unique position in the process of mutual knowledge building that interlocutors must go through in order to achieve meaningful dialogue. This does not imply that interpreters have special access to what interlocutors really mean—simply that they occupy a more significant seat at the negotiating table than is presently acknowledged.

Interpreters, like many other professionals, experience tensions between their everyday moral intuitions and the demands of their role within a particular institution. Professional codes and institutional demands do not make difficult ethical and moral decisions any easier, and they do not make immoral actions moral. These decisions are influenced by pragmatic, personal, and political realities which create various kinds of partnerships between interpreters and their interlocutors. Interpreters are active, key players in interpreted communication, facilitating open negotiations over meaning and maximizing the possibility that the communicative objectives of all participants are met; they require codes of practice in which principles like neutrality or impartiality are not taken to mean the abdication of personal and social responsibility in their role.

3 Morality and Im/Partiality on Trial

Toward a Justice-Seeking Ethics

The views expressed by interpreters working in national and international judicial and political contexts indicate that their decisions, about both whether to interpret and how to interpret in a particular situation, extend far beyond questions of semantic or pragmatic competence; even the simplest decisions can expose complex moral and ethical relationships which interpreters must navigate. Under these circumstances, tensions can emerge between the moral 'person' and the ethical 'professional', a distinction moral philosophers sometimes make between 'ordinary' morality, the moral obligations that bind individuals (whether these are understood to be based in rights-based liberal individualism, communitarian, or universalist ethics), and 'role' morality, the duties and loyalties that go along with various social roles. Whereas ordinary morality assumes an evolving moral code that is shaped within one or more cultures and societies, role morality applies to standards or codes of behavior expected by a professional group to which an individual belongs. This distinction parallels the relationship between the 'moral' which relates to individuals or communities and the 'ethical' which stresses a social system in which those morals are applied, tested, or refused.

Interpreters and translators are not unique in experiencing conflict between their own moral intuitions and the ethical requirements of their professional role. The question of role morality has been considered in areas as diverse as the law, the military, business, politics, the media, bioethics, and the medical profession (see Goldman 1980; Bowie 1982; Gert and Culver 1982; Luban 1988; Applbaum 1999; Gibson 2003; Tanovich 2005; P. Robinson et al. 2008). The distinction between ordinary morality and role morality is often positively understood within these professions as a means by which individuals and groups handle the tensions that arise between their everyday moral intuitions and the requirements of a professional role. This chapter examines this distinction more critically. It considers whether or to what extent the duty for interpreters to adhere to a specific role morality should outweigh their moral inclination to act ethically in ways that stand to violate professional codes of practice. Departing from the interpreting profession, by way of comparison, the chapter also examines ongoing debates of legal practitioners within the legal field on this topic. The legal profession is particularly pertinent because, as in the interpreting profession, language, interpretation, and questions of partiality and impartiality are central issues related to its challenge of ensuring equal justice for all.

ROLE MORALITY

The concept of role morality combines philosophical inquiry into moral behavior with sociological considerations of roles within particular fields and professions. The ethics philosopher Alan Goldman defines it in the following way (Goldman 1998: 576–577):

> Roles are positions in business or the professions to which different social functions attach; role morality is the assumption of different normative ethical systems for different roles. The central issue here is whether different social roles require distinct norms or moral frameworks to guide their behavior. For there to be truly distinct role moralities, it is not sufficient that those in different social roles or professions enter into unique relations with others. All social roles involve relations that uniquely define them to be the roles they are. Instead, moral considerations that arise elsewhere must be weighed differently, must be systematically augmented or diminished in their weight, against opposing considerations in proper moral deliberations in these social contexts.

Role morality makes moral criticism of an action from outside a practice—from the perspective of 'moral decisions that arise elsewhere'—irrelevant or even impossible; it implies that ordinary moral judgments are too subjective to ensure the fulfillment of certain professional duties. The concept of role morality presupposes that particular actions taken in the name of an institutional practice are justified and can be evaluated only by standards internal to the practice. From the point of view of moral theory, a crucial issue is whether role morality is a morally acceptable, coherent concept. Goldman considers, for example, whether moral rights should be overridden in the business field to maximize profits or in the legal field to defend a client zealously "if the aim is not to protect more central or important rights in a particular situation, or to prevent greater harm or to realize a collective good" (*ibid.*). He suggests that any justification of special role moralities, even if coherent, must be subject to scrutiny, given that other important moral factors may be sacrificed.

The legal philosopher David Luban has argued that creating a distinction between ordinary morality and role morality deflects ethical judgment away from personal responsibility. To favor role morality to resolve a conflict through an appeal to a role or the institution that creates that role, even a "morally good one", he claims, too often excuses individuals from considering their personal moral obligation in a conflict. He characterizes a number of moral dilemmas which an 'institutional excuse' creates (Luban 1988: 130–131):

> The structure of this institutional excuse may be spelled out as follows: she points out that the role act of complying with P is required by her role obligation, which in turn is necessary to perform the role's institutional task, which (finally) is justified by the positive moral good of the institution. Taken together, these obligations for the role act outweigh the obligation to do X. [. . .] The general problem, which creates the dilemma, is that the propositions "The institution is a morally good one" and "The institution imposes role obligations on its officers, some of which may mandate morally bad role acts" can both be true. In fact, the problem is more complicated than that because the structure of the argument I have just described contains two terms between institutions and role acts (namely role and role obligations) and the general problem that moral good can authorize moral wrong is replicated at all stages. Good institutions can require unsavory roles; good roles can have unwelcome obligations attached to them; and honorable obligations can require awful actions.

Luban maintains that institutional excuses do not absolve individuals from moral criticism even in relation to morally good institutions. Role morality assumes a 'policies' over 'acts' approach that he considers untenable. He suggests that in taking their role seriously individuals must also acknowledge the moral limitations of the role and refrain from the mechanical application of duties that are institutionally imposed. Moral judgments or decisions made by occupants of a particular role should not be evaluated in the abstract in relation to a set of policies or a code of practice, for this ignores the contextual factors and particularities of each situation (*ibid.*: 116–120). Luban argues for what he terms a 'morality of acknowledgment' which grants occupiers of a role the freedom, given the particularities of a case, to respond to the specific moral demands of others (persons qua persons) regardless of the normative ethical demands of the role (*ibid.*:127). This does not make roles or the policies underlying them irrelevant or without force and it does not suggest that 'role morality' should never prevail. It simply means that no role can demand that its occupant be blind to the moral worth of others regardless of the situation.[1]

The decision to interpret or refuse to interpret in a particular social or interactional context involves a significant moral decision that can have wide-ranging personal and pragmatic consequences. Role morality, however, is more specifically concerned with the moral dilemmas that arise once the decision to act in role has been made. Role morality prescribes moral behavior in acts undertaken within a practice; it refers to an institutionally established fixed distinction between the moral justification of an action taken in role and that taken outside of the role. Though individuals across a range of professions will exercise different degrees of autonomy regarding their adherence to this distinction, it is generally accepted as a necessary requirement and one which helps to shield members of a profession from ethical conflicts that may arise between their personal intuitions and professional obligations. Within the interpreting profession, the principles of neutrality, partiality, and confidentiality, coupled with the highly valued narrative of interpreters' social and interactional invisibility, are intended to act in this way. However, as has been demonstrated, these principles often prove ineffective in handling the complex task of responding effectively and responsibly to the moral imperatives that emerge in particular contexts.

Role Morality as Political Morality

Ethics scholar Arthur Applbaum disputes the inherent virtue of person-neutral roles in which individuals are "alienated from the projects, commitments and relationships that are worthy of self-respect and the respect of others". He questions the demand they make on individuals to exclude reasons for their actions that draw on personal resources or ones shared with others, including "extraprofessional projects, values, commitments, relationships" (Applbaum 1999: 64–65):

> The epithet "faceless nameless bureaucrat" is in this sense a virtue: actions of an official should not depend on her identity, attributes, or values. To varying degrees, the professional role of soldier, business manager, journalist, lawyer, and doctor also demands that actions taken within the role be faceless and nameless, in that the role occupant is required to ignore some set of personal resources. In return, the person-neutral occupant is to be spared personal judgments that do not bear on performing the role well.

Against the ethical demand for a role-relative, person-neutral morality, Applbaum recommends what he refers to as political morality, one grounded in civic virtues like justice, liberty, equality, utility, legitimacy, and democracy. Political morality, he suggests, offers individuals the justification, legitimation, and obligation to respond to a particular situation that supersedes person-neutrality on the grounds that the decision can be "justified to reasonable people holding different philosophical or religious views of the good life" (*ibid.*: 68). Political morality, in Applbaum's view, can provide individuals in professional roles with the critical distance to make valid moral judgments; it can allow professionals to be morally accountable to persons as persons, and not mere occupants of a role.

Applbaum's conceptualization of political morality may serve as a potential guide to the contradiction pointed out by Luban that institutions can be morally good ones yet impose role obligations on their professionals, some of which may mandate morally bad role acts, and to the question of individuals' authority to question as unjust the legitimate practices or policies of their professional institution. Applbaum's answer to the question "Who is to say that one's judgments about political morality are correct?" is this (*ibid.*: 71):

> One has no choice but to judge all things from where one stands. Once one has employed methods of reflection and evidence that withstand the tests of publicity and universalizability, so that one reasonably believes that one's inferences would be reasonable for a reasonable person to make, skepticism has been answered as well as earthlings can answer it.

The type of moral reflection Applbaum refers to here, where "tests of publicity and universalizability" occur, requires the creation of social and communicative contexts in which the reasonably arrived at perspectives of the relevant participants can be voiced. Importantly, however, as I argued in the previous chapter, the admission of personal or political judgments in the context of a role does not require a determined set of ideal, universal validity claims. The type of reflection backed up by evidence that withstands the scrutiny of a relevant public envisioned by Applbaum requires no more than a legitimate space for role occupants to reflect upon or challenge the rules and principles of their professional code and to enter into open and transparent dialogue in situations where gaps are perceived between the norms and interests of the profession and those attached to specific individuals, communities, or the wider society. The weaker distinction between a role and a person that such a dialogue can bring about acknowledges that professionals operate in a world of situated human practices, not abstract de-contextualized policies, where the benefits of a morality of acknowledgment would seem to far outweigh those of a morality of non-accountability. The firm line which the concept of role morality attempts to draw between professional judgments based on the requirements of one's role and the practical judgments of individual persons greatly oversimplifies the complexity of the ethical demand in social and interactional contexts. Its person-neutral prescription does not adequately distinguish between a perspective or a prejudice and a fraud or a deceit. Where questions of justice are concerned, the admission of moral subjectivity not only should be permitted to inform the decision to refuse a role due to an irresolvable conflict of interests, it should also be viewed as a legitimate resource with which to face the ethical demands of a particular situation within a practice.

It is not a simple matter for professionals to act reflectively in relation to the official policies that guide their occupations. As I have argued elsewhere (Inghilleri 2003, 2005), following Bourdieu, the collective understandings of the occupants of a role come to form a coherent rational worldview that can be difficult to penetrate from within. Members of established professions tend to reproduce with a good deal of certainty what they feel to be the goals and purposes of their role as well as the beliefs that underlie these. Attempts by role occupants to define or redefine their positions within a given profession are likely to be oriented toward the correction or adaptation of their individual practice rather than overt strategies designed to challenge or resist the official codes that guide them. However, the actions of individuals within an established practice can also serve to reconstitute the social; role occupants who manage to extend (and are permitted the space to extend) their subjectivity beyond the perimeters set by the role demonstrate the capacity of the role in a particular instance to integrate a more expansive morality of acknowledgment, particularly where questions of justice are involved. The principles, norms, and habitual actions associated with or prescribed by a role require constant innovative and creative interpretation, not abstract application, in order to respond to the ethical demands of particular situations. In circumstances where occupants of a role are propelled to act in more morally expansive ways than those prescribed by the role, the abstract principles underlying their role morality are likely to come under scrutiny.

There is a clear relationship between the philosophical concept of role morality and Bourdieu's more sociological conceptualization of the habitus-field relationship which I have explored elsewhere with respect to interpreters (Inghilleri 2003, 2005). Both recognize an ontological complicity between a role and its occupants and call attention to the difficulties involved in stepping outside of a role in order to reflect upon its codified rules and obligations. From a sociological perspective, however, role morality is more significant in how it serves to maintain structural hierarchies of power and knowledge, whereas from a philosophical standpoint, its significance lies in its potential to encourage moral closure. It is feasible, however, to view these perspectives as complementary where the aim is to consider how far the person-role-context relationship can also be considered as a force for moral, social, and political change.

ROLE MORALITY AND THE LEGAL FIELD

In debates over legal ethics, many, if not most, legal scholars and practitioners take the broad view that the institutions of the law and the democratic principles that inform them function to ensure impartial outcomes without the need to involve ordinary morality. Indeed, the two principal features of the 'standard conception' of the lawyer's role in the adversary system are: first, that lawyers should respect the law and its procedures; and second, that they should represent their clients 'zealously' within the bounds of the law. The procedures of justice decide the limits of what counts as legitimate zealous advocacy. Traditionally, a fundamental role of lawyers has been to fulfill the moral obligation of the legal system to protect the rights of its constituents. The adversarial procedures attached to the Anglo-American system of justice identify the professionalism of lawyers with the principles of partisanship, neutrality, and non-accountability. These principles are upheld through the zealous pursuit of the lawful objectives of clients without regard for an individual lawyer's personal views about the moral merits of a case or a particular client's character. Lawyers are deliberately not held to account for the moral worth of a client's actions or objectives as this might result in an individual not securing the legal representation required for the proper functioning of the adversarial system.

A standard defense of neutral partisanship—i.e., morally neutral, non-accountable partisanship—is grounded in their fidelity to the law and its institutions, both of which are deemed to embody the pluralist views and fundamental moral concerns of all individuals in a representative democracy. Lawyers must be committed to the principle of universal access to justice regardless of their own personal views of the actions of a particular individual (Freedman 1966, 1992; Yellen 1998/99). An increasingly contentious issue within legal ethics, however, has centered on the question of whether a professional ideology that treated lawyers' personal morality as relevant to their professional conduct would inhibit their ability to morally and ethically serve their clients within the adversarial system of justice (Postema 1980).

According to the 'standard conception' within the legal profession, in the name of 'zealous advocacy', lawyers' duty to their clients' interests must always be placed as high as or higher than third party interests even if it means acting in ways that would otherwise be morally impermissible. Both lawyers and judges are trained to interpret the law objectively as a body of historically and internally coherent rules. A primary concern regarding ethical practice is how to maintain fidelity to the 'objective' constraints of the law as an independent text and, at the same time, to act in ways that are morally and legally justified as well as politically legitimate (Dworkin 1986).

The neutral partisanship that underwrites the legal system has come under criticism by some legal professionals and scholars for sustaining an image of lawyers as professional hired hands who act with 'hyper-zeal' to employ whatever legal means available to pursue their clients' objectives, even where the ends extend beyond their clients' legal entitlements. This expectation conflicts with the idea most lawyers have of themselves as facilitators of justice whose role it is to protect the interests of their clients with 'mere zeal', that is, based on a fair and balanced understanding of their legal claims (Dare 2004). For many, the obligation that a lawyer lends uncritical support to a client's ends by "maintaining no voice of her own but instead continually working merely as a mouthpiece, speaking for her client" is viewed as a distinctively lawyerly virtue that cannot be evaluated from outside the profession without compromising the traditional role (Markovits 2004: 273; and see Freedman 1966, 1992). At the same time, the position of modern lawyers has increasingly become subjected to moral ideals that emanate from the world at large that can be at odds with the established traditions of the profession. As the boundaries between ordinary morality and role morality have weakened, attempts have been made within the legal field to reform, reconstruct, and/or re-describe the framework of professional responsibilities in ways that account for the effects on personal conscience and the broader social and political consequences involved in 'thinking like a lawyer'.[2] Unsurprisingly, most attempts at reform are designed to avert the type of existential crisis elucidated by Markovits rather than to develop strategies to challenge or resist the 'standard conception' of the lawyer's role.

Debates over the defining principles of the lawyer's role are structured around the distinction between zeal and integrity, analogous to the role morality and ordinary morality distinction; though not all legal scholars embrace or employ these terms. The problem of zeal refers to "the capacity of a theory [of legal ethics] to capture what in legal terms is known as the agency nature of the lawyer-client relationship—that is the right of the client to direct the lawyer as an instrument in attaining those ends", whereas "the problem of integrity refers to the ability within a theory of legal ethics to take account of the perspective of the lawyer, who remains a moral agent—as opposed to being legally an agent of the client—and who wishes to respect the demand of morality" (Wendel 2010: 262 n.39). The various ways legal scholars and practitioners have attempted to comprehend the impact on ethical practice of the potentially problematic relationship between zeal and integrity provides valuable insights into relevant thorny problems that can arise both socially and interactionally for interpreters and their interlocutors in seeking just processes and outcomes.

In order to explore these issues for their relevance to interpreting practice, I have selected three perspectives on the zeal/integrity debate for consideration. Each one addresses the relationship between lawyers' moral agency and integrity from a different angle: personal reflection, the interpretive community, and contextual judgment. The first two emphasize the fundamental principles of the law itself that serve as constraints on the profession, while the third perspective places more stress on the responsibility of individual lawyers to make complex and flexible judgments about the law, even invalidating aspects of it, depending on the context of each case. All reflect different components of the debates within analytical jurisprudence about the nature of the relationship between law and morality, and between law and society.

The primary purpose of this exercise is to make clear that the moral and ethical dilemmas which principles such as neutrality and non-accountability create for interpreters are not unique to their profession, and to demonstrate that such principles are no more adequately justified in legal codes of ethics than they are in interpreter codes of ethics from the point of view of role morality alone.[3] Neither profession fundamentally succeeds in fully resolving the question of how individuals reconcile their personal identity, autonomy, and integrity while operating as instruments of others' aims and objectives. For both lawyers and interpreters, when tensions occur between role morality and ordinary morality the appeal to role morality and the person-neutral stance is seen as a means to make the complexity of the ethical demand more manageable. However, the debates over legal ethics demonstrate that lawyers are unavoidably implicated as moral and ethical agents in their clients' objectives. The question that remains for lawyers concerns the means that are available for them to represent this experience to themselves and to determine their own agency within it. The question for the legal profession as a whole is to what extent society's interest is served by the neutral partisanship of lawyers.

The Reflective Individual and Fidelity to the Law

One suggestion is for lawyers to engage in an individual deliberative process, one in which their response to the ethical demand brought about by a particular client's actions or objectives is to engage in quality reflection over the demands of their role, and be willing to embrace the outcome of that reflection even when contradiction or conflict remain with respect to their moral agency. The primary emphasis is on the quality of the reflection, not the substance of the ethical demand or its outcome. The idea is that to remain persons of integrity, lawyers must find a way to justify the authority of the law and their role responsibilities to themselves—to bridge the gap between role morality and ordinary morality by exercising their engaged moral judgment (Dare 2010: 120):

> . . . what matters for integrity is not the outcome of the pursuit of integration-integrity—not the attainment of perfect integration—but instead the critical engagement with one's position, the acknowledgment of the tensions it contains, the participation in finding a way to live a satisfying life in the face of its competing demands. We should often be prepared to regard someone who has reflected upon their situation and decided what weight to give what preferences in what circumstances, who can describe her situation, who gives an account of why she has something other than a unitary ordering of volitions and desires—as a person of integrity.

The problem that the reflective individual attempts to solve is not the ethical matter as such, but the distance it creates between professional and private moralities. The purpose of such reflection is to permit lawyers to inhabit their role with less moral uncertainty, and to replace it with greater certainty of the character of the political processes and institutions of law. The desired outcome is the strengthening of the legitimization of the moral, ethical, and evaluative frameworks of the law and its institutions.

The Interpretive Community and Fidelity to the Law

Another suggestion is that, particularly under circumstances where procedural constraints on partisanship are absent, for example, where there are no judges to act as impartial referees, lawyers draw moral guidance from a unifying deliberative framework emanating from the "interpretive community" of legal professionals which acts as both a measure of their integrity and a check on their zeal (Wendel 2005). In this view, the legal community, not the isolated individual, establishes concurrence between a lawyer's moral values and the substantive meaning of the law. The community of legal professionals both establishes the criteria for a reasonable exercise of moral judgment and serves as a constraint on what counts as legitimate and illegitimate constructions of the law (*ibid.*: 1173):

> . . . there is no such thing as a self-interpreting legal text that regulates the actions of lawyers or clients apart from the exercise of judgment by a community of professionals. As a consequence, the law cannot operate as a device to settle normative conflict and coordinate activity without a commitment on the part of law-interpreters to respect the substantive meaning standing behind the formal expression of legal norms.

The interpretive community establishes the "higher-order standards" that help distinguish "artificial, abusive transactions that comply only formally with legal rules from those transactions that comply substantially with the law" (*ibid.*: 1209).[4] In this way, the interpretive community is seen to act as a stable justificatory support for ethical practice based in existing legal norms, and also to make lawyers publically accountable to one another for the ethical standing of their decisions. Importantly, the interpretive community does not expect to impose a consensus amongst lawyers on the substantive meaning of justice in any particular case; it merely acts as the deliberative framework within which the norms, standards, habits, and shared aims of the profession are exercised through both professional codes and the informal understandings built up within the profession over time.

In both of these conceptions of professional practice, the law and the institutions of the law are taken as the justification for zealous advocacy and the assurance of personal integrity. In the first approach, the responsibility is the individuals (recognized as a gendered, ethnic, religious, etc. self) to reconcile any tensions between ordinary morality and role morality. In the second, the interpretive community acts as an effective intermediary, a conduit even, standing between citizens or clients and their rights under the law. Both approaches restrict lawyers' reflexivity and responsibility to the limits of their role morality guided exclusively by the authority of the law. They are therefore never truly separated from their professional selves, whether they act as individuals or as a community. Moreover, given that lawyers are educated, trained, and derive their professional status within the same legal field that creates the ethical demand, their reflexivity remains grounded in their tacit faith in the established role morality of the field.[5] Additionally, because the same professional codes, legal rules, and principles to which the interpretive community is bound are routinely used strategically by its members to serve multiple and conflicting purposes, it is difficult to envisage this community operating effectively to set the threshold at which professional moral responsibility is met exclusively through fidelity to legal norms.

A partial resolution of these issues is offered in what can broadly be referred to as a contextualist approach to legal ethics. Proponents of this perspective attempt to reconstruct zeal and integrity by appealing to a more expansive view of the law, one that encourages a more explicit connection between legal norms and the wider society. Although supporters of this approach view this relationship in different ways, they are agreed that lawyers must assume greater personal responsibility for serving the interests of justice, and not merely the laws's or their clients' interests, by taking into consideration what societal norms require relative to a given situation. They reject the idea that morally good institutions cannot and do not legitimate morally bad acts, and insist on individual lawyers' obligation to question any unjust principles, practices or policies of their profession (see Luban 1988, 2007; Hutchinson 1995, 1998; Rhodes 2000).

Contextual Judgment and Fidelity to the Law

A leading proponent of the contexualist view, the legal scholar William Simon, believes lawyers need to redefine their professional obligations in terms of contextual judgment rather than categorical rules, to privilege the purpose of law over its form. He argues that lawyers should on certain occasions be free to "violate some legal norms to vindicate more basic ones" (Simon 1996/97: 252), for example, to betray a client's confidence or to take into account not just a client's rights but the legal entitlements of other relevant parties in order to prevent a significant injustice from occurring. Simon insists, however, that a lawyer's judgment be based in the sources of authority and methods of argument of the law, not in conceptualizations of justice issued in ordinary morality. Where he differs from the positions outlined above is that he advocates fidelity to the law only insofar as this does not conflict with a 'justice-seeking ethics' or a just ordering of the social world. According to Simon, an ethics oriented to justice requires lawyers to measure their zeal by taking into account the legal merits of their clients' claims or objectives (Simon 1988: 1083):

> Lawyers should have ethical discretion to refuse to assist in the pursuit of legally permissible courses of action and in the assertion of potentially enforceable legal claims. This discretion involves not a personal

> privilege of arbitrary decision, but a professional duty of reflective judgment. One dimension of this judgment is an assessment of the relative merits of the client's goals and claims and those of other people who might benefit from the lawyer's services. Another is an attempt to reconcile the client's goal and claims. In both dimensions, the basic consideration should be whether assisting the client would further justice.

For Simon, a lawyer's "professional duty of reflective judgment" should be directed at broadening the parameters of role responsibility to ensure that justice is advanced. Fidelity to the law involves the exercise of discretion in deciding not only what is formally or procedurally legally permissible, but what justice demands in substantive terms and in relation to societal norms. Rather than putting their resources into finding procedural loopholes in the law to protect their clients' interests, lawyers have a role obligation to ensure both that the legal process they submit to is fair for all relevant parties and that their own behavior contributes to rather than subverts that fairness (Simon 1999/2000: 1025). Though Simon maintains a clear distinction between "judgments based upon the law and naïve intuitions of fairness", others are somewhat more open to the use of resources and concepts from ordinary morality for the justification and articulation of professional judgments. The legal scholar Alan Hutchinson suggests that to expect lawyers to subordinate their personal morality to role morality amounts to a "two-dimensional moral universe in which lawyers are no more expected to intrude their own personal values than actors or butlers in the performance of their duties" (Hutchinson 1998: 178). Hutchinson also argues, from a pragmatist point of view, against the idea of interpreting moral responsibility solely through a body of rules or codes of practice that are applied universally across a range of different contexts (*ibid.*: 187):

> My approach suggests that legal ethics has more to do with a practice of situated reasoning and has more to do with the interests, purposes and consequences of the participants and their contexts. Reliance on codes atrophies the moral intelligence and leaves lawyers adrift without a moral compass when those professional rules run out or give conflicting advice: my approach encourages continual reflection and therefore better prepares lawyers for difficult situations.

Hutchinson's advocacy of a practice of 'situated reasoning' echoes my argument that interpreters be permitted to engage their moral intelligence to respond to the ethical demand in communicative contexts where significant mutual misrecognition and misunderstanding are at stake for an individual. For lawyers, this becomes necessary when a law appears unjust and the adversarial system ceases to operate to ensure justice for all. Under these circumstances, ordinary morality, operating publically and dialogically like 'political morality', can provide an additional voice for lawyers to respond to persons as persons in the interest of justice in a way that their role morality prohibits them from doing. As Luban expresses it, "Thus, when professional and serious moral obligation conflict, moral obligation takes precedence. When they don't conflict, professional obligation takes precedence" (Luban 2007: 63).

Political Morality and the Respect for Human Dignity

Deciding when a conflict is present is not, of course, something on which occupants of a role would necessarily agree. Luban suggests that "concern for human dignity" should serve as the overriding principle to make this determination (*ibid.*: 63; and see Donagan 1983). Importantly, though, Luban views the concept of human dignity not in a universal sense but as a "property of relations between human beings—between, so to speak, the dignifier and the dignified" (*ibid.*: 66) which permits individuals to tell their stories and be listened to in good faith. Elsewhere Luban states (Luban 1988: 86):

> If a lawyer serves as a surrogate or mouthpiece for the client in raising good faith claims about facts and law, then the lawyer's obligations are derivative of the client's. Precisely because the client is morally accountable for the means used and ends achieved in court, the lawyer is as well. Thus, the opposite of the principle of non-accountability follows from the human dignity defense of adversary advocacy. Indeed, the lawyer's behavior must on this view be imputed to the client, including actions on the lawyer's part that would be immoral for the client to perform; thus, for the lawyer to perform such actions is itself an assault on the client's dignity as a human being.

Interestingly, in this passage, Luban uses the terms 'surrogate' and 'mouthpiece' to define the lawyers' relationship to their clients as one of fidelity to their stories. He suggests that because lawyers translate their clients' stories into "facts and law" in order to present them in court, they have a responsibility to the courts, but more importantly, to their clients to ensure that they do not use their power to speak for their clients in ways that assault their dignity as human beings. This account of the lawyer-client relationship is not at all dissimilar from the relationship experienced between interpreters and individuals who are not adequately represented or not represented at all in situations where what is at stake is precisely their dignity as human beings, and where moral obligations take precedence for the interpreters present. This passage also suggests that regardless of the important differences that exist between lawyers and interpreters, the act of 'speaking for others' creates a similar ethical demand: to ensure that those others are adequately and justly heard.

As the re-tellers of others' stories, lawyers and interpreters are involved in their translation, whether this occurs from ordinary speech into legal discourse or from one language into another. It is not surprising that both professions appeal to neutrality and non-accountability in order to separate the professional tellers from the stories they present to others. This is assumed to protect and distance the professionals (whether lawyers or interpreters) from any responsibility for their content. At the same time, it is deemed to protect the stories' subjects from any potential biases on the part of the professionals. But lawyers can no more shield themselves from moral responsibility by appealing to fidelity to the law than interpreters can by appealing to fidelity to language. The law and language cannot be protected from manipulation by any of the parties involved; there is no such thing as a self-interpreting text of any kind. Though the law and language may operate effectively enough for 'professional obligations to take precedence' enough times to maintain the status quo of professional practice, the difficult situations experienced by lawyers and interpreters alike in representing less powerful others can frequently call established practice into question, leaving both groups of morally and ethically inclined professionals 'adrift without a compass'.

MORALITY AND IMPARTIALITY ON TRIAL IN POSTVILLE, IOWA: THE LAW, THE INTERPRETER, AND THE COURTS

An interesting example of the kind of moral and ethical dilemma that lawyers and interpreters confront in which professional and moral obligations come into conflict was the highly controversial U.S. immigration raid by Immigration and Customs Enforcement (ICE) on hundreds of allegedly undocumented workers at a meat-packing plant in Postville, Iowa, in May 2008. The raid gained the attention of the interpreting field due to an essay written and circulated to the profession by Erik Camayd-Freixas (Camayd-Freixas 2008a), one of the interpreters for the group of criminal defense attorneys appointed by an Iowa District Court. Camayd-Freixas also testified and submitted a written statement to the Congressional Hearings held in July 2008 (see Subcommittee on Immigration, Citizenship, Refugees, Border Security and International Law 2008 for a full record of the hearings) as an eyewitness to events that took place over the two-week period of the legal proceedings. His written statement along with those of representatives of the American Civil Liberties Union (ACLU 2008a), a representative of the American Immigration Lawyers' Association (AILA) (Leopold 2008), and a local attorney, Rockne Cole (Cole 2008), among others, catalogued numerous violations of due process with regard to the 'fast-tracked' detention, sentencing, and imprisonment of close to 300 of the detained workers, mostly from Guatemala.

The ACLU report describes the raid as a "preplanned and massive *criminal* prosecution of immigrant workers for allegedly using false documents to work" (ACLU 2008a: 2, original italics), a charge normally treated as a civil offense. Representatives from the U.S. Attorney's Office and the Department of Homeland Security suggested that the workers could be charged with 'aggravated identity theft', a felony crime that carried a mandatory two-year minimum jail sentence if they did not accept several possible plea deals which appeared to have been agreed with the District Court judge in advance of the raid and before defense attorneys had even spoken to the defendants (see ACLU 2008b, Preston 2008c). The deal proposed for the majority of the workers was to plead guilty to a lesser felony charge of 'knowingly' using a false Social Security number or a false employment document and receive a maximum of five months in jail. All charges would be accompanied by a judicial order of deportation following completion of the sentence. A decision to plead not guilty would mean that the 'aggravated identity theft' charge would be applied, a charge that implied a six- to eight-month wait in jail for a trial with no possibility of bail because of the deportation order (Preston 2008c: 4). The workers were given seven days to accept the plea agreement; one attorney was appointed for every seventeen defendants on average. The report states (*ibid.*):

> Under the circumstances of Postville, with multiple defendants represented by a single lawyer, complex immigration issues, and significant language, educational and cultural barriers, the extreme time limit made adequate legal defense, investigation and counseling almost impossible. Within days, defendants routinely waived all of their rights—including their right to indictment, to court reporters, to review the pre-sentence investigation report, and to appeal their convictions and sentences—and pled guilty . . .

The Lawyers

Within ten days of the arrest, a letter was sent from the national president of AILA to the U.S. Department of Justice, and in a written statement to the Congressional Hearings, the immigration attorney and national vice president of AILA at the time, David Leopold, raised doubts about the adequacy of the workers' defense due to the absence of court-appointed lawyers who were specialists in both criminal and immigration law. Given that most of the public defenders were criminal lawyers, defendants were not provided specialist immigration counsel regarding the immigration consequences of their pleas or their individual eligibility for various forms of relief from deportation (Leopold 2008: 6).[6] Though Leopold maintains that "[b]y all credible accounts, the CJA [Criminal Justice Act] defense counsel did a valiant job defending the workers under the extremely difficult circumstances created by the government and the court", he nevertheless concludes that with regard to their immigration rights:

> The workers were essentially coerced into giving up procedural and substantive rights under the immigration law, including the right to a full hearing before an immigration judge which would have required the government to meet its statutory burden and afforded the defendants an opportunity to apply for relief from deportation.[7]

In the end, despite or because of the numerous contextual factors that significantly reduced the possibility of an adequate legal defense of the workers, the court-appointed lawyers advised their clients that pleading guilty to the lesser charge was in their best interest, although it was recognized, as one of the lawyers is quoted as saying, that the government used the threat of aggravated identity theft "as a mechanism to pressure people into taking the plea agreements" (Popper 2009). At least one criminal defense lawyer, however, is on record for refusing to participate in the proceedings. Rockne Cole, who submitted a written statement to the Congressional Hearings, had been called to the Iowa District Court on the day of the raids but, learning of the nature of the raids and the apparent coordination of the plea deals between prosecutors and court officials months earlier based on a presumption of the workers' guilt, decided that he could not participate in what he termed a "mass violation of rights" (Cole 2008: 4) Under the circumstances, he wrote in his statement, "[t]he court appointed attorney's role appeared to be only to act as a guilty plea processing clerk, and served only to expedite the mass waiver of rights" which was characterized by the "mass detention, roundup, representation plan, plea deals, and sentencing PRIOR to one single attorney consulting with a client" (*ibid.*)

The Postville prosecution is a clear example of the adversarial system ceasing to operate to ensure justice. Yet, there is little evidence in the public records that any of the perspectives on the zeal/integrity issue discussed above served the court-appointed lawyers in addressing what were, for some, clear ethical and moral concerns. Instead of the law monitoring the partisan advocacy of the lawyers, the defense lawyers became mere instruments of the zealous aims and objectives of the government. 'Fidelity to the law' in this case served the willful interpretation by ICE and the Department of Justice of the federal aggravated-identity-theft statute.[8] The justification of the authority of the law under these circumstances prevented members of the legal community from ensuring that due process prevailed.

Within the bounds of their role morality, it may be said that the lawyers 'did a valiant job' under the circumstances. However, the circumstances at Postville were arguably of the sort that required moral obligations to take precedence over professional ones. As Luban argues, where judgments based upon the law no longer prove reasonable, especially where the law is manipulated to serve a wider political and ideological agenda, the moral obligation to defend human dignity becomes a necessary part of legal practice. Under such circumstances, role morality must become politically and morally oriented toward the kind of 'justice-seeking' ethics that scholars like Simon and Luban support—one that allows the occupants of a role the critical distance necessary to make situationally informed moral judgments. It may be argued that the lawyers exercised their neutral partisanship in order to respond directly to their clients' expressed wishes to plead guilty to the lesser charges so that they could return home as quickly as possible. However, it is certainly worth considering what may have happened if out of concern for their clients' human dignity, the legal community—lawyers and judges alike—sought a way, when the professional rules ran out, to demand that the defendants were allowed to tell their stories and be satisfactorily heard. Instead they became caught up in a government agenda that injudiciously sought to conflate illegal immigration with criminality, terrorism, and national security. As one of the defense attorneys said of the plea agreements, "That's not the defense of justice. That's just politics" (Preston 2008a: 3).

The Interpreter

There is no question that Camayd-Freixas played a significant role in bringing many of the questionable practices that occurred during the two-week legal proceedings that resulted in the workers' imprisonment to public attention. An essay he wrote in June 2008, shortly after the proceedings ended, is cited in both the ACLU and AILA reports submitted to the Congressional Hearings, and after sending it to the *New York Times*, was the basis for his interview in July 2008 with Julia Preston, the *Times* national correspondent covering immigration, who wrote a series of articles on the Postville prosecutions (Preston 2000a, 2008b, 2008c). From his position as a Spanish-speaking interpreter, Camayd-Freixas was able to speak in detail about many of the workers' lack of understanding of the complexities of the legal proceedings, including the plea agreements they were persuaded to sign. According to Camayd-Freixas, many of the clients were illiterate in Spanish and some had no idea what a Social Security number was or what purpose it served; in some cases, their work papers had been filled out for them at the plant.[9] This suggested to him that they could not be guilty of 'aggravated identity theft' or the lesser charge of 'knowingly' using a false Social Security number for which they had pleaded guilty. Camayd-Freixas' investigation essentially confirms what Rockne Cole had suspected from the outset (Camayd-Freixas 2008a):

> Not only were defendants and judges bound to accept the Plea Agreement, there was also absolutely no defense strategy available to counsel. Once the inflated charge was handed down, all the pieces fell into place like a row of dominoes. Even the court was banking on it when it agreed to participate, because if a good number of defendants asked for a grand jury trial, the system would be overwhelmed. In short, "fast-tracking" had worked like a dream.

Camayd-Freixas' decision to expose the injustices he observed in his role as interpreter was unquestionably a welcome and highly commendable act. Under the circumstances, he did not accept that the principle of impartiality meant the abdication of his personal and social responsibility. On the contrary, Camayd-Freixas has insisted that it was his "interpreter's perspective as an impartial and informed layperson" that allowed him the "unique vantage point" from which to perceive the violation of the workers' legal right to due process and to exercise his civic duty to speak out, as he suggests in the following passage:

> . . . the interpreter is the only one who gets to see both sides of the coin up close, precisely because he is the only participant who is not a decision maker, and is even precluded, by his oath of impartiality and neutrality, from ever influencing the decisions of others. That is why judges in particular appreciate the interpreter's perspective as an impartial and informed layperson, for it provides a rare glimpse at how the innards of the legal system look from the outside. I was no longer sorry to have participated in my capacity as an interpreter. I realized that I had been privileged to bear witness to historic events from such a unique vantage point and that because of its uniqueness I now had a civic duty to make it known.

Here as in other statements (see 2008b) Camayd-Freixas likens his impartiality to the position of the outsider, the participant observer who, unlike the lawyer, remains outside the web of interlocution that comprises the legal system. This seems to me, however, to distort what actually happened in Postville where the adversary system essentially broke down and, on this occasion, took the lawyers and the judges with it, willingly or not. Camayd-Freixas has attempted to defend their participation by suggesting that they, unlike him, were unaware of the unfolding consequences of their individual actions. He writes (*ibid.*: 5):

> What was most peculiar about the Postville case is that, on paper, everything seemed to be following the law, but in actual practice there were shortcomings in due process at every step of the way. Each shortcoming, taken by itself (which was how the officers of the court would see it) did not appear so monumental, but put together (as the interpreters saw it), led to the most unjust results.

Camayd-Freixas is right to suggest that the presence of interpreters across the multiple contexts of legal proceedings provides them a distinct vantage point. However, their duty to remain impartial is normally understood as a duty to remain silent, even in the face of injustice, as presumed outsiders to the legal system. For interpreters working within this system, it is considered part of their role morality to leave the lawyers and the judges to question the unjust principles, practices, or policies of the judicial system. Contrary to Camayd-Freixas' statement that the interpreter is "the *only* participant who is not a decision maker, and is even precluded, by his oath of impartiality and neutrality, from ever influencing the decisions of others", in the Postville case, he was one of the only informed participants to decide to influence the decisions of others. (The only public record of a lawyer's proactive ethical stance in relation to the proceedings is Rockne Cole's decision not to participate.) In my reading of events, Camayd-Freixas' decision cannot be seen as an outcome of his professional duty of impartiality, at least not as this is normally understood, nor as a consequence of his position outside the legal system. Rather, it was his presence as an informed participant within the legal process that compelled him to promote the kind of 'justice-seeking ethics' that Simon and others have called for the legal community as a whole to embrace—an ethical approach that requires the abandonment of one's professional neutrality and non-accountability, the disclosure of one's partiality toward the less powerful, and the acceptance of one's moral responsibility for the fact that justice has not been served.

Camayd-Freixas' decision to exercise his civic duty reveals the extent to which he felt responsible for the wider social and moral implications of the public deliberative event he helped to facilitate. Though he may have strategic reasons for attributing his actions to his 'oath of impartiality and neutrality', if notions like impartiality and neutrality are to persist as guiding principles for the role morality of interpreters, his actions demonstrate that they need not imply the neglect of personal and social responsibility toward others where questions of justice and fairness are concerned. His actions also provide further evidence that interpreters' role morality can be freed from the neutralized morality that has traditionally defined it in the name of impartiality.

THE QUEST FOR INTEGRITY

The structure of the institutional excuse which justifies certain limits on reflection or expansion can make it difficult for lawyers and interpreters alike to perceive significant gaps between their personal integrity and their professional obligations. Where fissures do appear, principles like im/partiality, neutrality, and non-accountability create a distinction between rational judgments and subjective intuitions that is designed to restore the balance between individuals' actions in role and their personal beliefs and values. Ultimately, however, whatever the degree of reflection or expansion individuals undertake in order to manage ethical uncertainties in relation to their role morality, some moral 'residue' may always remain, leaving integrity only partially or temporarily intact. It may be the case that some form of compromise between the ideal and the real is always required in performing a role.

Interpreters' moral proximity to the less powerful individuals for whom they speak is not mediated by the 'facts and law' that help to shield lawyers from dilemmas that emerge between their role morality and ordinary morality. Interpreters have no comparable 'text' mediating their relationships with their interlocutors. As a result, their role morality may not necessarily shield them effectively from the ethical demand, particularly in the face of a clear injustice. Under these circumstances, interpreters may relate strongly to their less powerful interlocutors. At the same time, however, despite the claim of interpreters' neutrality with regard to the institutional contexts in which they perform their role, different institutions and their accompanying role moralities can play a part in the development and management of interpreters' ethical practice. Interpreters can come to adopt (and feel shielded by) the same role-based beliefs and values as the professionals with whom they work. Most of the time interpreters maintain a fair and balanced position between the different interests of their interlocutors. However, in some situations, as in Postville, an ethical response beyond their own or other's role morality may be deemed necessary.

The next two chapters consider the relationships between interpreters and the professions for whom and to whom they speak in two different contexts where interpreters have played a central role: the political asylum application process in the U.K. and the U.S. military occupation of Iraq. The discussion considers the tension between ordinary moralities, role moralities, and the political and structural influences of the institutional contexts in which interpreters, legal professionals, and military personnel are embedded; it considers the alliances that form amongst these role occupants and the challenges and changes to established role moralities that emerge as a result.

4 Linguistic Hospitality and the Foreigner

Interpreting for Asylum Applicants

The multicultural and multilingual public procedural contexts in which interpreters work involve them in webs of interlocution where differing descriptions and discourses compete for the most comprehensive account of a matter or event. Their role is to coordinate various interlocutors' interpretive theories, helping them reach sufficient inter-subjective understanding to achieve their respective communicative aims. Although interpreters' actions cannot be directly linked to outcomes in public procedures involving questions of justice, they nevertheless help to determine the ethical environment in which communication amongst the relevant participants occurs.

This chapter examines asylum adjudication in the U.K. in order to demonstrate the specific communicative and ethical demands on interpreters and their interlocutors in the juridical-political field. It considers the relevance of communitarian and universalist theories of ethics and justice in a context where national policies of exclusion predominate, and revisits Kant's notion of hospitality toward outsiders in the light of contemporary international migration. The chapter considers the universal criteria of eligibility and credibility upon which asylum claims are settled and their potential to create contradictions in the adjudication of politically and culturally embedded individual claims. The interviews, consultations, and hearings that take place in the array of contexts involved in asylum adjudication serve as key communicative sites for encounters between interlocutors' capacities for mutual understanding and different forms of discursive constraint. Interpreters play a pivotal role in each of these contexts by indicating, negotiating, and challenging the boundaries of communication amongst interlocutors and between the competing agendas of inclusion and exclusion.

SPHERES OF JUSTICE AND THE BOUNDARIES OF HOSPITALITY

Communitarian and universalist theories of justice form part of the discourse on human rights where different perspectives compete to formulate the criteria that will define who is a moral subject, who has ethical standing, or who merits ethical consideration. For communitarians, human rights make sense only in the context of a particular society or ethical community; the justifiability of a particular belief or practice is always contextualized. Rights have no separate ontological status; they are products of a particular kind of society. There are, however, situations where a 'thin' moral code is enacted for humanitarian reasons perhaps, when members of one ethical community are moved to bring members of another ethical community within their own ethical 'jurisdiction' without any subjective distinctions between 'them' and 'us'. With regard to international human rights, the 'culturalist' position has been criticized on a number of inter-related fronts, including its tendency toward cultural relativism and the accompanying view that it is impossible to interpret or evaluate an ethical community other than one's own; its readiness to refuse ethical judgment or responsibility toward those outside its own ethical community, thus preventing possible action against injustice elsewhere; and its assumption of and reliance on homogeneity within ethical communities themselves.

In contrast, universalists view the ethical self as defined by its rational capacity to adopt an impersonal point of view within a framework of a common moral community. Universalists emphasize the interconnectedness of domestic and international structures of norms, power, and authority rather than their mutual exclusivity. They assume that moral consensus can be achieved dialogically, under ideal conditions, within a rights-based political system. With regard to international human rights, the 'universalist' position has also been criticized for reasons that include its misrepresentation of or insensitivity to salient cultural issues when identifying certain practices as human rights violations; its imposition of hegemonic Western values on non-Western societies under the guise of universalism; and its appeal to objectivity and acceptance of the existing order as given and absolute.

Universalism and Particularism in the Asylum System

In refugee and asylum adjudication across the globe, features of both of these positions can be found, together with the limits and promise for justice they suggest. For example, although the universalist embrace of reason seeks universal and unconditional moral obligations regarding human rights, it has proven impossible to achieve international or domestic agreement over what constitutes cruelty or suffering with regard to specific individuals or groups in specific contexts. And though it may be plausible to think with communitarians that ethical bonds emerge out of loyalties to particular ethical communities, the boundaries and bonds that constitute such communities can be fragile and unpredictable. Expressions or extensions of sentiment and solidarity toward others are usually contingent on a strong sense of security which may weaken when individuals, groups, or nations who feel some sort of ethical bond are threatened by an economic crisis or a civil war, or fear the erosion of hard-fought-for social or cultural cohesion. The absence of universal consensus or the presence of contingency are not simply matters of cultural or geo-political divisions between the West and the non-West or the North and the South, fissures can also occur within continents, regions, cultures, or social groups, as the following examples reveal. The first is taken from an account of a Sudanese refugee describing his encounter with an Egyptian resettlement official in Cairo (Marfleet 2006: 235):

> When he asked how I arrived in Egypt I said that I had no money so I walked. He laughed and said that nobody could walk that far and that this story would not help me. He thought I was lying and although he asked me some other questions, I knew that was the end of my application.

The next two excerpts are taken from the accounts of a Colombian man and a Ugandan woman, both displaced persons who were eventually resettled in London. In the first example, Antonio describes the circumstances in Mexico City upon arriving from Colombia (*ibid.*: 232):

> When I got there in 1994 there were refugees from all the nearby countries. Some people, like the Chileans, had been here for over 20 years. People were arriving all the time, especially from the south, countries like Peru. Those who arrived last had the toughest time. We had to start from the beginning in putting together our communities: getting jobs and homes, finding out about our rights, bringing our families. No one gave much help: actually the refugees who had been there a long time guarded important information. When you are living a refugee life, information can be more important than anything else and people protect it. This made our lives more difficult.

In the second example, a Ugandan woman, Elizabeth, who is waiting in Kenya to be resettled outside that country, discovers competition and a lack of camaraderie amongst her fellow refugees (*ibid.*):

> When a lot of people who had recently arrived were taken on a [resettlement] programme, we were angry. Some of us had already applied to that country and we had been refused. We asked them about how they had been accepted. Once they were friendly but now they would not talk to us. Relations got very bad.

The refugee and asylum adjudication process, and the social and economic realities of a refugee life can test the willingness of members of one ethical community to recognize others as fellow human beings entitled to the right to seek sanctuary and as future, either temporary or permanent, members of their ethical community. In formal applications for refugee or asylum status, attempts to establish one's right to recognition take place at crucial points through interpreted spoken communication. Interpreters play a crucial role in facilitating this process at the institutional level.

Paul Ricouer has referred to our willingness to reside in more than one language and play host to another's culture as 'linguistic hospitality'

(2006: 23). He views this as an ethical as well as a communicative task, requiring both responsibility and sympathy for listening to and interpreting others' stories. Linguistic hospitality, according to Ricouer, is grounded in a commitment to the belief in the translatability of all languages (Ricouer 1965: 282):

> Certainly everything does not come out in a translation, but something always does. There is no reason or probability that a linguistic sign is untranslatable. The belief that the translation is feasible up to a certain point is the affirmation that the foreigner is a man, the belief, in short, that communication is possible.

Here Ricouer echoes Davidson's claim that all that is required to translate is the assumption that our conversational partners hold various beliefs, desires, and attitudes that are causally linked to the same world—or as Ricouer expresses it, 'the affirmation that the foreigner is a man'. To make a rational choice about the meaning of another's utterances requires no more than the knowledge that the basic truthfulness of his or her beliefs, like ours, is rooted in the world. Though, as Davidson suggests, nothing guarantees we will "understand those with whom we differ on vast tracts of physical and moral opinion . . . there are no definite limits to how far dialogue can or will take us" (D. Davidson 2001: 219). Where social and institutional conditions are in place for the extension or exchange of 'linguistic hospitality', interpreters facilitate this communicative task with relative ease. However, in inhospitable communicative environments where the participatory rights of some individuals or groups are constrained or require some form of negotiation, the communicative and ethical demand on interpreters is greater.

The different ways complex ethical relationships play out on a global scale can be seen in the judicial and political realm of asylum adjudication. In the determinations of applicants' claims of persecution, ethical considerations fuse with social, political, and discursive instruments of power that determine whether the 'universal' right to hospitality is denied or granted. Across the array of contexts that make up the asylum system, the interactions between asylum applicants and government officials, legal representatives, immigration judges, and interpreters demonstrate different degrees of linguistic hospitality. At some point each of these participants will be required to reflect on their personal and professional ethical commitments, reaffirming some and abandoning others, depending on how they stand up to scrutiny in particular instances. Within this web of interlocution, interpreters are actively involved in helping to ensure that mutual recognition amongst the relevant interlocutors is attempted, if not achieved.

International Migration and Thresholds of Hospitality

The question of hospitality as a means of sanctuary for foreigners based on their universal right to hospitality rooted in human reason was notably explored in

Kant's defense of cosmopolitan values in his 1795 essay, 'Toward Perpetual Peace', in which he argued for a set of common principles in the treatment of strangers shared by individuals as well as states (Kant 1795/1957: 20–21):

> Hospitality is the right of a stranger not to be treated as an enemy when he arrives in the land of another. One may refuse to receive him when this can be done without causing his destruction; but, so long as he peacefully occupies his place, one may not treat him with hostility. It is not the right to be a permanent visitor one may demand. A special beneficent agreement would be needed in order to give an outsider a right to become a fellow inhabitant for a certain length of time. It is only a right of temporary sojourn, a right to associate, which all men have. They have it by virtue of their common possession of the surface of the earth, where, as a globe, they cannot infinitely disperse and hence must finally tolerate the presence of each other.

Derrida has characterized the Kantian conception of hospitality as a paradoxical, aporetic relationship between an unconditional 'absolute hospitality'—i.e., giving to an absolute and anonymous other without asking for reciprocity—and a conditional 'right to hospitality'—making this unknown other recognizable and responsible before the law. For Derrida, Kantian hospitality functions too much like a charity; it can be granted or withdrawn at any time by the donor, in this case the sovereign nation, which is protected by law, protocol, and power. He argues that individuals and states cannot protect themselves from the ethical demand of a foreigner's request for hospitality by embracing one form over another as the two are heterogeneous and inseparable. Once foreigners identify themselves as in need of hospitality, they are 'named' and become responsible before the law, subjects in law and subjected to the laws that will determine whether they are granted or denied the hospitality they seek. A request for hospitality thus forces a decision on the morally and ethically undecidable; it is a reminder of the irresolvable in ethical-political life (Derrida 2000: 55):

> No hospitality, in the classic sense, without sovereignty of oneself over one's home, but since there is also no hospitality without finitude, sovereignty can only be exercised by filtering, choosing and thus by excluding and doing violence. Injustice, a certain injustice, and even a certain perjury, begins right away, from the very threshold of hospitality.

Within the asylum system, interpreters play a major role in the paradox of hospitality. On the one hand, they participate in the 'filtering, choosing and excluding' practices that serve nation-states' desire to maintain tight control over their sovereignty while accepting their international obligation to acknowledge the political and economic reality of international migration. On the other, as purveyors of linguistic hospitality, they bear witness to the histories and narratives of events that have given rise to an asylum applicant's fear of persecution, and serve as their agents for the retelling of events. At the same time, however, where persecution has resulted from regional or ethnic conflict, interpreters who are fellow nationals may be viewed with suspicion or alarm, justifiably or not. This paradoxical role can give rise to both ethical and unethical interpreting practices within the system as a whole.

The motivations for late twentieth and twenty-first century migration have been articulated in the press and in political debates in either economic or political terms, within the terms of national sovereignty, and rarely accompanied by any reference to hospitality. The persistence of this either/or interpretation of the causes of migration is evident in the pejorative categorization of the 'bogus' asylum seeker in cases where an asylum claim is believed to be based on economic reasons alone. This charge is highly problematic. It is increasingly difficult to make a distinction between political refugees and economic migrants (Crisp 2003: 81) as most individuals and groups seeking asylum migrate as a result of a combination of factors deriving from the consequences of civil war, ethnic conflicts, and other forms of social and political violence. Demetrios Papademetriou, president of the Migration Policy Institute, has argued that both our existing conceptual and analytical tools and the administrative categories and structures used to understand international migration are sorely in need of review (2003: 42):

> Such a review suggests that, the danger of oversimplification notwithstanding, the existing international migration system is organized around ideal constructs that are both dated and disturbingly binary. States are designated as either 'sending' or 'receiving'; people who move are classified as either permanent settlers or temporary residents; and reasons for flight are categorized as either the improvement of one's economic condition or protection from various forms of persecution.

Over the past several decades numerous scholars have shared this concern and questioned the significance of territorial boundaries and the effectiveness of national laws to organize and control the increasing movement of peoples in a globalized world. They point to the changing nature of migration in which complex local, regional, and global associations and allegiances are formed and suggest an end to traditional dichotomies such as citizen/noncitizen, national/non-national, permanent/temporary (see Soysal 1994; Sassen 1999; Papastergiadis 2000; Vertovec and Cohen 2003; Marfleet 2006). But even as these dichotomies continue to be debated in contemporary political debates as both an empirical and a philosophical matter (see Mertens 1996; Bohman and Lutz-Bachmann 1997; Kleingeld 1998), 'universal personhood' remains largely unrecognized as a normative category within international migration policy. The decision over who is granted temporary or permanent rights of residence remains with individual nations which, in recent decades, have tightened control over immigration through stricter border controls, mass deportation, and the construction of detention facilities designed to cordon off asylum seekers from the rest of the population under the guise of protecting national security and stability. The granting or refusal of an asylum petition is decided by a conflux of sometimes contradictory or opposing factors: national immigration laws and treaties, foreign policy and international relations, international human rights laws and conventions, and the perceptions of refugees and asylum seekers that are articulated by policy makers and the media. International agreements regarding refugees and asylum seekers are typically established with other 'receiving' nations in order to establish 'thresholds of tolerance', not with 'sending' countries from which large numbers of people are seeking temporary refuge or permanent asylum.[1] Within the asylum systems of major 'receiving' nations, not all individual claims count as equally legitimate. A request for asylum invokes a number of different responses at the 'very threshold of hospitality', ranging from hostility to ambivalence to openness, each of which occurs within a legal process characterized by inconsistency, uncertainty, and contingency (see Asylum Aid 1999; Jarvis 2003; Kidane 2006; Ramji-Nogales et al. 2007; Thomas 2008).

THE POLITICS OF ASYLUM ADJUDICATION

Asylum decisions are based on assessments of whether an applicant is telling the truth about his or her personal experiences of actual or threatened persecution and on whether an applicant's story, if credible, would make the applicant eligible for asylum under the law. While the more subjective assessment of credibility may be expected to produce inconsistent responses from one immigration officer or judge to another (Legomsky 2007) even in cases where the same facts are presented, there can be tremendous variation in the assessment of an applicant's legal eligibility. Catrina Jarvis, an immigration appeals judge in the U.K., interviewed her colleagues about the factors involved in their assessment of credibility in an asylum claim. She found that the judges she interviewed had very different attitudes toward human rights, the role of international law, and so-called 'extraneous' factors such as race, ethnicity, gender, and class (Jarvis 2003: 10; and see Thomas 2005):

> In general interviewees state that they endeavour to start their assessment of credibility from a neutral standpoint but most are aware, to varying degrees, that they are swayed, potentially or actually, by their own characteristics, upbringing, views of the world, and, subconsciously or otherwise, by the demeanor of a witness. It is clear that here, as in other aspects of the assessment, there is a lack of consistency in approach. Some respondents realize that they are looking into a mirror and, recognizing the effect of who and what they are upon their ability to fairly assess credibility, try to look through the glass in order to carry out the exercise whilst acknowledging that sometimes they forget the mirror is there. Others have not yet seen the mirror, or if they have, are not admitting to its existence.

In a recent U.S. study, Ramji-Nogales et al. found that immigration judges in the U.S. who had previously worked in the private sector, especially those who had worked in academia, for other non-profit organizations, or for private law firms, had significantly higher asylum approval rates than those immigration judges who had previously worked for the federal government, particularly those who had worked in a law enforcement capacity for the Department of Homeland Security or its predecessor agency, or in the military. In fact, the longer the prior government service of judges, the lower their asylum approval rates were. They argue that (Ramji-Nogales et al. 2007: 305: and see Legomsky 2007),

> Human judgment can never be eliminated from any system of justice. But we believe that the outcome of a refugee's quest for safety in America should be influenced more by law and less by a spin of the wheel of fate that assigns her case to a particular government official.

Asylum cases can be won or lost based on the competing public narratives of applicants and the receiving nations (Barsky 1996; Jacquemet 2005; Maryns 2006; Blommaert 2009; M. Baker 2006, 2010). Although in principle the asylum application process is the means by which receiving nations extend universal rights to asylum seekers, in practice it is the particularity of each individual claim that is treated as suspect. Even where a receiving country acknowledges that rape, torture, or illegal detention are currently and commonly practiced in a claimant's country of origin, the burden of proof is on asylum seekers to convincingly demonstrate the credibility of their individual 'well-founded fear' of future or continued persecution. In order to accomplish this, claimants must create coherent links between the 'subjective' elements of their claim, which often rest on no more than their word alone, and the 'objective' ones, which include the 1951 Refugee Convention criteria for what constitutes justifiable fear and supporting documentary evidence reporting on the human rights record of their country of origin or country guideline determinations intended to provide authoritative guidance on existing conditions.[2]

Despite the existence of the International Refugee Convention and, in Europe, the European Convention of Human Rights, the fact that both legal and political recognition of persecution depend on the views of the receiving states means that 'objectivity' is difficult to sustain. Applicants from states with an internationally recognized weak record of human rights, for example, can have a difficult time getting their claims approved because the receiving country wishes to maintain strong political and economic ties to their countries. And although the Convention definition of the phrase 'well-founded fear' is aimed at qualifying the subjective nature of the fear of persecution at the same time that it seeks to lower the 'objective' standard of proof for applicants, it is unclear what counts as 'well-founded' in practice (Kidane 2006: 130):

> The term well-founded is a manifestation of the state's desire to maintain the objective assessment of both the genuineness and justifiableness of the claimant's subjective perception of the situation in his country of origin. According to this definition, what the claimant feels about his situation is only the first step. Anyone who claims refugee status may have his own "fear," whether it is well-founded or not; however, legal recognition depends on the views of the authorities of a receiving state. The main question remains whether or not an objective assessment of a subjective fear is practicable in refugee situations. Although the Convention provides this criterion, it does not outline a clear standard of adjudication. As a result, it has remained a subject of inconsistent interpretation and application.

When placed within the Convention itself, the phrase is taken to mean a 'reasonable degree of likelihood' or 'substantial grounds for thinking' that an individual will suffer persecution for a Convention reason if returned. Although the use of the term 'reasonable' in the Convention is intended to reflect a lower standard of proof in refugee cases given the inevitable difficulties of supplying conclusive evidence in the majority of cases, it is common for immigration officials in receiving countries to demand proof to a standard that cannot be met by asylum applicants (Hathaway 1991; Asylum Aid 1999). Given the significance that credibility plays in the assessment of an asylum claim, the fact that claimants' accounts of persecution are frequently met with doubt and suspicion by decision makers can interfere with applicants receiving a fair hearing (Coutin 2001; Jarvis 2003; Juss 1997, 2005). As U.K. immigration judge and legal scholar Satvinder Juss notes (Juss 2005: 29):

> The applicant is likely to face a 'culture of disbelief'. Country information (even if incomplete) may be overlooked. Wrongful assumptions may be made to undermine the applicant's claim. The prevalence of bribery in poor countries may routinely go unrecognized. Knowledge about how police and prison officers work in foreign countries may be falsely claimed; worse, instances of casual brutality, rape and torture may go unrecognized. However, these are the very reasons why the applicant fears persecution.

In asylum interviews and hearings, applicants or their legal representatives attempt to present their case for asylum based on the cultural norms and practices and socio-historical conditions of the applicant's country of origin with respect to understandings about what constitutes rape, how state authorities such as the police function with respect to the protection of the public, and the extent to which civil order is maintained. The response of immigration officials to such statements is to argue for or against the inherent logic or plausibility of the claims and their relevance to each individual applicant's story. To determine what counts as a legitimate reason to fear persecution or a legitimate reaction to that fear, they will often rely on normative criteria which, though in each case can imply something very different, is universally evaluated. Statements like "the fact that you were able to leave on your own passport indicates that the authorities had no interest in you" and "the police actions you describe are random in nature and are as the result of individuals abusing their official position rather than from any concerted policy on the part of government authorities" (Documentary sources, 2005) are typical of the reasons commonly given by a receiving country authority for denying a claim. The negative approaches to credibility displayed by some immigration officials and judges are designed to undermine the relevance of the socially, politically, and historically motivated beliefs and practices of applicants. These are treated as only minimally significant or are subsumed within a universalizing discourse that does not benefit claimants (Coutin 2001: 83):

> Asylum law, like liberal legal theory, presumes the existence of a generic or universal personhood that is essentially devoid of cultural, class, ethnic, or other content. Thus, the judge who assesses an asylum application and the individual asylum applicant are presumed to share basic assumptions about risk, reality, and fear.

The presumption of a shared 'universal personhood' is often no more than the worldview of more powerful interactional players represented as 'universal' and 'impartial'. This presumption acts to de-contextualize acts of persecution, raise suspicion, and undermine the validity of applicants' motivations for fear leading to flight (Kidane 2006: 140):

> It is much easier for the adjudicator to decide that a certain act does not amount to persecution than for the claimant to convince a court that it does, unless the act is manifestly atrocious and barbaric by nature. Even when manifestly atrocious acts such as rape are concerned, some adjudicators seem to have found a way to deny status, as in the case of the Bosnian Serb victims. Again, the use of the term "persecution" to denote a wide range of possibilities of jeopardy that a person may face directly reflects nations' desire to retain a flexible policy of judging every instance according to their own standards.

INTERPRETING IN THE JURIDICAL-POLITICAL FIELD

The task of reaching accurate decisions on the basis of credibility or the conditions in the countries generating asylum applicants is, ultimately, an interpretive and evaluative exercise. For this reason, as each side attempts to strategically control their own communicative objectives, the type and extent of interpreter input that occurs in the asylum context can have considerable impact on outcomes. In addition to their linguistic input, interpreters help to negotiate the ethical demand to situate the legal contest of the asylum claim within as broad a context as possible, particularly where legal representation is lacking or inadequate. They act as monitors and mediators—and sometimes even instigators—of the clashes and convergences that originate in different sets of values and beliefs and the competing communicative objectives to which they give rise. In these roles, interpreters work actively to connect the universalizing tendencies of the state with the particular experiences of the applicants. However, given the contingent nature of the interpreter role and their perceived professional obligations, the extent to which they are willing or able to perform this function varies considerably.

Skills-Based Approaches and the Interpreter Role

Research studies on interpreter influence over communicative exchanges have tended to focus on the potential for interpreters to impact on both the meaning and flow of utterances in interpreted communication by highlighting instances where an interpreter has (unintentionally) misinterpreted a word, phrase, or the apparent pragmatic intention of an utterance (Berk-Seligson 1990; Hale 2004; Pollbauer 2004). Although the various findings of this research have successfully challenged the view of the interpreter as an invisible interactional presence, they often reveal more about the particular realizations of discourse processes within interpreted interactions than about interpreters as active and visible agents in broader communicative, social, and political processes that inform these micro-interactions. The conclusion generally drawn is that interpreters must become more aware of the semantic and pragmatic aspects of communication and better trained in a number of specific interpreting skills in order to ensure greater accuracy and transparency of meaning across cultural and linguistic boundaries. The skills necessary to achieve this are (Dunnigan and Downing 1995: 111):

> The ability to hear and understand exactly what another person has said, to recognize contextual meaning, implication and ambiguity as well as social meaning conveyed by one's manner of speaking and stylistic level: to retain the message in memory or, in simultaneous mode, to articulate the message in a second language while still attending to the speech as it is produced; to convey the understood message completely and accurately, without commentary or elaboration, while conserving the speaker's intent, tone, stylistic level and meaning (presupposition, assertion, implication, reference) to the extent possible.

While these skills are an important part of the interpreter role, there are a number of limitations with the overall conclusions of research of this kind which prioritizes linguistic and cognitive skills over ethical and moral responsibility. Placing sole or primary emphasis on skills reinforces the idea that well-trained interpreters can ensure that interlocutors' communicational intentions are precisely captured and conveyed to one another without the need for discussion or negotiation over possible or probable meaning. This commonly expressed view paradoxically reinforces interpreter invisibility in the event and ignores the fact that many interpreting scholars have long recognized: that mutually effective communication under most circumstances requires some degree of prior or 'on the spot' collaboration over meaning before a pair or group of interlocutors feel satisfied that they have understood one another sufficiently and effectively (see Laster 1990, 1994; Morris 1995, 1999, 2010; Mikkelson 1998, 2008).

A reduction of the interpreter's task to a list of sociolinguistic and cognitive skills also abstracts interpreted utterances from the wider social and ideological processes that inform communicative behavior. Although Dunnigan and Downing stress that professionals who work with interpreters should have some appreciation of what interpreting involves and be prepared to "collaborate fully in the process of making justice available to those who are language handicapped" (*ibid.*: 110), this stated objective fails to acknowledge that in many interpreting settings sociolinguistic collaboration toward just outcomes is not necessarily a shared or guaranteed goal. In the asylum process all interlocutors are 'language handicapped' with respect to one another, hence the need for interpreters, but it is the applicants—the linguistic and cultural 'others' in this context—who are obliged to make their accounts of persecution intelligible and commensurable to the linguistic, cultural, and political realities of their official 'hosts'. Despite the reality of multilingualism implied by the asylum process—and which may be evident in the society in which an immigration court is located—there is an overarching assumption of monolingualism that goes well beyond the reasonable acknowledgment of the relationship between the language in which the law is written and what should be the official language of the court. This impacts the care and attention paid to precise meanings expressed in languages other than that of the receiving country, and the status given to the cultural knowledge required to unpack those meanings in such a way as to ensure as far as possible that sufficient understanding is achieved. It is precisely in such contexts that restricting the interpreter function to conveying the understood message "completely and accurately, without commentary or elaboration" can actually work to prohibit open dialogue over meaning and shelter members of the juridical-political field from the inevitable interpenetration and transgressions of linguistic, cultural, and political borders.

Translating Trauma

Skills-based approaches also fail to acknowledge the psychological and emotional dimension of interpreting both for the victims and for the professionals who bear witness to asylum seekers' accounts of 'unspeakable' atrocities (see Tribe and Raval 2003). Although judges, attorneys, clinicians, immigration officers, and interpreters all have an ethical duty to listen perceptively to applicants' re-telling of their trauma, only interpreters fulfill this duty by re-voicing applicants' accounts of rape, murder, and torture as though the words and experiences they attempt to describe are their own. As one Iraqi interpreter explains (Interpreter interview, 2002):

> I would do my best to be that person who's in the session with the clinician, and not just by speaking the language but also by trying my best to feel his feelings, and putting myself in the situation, being in this country, alone, nobody around, they are totally blind and deaf and they need somebody who can represent them, and convey the accurate message.

By this account, interpreters do more than convey the accurate message through linguistic and cognitive skills, they embody the experience of the applicants—both their past trauma and their efforts to re-tell it in the present—while maintaining a delicate balance between empathy and critical distance. As a UNHCR interpreter recounts (Dawes 2007: 85):

> It is hard. You should not show sympathy to the ICs [individual claimants]. They will say what they think is affecting you and you will not get the facts. They will try to make pressure on you. They will try to manipulate you; they will hold you responsible. People cry and you must sit there.

Interpreters who work throughout the refugee and asylum system are aware that the applicants' accounts of trauma are evaluated within the judicial-political framework of a particular nation state's immigration policies that influence the determinations of their legitimacy and credibility. In the asylum system, trauma as a categorical moral subject is not doubted, but the particularity of a single person's stories and claims is often suspect. Immigration officials and judges are ready to believe in the truth delivered by trauma when it refers to a general fact about persecution but much less when it refers to the particular cases of the persecuted.[3] Trauma discourses—involving both psychic and physical suffering—can gain or lose priority at any given time in bureaucratic and judicial systems designed to maximize the exclusion of some and the inclusion of others (Das 2007). Where legal representation is lacking, interpreters can feel an increased responsibility to translate the applicants' stories into the officially sanctioned vocabulary of the asylum system.[4] Interpreters who put themselves on the line to represent the 'unspeakable', despite the fact that the applicants' claim may be inhospitably received, demonstrate a professional commitment that is insufficiently acknowledged in skills-based approaches. For interpreters who have undergone similar trauma, getting others to understand the real and symbolic violence that asylum seekers suffer can be a painful form of bearing witness. In these events, interpreters do not demonstrate ethical and professional behavior by acting as conduits of language, but by serving as "conduits of history", assisting in the process whereby a trauma victim's personal testimony is transformed into a call for historical truth (McKinney 2007: 277) within a system in which the 'truth' of individual persecution narratives is consistently called into question.

EXPANDING THE SCOPE OF MUTUAL RECOGNITION

Interpreters are frequently the only ones present in the legal system who speak the relevant language, understand the culture, and know something of the circumstances of applicants' motivations for fleeing their countries of origin. As a consequence, the relationships that develop between interpreters and applicants, interpreters and legal representatives, interpreters and immigration officials, and interpreters and judges extend beyond the type of practice envisioned in interpreting codes of ethics, creating both holy and unholy alliances.

By law and depending on the individual country, asylum seekers must either provide their own or be provided an interpreter before a formal interview can take place with a specialist immigration officer. There are no similar laws that guarantee the provision of professional legal advice or representation for applicants at any stage in the process, whether the point of entry, the formal interview, or, if a claim is refused, the appeal hearing.[5] Most applicants depend on pro bono, reduced-rate, and government-funded legal services provisions for formal representation. Where such resources are scarce or unavailable, they tend to rely on the advice of members of their own communities. Many applicants attend interviews with little or no information about what they will be expected to recount about their experiences, including what type of information and level of detail they will be expected to provide about prior or anticipated persecution. Torture and trauma victims often lack the necessary medical evidence to corroborate their claims.

A recent study conducted in the U.S. found that legal representation "plays an enormous role in determining whether an asylum seeker wins her case" (Ramji-Nogales et al. 2007: 340; and see Thomas 2005 for a similar claim about the U.K.). Practical access to competent counsel—attorneys or other qualified representatives—has repeatedly been shown to be one of the highest correlates of asylum approval rates. The complexity of the cases and the amount of corroborating evidence and other preparation required to win an asylum case make it highly likely that representation clarifies the issues and presents the judge with critical information. On that assumption, practical access to counsel at least improves the probability that the judges will reach more informed decisions (Ramji-Nogales et al. 2007: 376):

> Advocates are able to collect affidavits from lay and expert witnesses and other corroborating documents; are familiar with the Immigration and Nationality Act, the voluminous regulations promulgated under that law, and the volumes of case law interpreting it; understand the court's exacting standards for the corroboration of testimony and authentication of documents; know the court's timetables and formal requirements for filing papers; are aware of the procedures for pleading and motions; and know how to conduct direct and cross examination of witnesses and make closing statements that tie together the facts and law.

While the importance of advocacy cannot be overstated, incompetent legal representation can impact an applicant's case more negatively than no representation at all (Thomas 2005: 482–483):

> A further obstacle to the operation of an effective appeal process arises from the standard of representation which is, according to the Council of Immigration Judges, 'very variable in quality'. There are certainly a substantial number of representatives who provide high-quality services and many are members of organizations that are key players in the broader asylum debate. At the same time, there are those who provide either incompetent, unscrupulous or exploitative services; while good representation may assist the appeal process, bad representation may positively hinder it.

Incompetent legal representatives also tend to reflect very badly on applicants. In my observations in one U.K. appellate court, representatives frequently arrived in court with little or no knowledge of their clients' cases, indicating little commitment to their experiences of persecution, their current well-being, or the final decision on their claim. They phrased statements and questions incoherently and showed little regard for the instructions or requests for clarification of the judges regarding a specific point to do with a client's case. This lack of preparedness and careless commentary also made it very difficult for interpreters to provide quality translations. In the absence of adequate counsel, or any counsel in some cases, immigration judges were more likely to speak directly to interpreters in an attempt to engage in some form of fruitful dialogue with the appellants. As a result, interpreters came to be seen by the appellants (and effectively were in some cases) as the only guarantors that due process had taken place.

Interpreters and the State

Unlike legal advocates, interpreters are present from the very start of an applicant's involvement with the immigration system. In the U.K., asylum applicants are obliged to use freelance interpreters supplied by the immigration service, a branch of the Home Office, at their immigration interviews.

Many interpreters refuse this work on moral and ethical grounds given the Home Office's reputation for having a hostile and biased view of asylum seekers. Although Home Office interpreters operate as self-employed external resources for the government, they are met with a mixture of trust and suspicion by many asylum seekers and their legal representatives. Whether this suspicion is valid in all cases, it can be a matter of guilt by association, as the following statements suggest:

> One of the problems is that the Home Office interpreters quite often get sucked into the Home Office system, so they are part of the Home Office machinery, they've got a vested interest in weeding out the ones to be refused and they're part of that culture, because they're all behind the locked door and they all come in at the same time, and so I think that there's that additional pressure in terms of the Home Office interpreting which you don't get in court. (Attorney interview, 2004)

> A Home Office interpreter might feel obliged to be obliging to the people from the Home Office, for that is where their money's coming from. Would an interpreter who is working five days a week at X pounds an hour look the other way if the Home Office person had a go at a client or called him a name or something like that. It's human nature that they might wish to look away. (Attorney interview, 2004)

> I think attitude comes into it because there is this sort of notion of swaggering about Home Office corridors, you know, being almost part of the State apparatus. It's a political thing that you come from a country and you can either interpret for other fellow asylum seekers or you can go and work for the enemy as it were, you know, that is—that's certainly the perception with some languages. And I suppose you've got to look at the political histories of countries. And if there were a colonialism element, you know, so you can quite understand where that comes from. (Interpreter Coordinator interview, 2002)

The real or imagined scenarios described in these excerpts suggest the convergence of interpreters' role morality with those of the state bureaucracy. There are also cases in which interpreters use the state for their own personal/political morality, particularly where an applicant's fear of persecution is a result of an internal ethnic or tribal conflict. In these situations, interpreters use the insensitivity and ignorance that some immigration department officials display with regard to the cultural or political histories of countries to their own political advantage by colluding in behavior designed to weaken the credibility of a rival political faction, clan, or oppressed ethnic minority from their country of origin, or by remaining silent about what they perceived as an obvious falsification in an applicant's testimony. In the following examples, an attorney describes two situations of interpreter interventions of this kind: the first involves a Kurdish asylum seeker who is provided with a Turkish interpreter for an interview at the Home Office, and the second involves the use of Polish nationals to interpret for Roma Gypsies seeking entry at the port of Dover:

> We put them on notice that he was a Kirmanji speaker [a Kurdish dialect] and needed a Kirmanji interpreter. For whatever reason, they obtained the services of a Turkish interpreter who approached our client to say his interview was about to start. [Our client] informed the guy he didn't really understand him as he was Turkish. An argument then ensued where the interpreter tried to force him to enter the interview room because, in his opinion—the Turkish-speaking interpreter's opinion, again there's racism involved here—the guy could understand what he was saying, he was just being difficult. So that continued into the interviewing room, when he was threatened by the interviewing officers there and this was rubbing off from the interpreter, the interpreter's saying to the interviewing officer, 'of course, he understands, he's just making it up'. (Attorney interview, 2004)

> A classic example used to be the Polish interpreters down at Dover; there was a period when there were a large number of Roma Gypsy asylum seekers, if you remember, a few years ago. And of course the interpreters being used were Polish nationals, what I mean by that is non-Roma. And they find the stories that the Gypsies are telling about racism in their country to be offensive against their national pride, and so they would refuse to translate what the person was saying, they would threaten, they'd say, you know, that's just lies, what you're saying is just lies and I'm not going to do it, start telling the truth kind of thing. They would also indicate quite robustly to the interviewing officers that the person is plainly lying. That kind of thing went on all the time. (Attorney interview, 2004)

Whether or not asylum officers' evaluations of asylum claims are influenced by this kind of negative feedback, verbal or physical expressions of incredulity and hostility from interpreters can contribute to the 'collective wisdom' of immigration officials about the overall credibility of claims from certain national or ethnic groups. For asylum applicants, inhospitable encounters of this kind reproduce rather than redress the conditions of fear and intimidation which prompted them to seek asylum in the first place, as illustrated by one Kurdish applicant's remarks with respect to his interpreter:

> We were able to communicate in Turkish but I felt as if I was right in front of the Turkish government, I was not feeling comfortable. He was standing there like the Turkish government. So when I said something against the Turkish government, he was shaking his head implying that

> I was lying. He was telling me off and telling the judge the opposite of what I was saying. I was not able to do anything and he had such an attitude that I felt I had to speak highly about the Turkish government. (Asylum applicant interview, 2006)

The statements that applicants provide to immigration officers at this point in the process are highly significant. They serve as the basis for the decision to accept, refuse, or refer a claim to the courts, and they are the first formal written record of their asylum claim. Any subsequent statements made on appeal will be measured against these accounts and used to determine an applicant's overall credibility. The lack of any legal requirement to assign asylum applicants competent legal counsel creates the conditions for unethical practices on the part of interpreters and legal professionals alike, both of which are capable of impeding an applicant's access to due process.

Interpreters are situated socially and politically in much the same way as are immigration officers and judges. Like other professionals with whom they work, interpreters are sometimes only as ethical and impartial as the juridical-political system requires. There is a spectrum of attitudes and beliefs toward asylum seekers that is manifest in the asylum system ranging from hard-edged cynicism and contempt to an unquestioned sympathy and provision of sanctuary. Both of these responses may be seen as eliciting 'partiality', and neither comes with a guarantee of legitimacy. Although a minority of interpreters represents the worst extremes, the vast majority occupy the middle ground of this spectrum, balancing their own attitudes and beliefs with those of their interlocutors against the backdrop of the institutional and political context of the asylum system.

Extending the Boundaries of Trust in Court

One context in which negotiation over the interpreter role is evident in the asylum system is the immigration courts, which like most courtrooms generally prefer to restrict the interpreters' communicative functions. However, due to the lack of competent representation and the unique nature of asylum adjudication which demands more than traditional, passive adjudication, immigration judges can come to look to interpreters for additional input. Despite the fact that asylum adjudication is situated within the adversarial system in which an impartial judge or jury decides in favor of either side, immigration judges often function as both judge and prosecutor, making it more like an inquisitorial system. This can create uncertainty for applicants as to whether the judge is a judge or an adversary.

Immigration judges, particularly in the absence of adequate legal representation, will often question applicants directly in order to elicit the necessary facts, clarify confusion, or corroborate previous oral and written statements. At the same time, they are expected to support the applicants in ways which give them confidence to participate in the process and compensate for the absence of legal representation and the knowledge of the operations of the legal system (Blake 2001). Though this dual and potentially contradictory role is intended to assist judges in determining refugee eligibility under the Convention, it also opens up the possibility that judges will adopt an accusatory style of inquisition. As U.S. attorney and legal scholar Deborah Anker has noted (Anker 1991: 270),

> In practice, immigration judges actively participate in the hearing, sometimes helping the applicant in preserving limited procedural rights, but frequently 'testing credibility' in a manner that resembles the cross-examination techniques of the government's attorney.

However, a potentially more positive consequence of their increased direct communication with applicants is that many immigration judges have come to recognize an increased need for interpreters to extend their role during proceedings. For example, interpreters may be asked to offer information about a country's history or geography that may have a bearing on the case:

> Well it has happened on occasion an interpreter has provided geographical information and I must say I have welcomed such intervention. For example I had an Eritrean case and as you know Eritrea has only recently become a country and the interpreter said Eritrea became a country in 1970 or whatever it was and that was very helpful. Occasionally the interpreter has said 'Oh the town is quite near such and such a place in the northern region of that country' which is helpful but it shouldn't really be subjective, that's obviously just giving information which is clearly to help the court but I wouldn't ask for it more than is necessary. (Immigration Judge interview, 2004)

Particularly in the absence of an independent legal advocate for an applicant, some experienced interpreters feel justified in querying a question posed by an immigration officer or judge, to clarify applicants' responses to ensure greater understanding, or to lessen the emotional effect on an applicant of a particularly hostile or intimidating form of questioning by a judge. Some immigration judges welcome such interventions as they greatly reduce the likelihood of time-consuming tangential statements or arguments and facilitate understanding:

> The interpreter, if he's wise and bright and following the proceedings, by re-asking the question or querying something with me, that might ring a bell for me, 'yes, maybe that wasn't right'. Through querying the clarity of a question, you can think yes, that wasn't actually a proper question at all or that wasn't a question. (Immigration Judge interview, 2004)

Other immigration judges recognize the support an interpreter can provide in the strained and, for some, completely alien environment of the courtroom:

> You can see someone from their own country who, in a very difficult situation they [the applicants] do lean on tremendously. And most interpreters are excellent; they obviously explain court procedure to them and put questions to them. Some of them can be very difficult, some can be very sensitive and we do have women who have been raped and men who have been raped as well. This is not easy. They have to discuss very intimate aspects of their life, even how much they earn, what they've been doing, their family life, and that's not easy in a strained cultural atmosphere. So I think they are a prop in many ways and the experienced ones are used to doing that. And I can see that many appellants are pleased to see the interpreter as someone who speaks their language and understands. (Immigration Judge interview, 2003)

These comments suggest recognition of the value of an expanded role morality for interpreters, even as one judge insists on distinguishing between objective facts and subjective knowledge. The more open participatory frameworks they describe are arrived at through the type of transparent dialogue which is justified by a 'political morality' as discussed in the previous chapter. The judges are responding to gaps they perceive between the norms of the courts and the needs of the appellants that appear before them. They perceive the value, in certain cases, of a convergence of professional roles through the development of professional partnerships to achieve a more effective judiciary, to humanize the law, and to ensure greater dignity for the appellants. This recognition allows both the judges and the interpreters to be morally accountable to the appellants as persons; it allows justice to proceed by way of a culturally situated, inter-subjective approach to ethical practice.

Professional Partnerships between Lawyers and Interpreters

Both types of interventions discussed above take place in the public procedural contexts of the asylum system: the immigration services and judiciary. Another key site in which interpreters work within the system are the legal firms and advisory centers that provide legal representation and advice to asylum seekers. The professional partnerships that interpreters develop with legal representatives in the preparation of an asylum case form a crucial part of the construction of an asylum case. Legal representatives often rely on interpreters to help them build rapport with their clients, making it easier for them to speak openly and without fear. Quality independent input by an interpreter into the elicitation of a narrative can help legal representatives understand cultural practices or linguistic nuances that may lead to confusion either at the time of the preparation of a case or later at an immigration interview. Interpreters can suggest different ways an attorney might phrase a question and also help prepare applicants to predict what an immigration official might mean when asking a particular question and to adjust their statements accordingly. In interviews with experienced immigration attorneys, many acknowledged this type of interpreter input as invaluable to their practice:

> An interpreter can be useful in explaining what the client means when he's referring to a relative. He might simply describe them in generic terms as brother and cousin. All those issues are very very important. Interpreters are very useful in describing to me the importance of kinship, and why what I would consider to be unusual would be usual in other countries, or why being severed from their kin is so significant. (Attorney interview, 2004)

> I mean each language is different but like a typical Turkish client might use the word for arrest, detain, arbitrarily arrested, charged, all interchangeably, and the Interviewing Officers don't use those words interchangeably. You are either picked up, you're either charged, you're arrested, you're put in prison. They're all different things. Some interpreters will actually, although their role is supposed to be passive, actually know what the client means and say, "When you asked him 'have you ever been arrested' and he said no that doesn't mean that he's never been grabbed by the police", so asking it a different way is kind of important. (Attorney interview, 2004)

> A good interpreter will understand the nuance of the language, it will be their first language hopefully, and they'll have a strong enough grasp of English to understand the nuances not being translated, this thing resembles that. And I'm just thinking I have a Nigerian client here in court, I mean one of the issues which is often put to people is that they're economic migrants and they've just come here for a better life, and so this sort of question was put around in court to try and raise that in front of the judge and he was asked what were his economic circumstances in Nigeria, and his answer was "we were eating". Now to Western eyes, that sounds like someone who's living hand to mouth. That was not what it was, the reality of it, what he was saying was that 'we were eating' means 'we were okay, we were doing all right, you know'. But you would have to have an understanding or feeling for West African culture, nuance of language to understand that. It just wouldn't come across. (Attorney interview, 2004)

Another important role played by interpreters is to facilitate the establishment of trust and rapport between applicants and their legal representatives, making it more likely that the full details of an applicant's experiences will be revealed. For many asylum seekers, opening up to any authority figure, even one advocating on their behalf, can be difficult. Under these circumstances, experienced interpreters may be more likely to elicit their trust, as they are likely to know something of the situation from which an applicant has fled and can convey this to the authorities in English. For this reason, some legal professionals view the professional relationships they develop with qualified and committed interpreters as invaluable. These relationships extend beyond those envisioned in conventional codes of ethics. The multi-layered relationships that develop in the triad of attorney and interpreter, attorney and client, and interpreter and client in the asylum context are characteristic of client-centered approaches to practicing law which challenge the dyadic norm of one-attorney one-client, allowing the subjectivity of a third person, in this case the interpreter, into the bond of communication (Ahmad 2007: 1002). The aim is to develop a more dynamic, trusting, and transparent communicative environment for clients (*ibid.*:1057):

> Once we accept the insight of client-centeredness that lawyers must explore both legal and non-legal dimensions of clients' problems, the active involvement of the interpreter in facilitating trust, providing information and perhaps even strategizing with the lawyer and client may seem more palatable and even desirable. Lawyers may wish to define primary areas of responsibility and reassert claims to specific areas of expertise. However, the collaborative co-counsel model suggests that the lawyer, client and interpreter relationships maintain fluidity, permit debate and contestation, and recognize that all three parties may bring expertise to the table.

In the following interview, an immigration attorney in the U.K. with ten years' experience reiterates this view to me (Attorney interview, 2004):

L: The classical view of an interpreter is known simply as a medium to relay information from one to the other. What I want from my client is for the client to speak from the heart, to tell the truth. And I don't think that this classical rule is particularly useful because it's not very good for engineering an intimate conversation.

I: So does that mean that you're comfortable and actually would encourage the interpreter and the client to establish a rapport, even if it meant you were excluded from some of the communication?

L: Yes because that would be dependent upon the rapport that I have with the interpreter.

I: So it starts really from you trusting the interpreter.

L: Yes. Well you know when the rapport has been developed here it makes my client a lot happier at court or wherever they have to go.

I: Right, yes. And do you feel that the interpreter plays that role more than you?

L: No, um because the clients ultimately in a sense look to the lawyer in order to obtain status and that's really all that they care about but a lot of the rapport has got to be done through the interpreter. It's really quite hard to, to really separate the role, because the body language between the client and the interpreter, when they're describing something that is very traumatic when, when in a sense they are lost in, lost in their recollection, is between the interpreter and the client, so the confidence, or the confiding is between the two of them. But after the end of such a session, the client tends to be, acknowledges the lawyer as well as the interpreter. So, so I don't think anyone's actually quite forgotten from the triangle.

In this kind of partnership between attorney and interpreter, both parties learn to negotiate the appropriate response to the client based on their mutual recognition of the specialized knowledge each possesses and on whatever role hierarchy has been mutually established. For example, for some legal practitioners it might be normal practice for an interpreter who knows the answer to an applicant's question to directly respond without first consulting the attorney or to enter into a purposeful dialogue about an upcoming interview or hearing with the applicant that is not translated. Alternatively, an interpreter might prefer to say each time 'They just asked me such and such', or 'Do you want me to explain what happens in the interview?' before proceeding. These normative practices are arrived at through open negotiation based on trust between the relevant parties. This trust is grounded in the shared belief that a well-informed and committed interpreter will communicate as effectively and appropriately as possible. It is strengthened over time through the repeated achievement of mutual understanding in the triangle of communication. In a fundamental way, this is similar to the trust which interlocutors develop with one another in monolingual conversations; it is what makes meaningful communication possible.

THE PERSISTENCE OF THE CONDUIT

Despite acknowledgment within the legal profession of the value of an expanded interpreter role, the conventional view of interpreters as passive conduits and the ideals of neutrality and impartiality that accompany this view persist in their images of what an interpreter ideally 'should be', though not without qualification:

> Well, strictly speaking the interpreter should be just an absolute direct and perfect conduit between client and legal representative, or client and adjudicator, or client and the Home Office. Of course that's exactly

> what it should be, transferring all the nuances involved, double meanings in any language. That's strictly speaking what it should be, and it's what you would always hope to strive for. There'd be no advising involved, there'd be no peripheral extra information of interest, directly deliver the information as it comes from the client or from the solicitor. You know just smooth out the enormous barrier that language creates. But good interpreters can provide a lot more, bad interpreters can do untold damage. (Attorney interview, 2004)

> Regular interpreters there know the spiel by heart really almost. And it's a help to our caseworkers because the interpreters go through it, they explain in no uncertain terms exactly what needs to be explained to the detainees. So it's really not advocacy, but you can see where there is scope for some kind of blurring where the interpreter can actually sort of push things along, and hopefully and probably, ninety-nine percent of the time actually help the caseworker. The experienced interpreters there know what standard [Home Office] documentation needs to be read out to the client. So they can sort of perhaps take the lead a bit there, where you wouldn't under any other normal circumstances expect the interpreter to take the lead in procedures. (Interpreter Coordinator interview, 2002)

> Sometimes I find an appellant who is unrepresented has a better chance to put his case than someone who is represented by a poor representative because I can tease out of him in a more logical order and get better reasons. Really the interpreter shouldn't have that role because how should he, he should be interpreting, he should be simply saying what is said. But I think probably, for example, some interpreters are very good and careful in repeating questions, if they think the appellant hasn't quite understood where you're coming from, whereas certainly the rep might not have picked that up and would just let it go. (Immigration Judge interview, 2004)

There are a number of possible reasons for the struggle between the 'ought' and the 'is' with regards to the interpreter role evident in the above statements. Given a choice, most professionals prefer not to work with interpreters as it disrupts traditional dyadic (legal, clinical, pedagogic, etc.) models in which clear rules of duty are in place and the power of decision making and judgment lies with one professional or a team of similar professionals. The conduit image makes it possible to proceed as if the interpreter is not really there. Second, professionals tend to trust interpreters with whom they have worked over a period of time. However, the freelance nature of the interpreting profession makes it difficult to establish relationships with interpreters that endure over time. Law practices and other private or public institutions generally do not maintain a permanent interpreting staff as it is not always economically feasible or practical. Related to this, the absence of job security, insufficient remuneration, and little opportunity for professional advancement mean that many experienced public service interpreters leave the profession after a relatively short period of time. As this U.K. attorney observed,

> Good interpreters, that means not only good at the interpreting but good at interpreting the way you're proceeding, good at dealing with cultural references, good at dealing with the clients, good at dealing with you, these people are rare and don't stay at X pounds an hour for very long. Typically they'll move on to better things. (Attorney interview, 2004)

Where collaborative partnerships are discouraged or unattainable, the classic rule of the conduit seems to function as an important safety net, operating in lieu of trust or perceived professional competence as a kind of reassurance that misunderstandings will not occur. This view is reinforced by the norms of impartiality and neutrality that continue to dominate existing professional codes of practice despite the fact that such norms involve a number of misconceptions about language, communication, and ethical practice. These norms and the ideals they support—namely, that interpreters can act as "absolute direct and perfect conduits"—operate on the erroneous assumption that the 'right' words alone can smooth over communicative barriers. This suggests that words, and whatever meanings emerge from their use in a particular context, somehow operate independently of other significant aspects of communication that can also contribute to understanding, sometimes through misunderstandings, that emerge in social interactions, due to, for example, individual or institutional beliefs and motivations, political and ideological privilege and power, prior conversations, or greater and lesser degrees of cultural knowledge.[6]

What is clear is that misunderstandings do not normally occur because interpreters have ceased operating as impartial and neutral conduits. They are most likely to occur on a regular basis in public and private institutions with weak and ineffective criteria of selection or training for interpreters and which offer poor pay and work conditions that in such contexts attract unqualified interpreters willing to work for less than their more qualified colleagues. They may also occur due to inadequate understandings of the legal or other institutional contexts in which an utterance is situated, confusions over the role of the interpreter, or where a language appears for the first time in the system. The source of the violation of professionally sanctioned models under these circumstances is not the individual interpreter but the system which permits the legal procedure to advance and to be valid in the eyes of the court—the very presence of an interpreter being seen to guarantee due process—without regard for the quality of the service that the interpreter is able to provide.

Moreover, proactive and individually enacted transgressions of impartiality and neutrality where interpreters add, alter, or omit utterances are not necessarily unethical. Interpreters who intervene to improve understanding amongst interlocutors or protect an applicant's human rights or because an applicant has no legal representation or is being treated inhospitably by an immigration official are arguably not acting in the same way as interpreters who create a hostile environment in which the validity of an asylum claim is evaluated. Under certain circumstances, an interpreter who acts as a passive and impartial conduit may actually contribute to the reproduction of deeply unethical systemic failures and miscarriages of justice, while an interpreter who actively intervenes in order to ensure that all parties can exercise their communicative rights improves both the system and the possibility of more just outcomes. In either case however, the source of the professional violation is not the interpreter alone but has links to the juridical-political system in which the intervention occurs.

Converging Moralities: Cracking the Conduit Code

The political goal of exclusion and the higher standard of proof required to obtain refugee status help create the conditions for the doubt and suspicion of asylum officers regarding the truthfulness of applicants' claims. In the bureaucratic routines of the asylum system, the rules and goals of communication are less dialogic and more inquisitorial—the presumption is that applicants are not necessarily speaking the truth, and the primary goal for government officials is to prove this. In order to adjudicate what nation states treat as a scarce resource—a grant of refugee status—interviews become opportunities to undermine applicants' credibility, rather than to extend them sympathy or charity. Applicants' utterances are not treated as 'holding true' with respect to the particular contexts to which they refer, including the immediate one. Instead they are evaluated in increasingly restrictive terms against the criteria of a Convention that sustains its legal legitimacy and moral standing through its assumed neutrality. The absence of a clear standard of adjudication in the current climate however has left the Convention open for interpretation and application that favors government policies, not applicants' genuine claims. There is little scope for the type of 'discursive will formation' envisioned by discourse ethics in the public deliberations involved in the granting of asylum. Asylum interviews and hearings do not serve as opportunities for reasoned deliberation in which different perspectives can emerge dialogically. Instead, they work to constrain communication and withhold recognition in the interest of the pragmatic and ideological agendas of nation states.

The convergences of role moralities between interpreters and legal professionals, however, does indicate the potential for a more effective response to the moral responsibility toward the dispossessed seeking justice in the asylum system. Where this is the shared objective, abstract principles like partisanship, impartiality, and neutrality are largely irrelevant as these are normally understood. These principles do not guarantee the judiciary or the individuals within it protection against the potential manipulation of the law or of language in the stories that are told—a lawyer's zealous partisanship can just as easily serve to distort as to reveal certain 'truths'; judges' impartiality does not make them impervious to their own subjectivities; and an interpreter's impartiality does not prevent the lies or protect the truths in others' utterances. The clear boundary between rational judgment and subjective intuition that such principles are believed to ensure is indeterminable without taking contextual factors and the particularities of each case into account. To do this, especially in the complex cultural, political, and legal maze of an asylum claim, nearly always requires open and continuous dialogue amongst all the relevant parties, including interpreters.

Existing codes of interpreting practice do not sufficiently acknowledge the decisions and actions interpreters take as a normal part of their task under these circumstances. What guidelines do exist presume that ethical decisions are taken by interpreters unilaterally, ignoring both the relevant agency of their interlocutors and the institutional contexts in which these decisions are made. They also deny the fact that the ongoing interpretative process of evaluating 'means to ends' with respect to interpreting activity is far from being decided by interpreters alone. Interpreters together with their professional partners frequently abandon unproductive norms and principles and reconstruct new ones in the event. This involves an acknowledgment on their part of both the interpreting skills that interpreters possess as well as their freedom and ability to exercise independent judgment regarding their professional practice. Although on occasion this may give rise to unethical behavior, the 'good interpreting' that interpreters demonstrate in collaboration with others in the asylum system indicates the need for alternative normative practices.

5 Just Interpreting

Local and Contract Interpreters in Iraq

Though the conditions in war zones may appear radically distinctive and without equal to most contexts in which interpreters work, the ethical challenges interpreters face in violent conflict zones are not entirely dissimilar to those encountered in other situations. The ethical decisions taken by interpreters in the asylum system are influenced by the wider juridical-political system in which interpreted interactions occurred. These involve ethical choices regarding not only the types of communicative interventions that interpreters make, but also the specific contexts in which they choose to work and the individuals for whom they choose to interpret. Some interpreters refuse to work for the government branch of the asylum system, for example, because they view it as intrinsically hostile to asylum seekers and refugees, while others feel they can make a positive intervention in what they view as an essentially just institution, even if the local effects of exclusionary asylum policies often lead to unjust outcomes. Some interpreters decide that professional codes of impartiality and neutrality relieve them of the obligation to consider the consequences of working in a particular context, while others feel they have little or no choice at all regarding for whom, what, or where they interpret.

This chapter focuses on the ethical choices involved in the decision to interpret, not the relationship between interpreters' motivations to serve with the U.S. military and the quality or authenticity of their translations, though the question of motivation does raise important ethical questions at the interactional level as well. It examines the nature of the relationship between interpreters and U.S. forces in the Iraq war, including the assumed role, in certain instances, of interpreters as combatants, and raises questions regarding any potential conflict between interpreters' moral intuitions and their participation in military actions. The chapter also considers the ethical implications for interpreters in their role as 'cultural brokers' in armed conflicts. From the standpoint of Just War theory, it raises the question of whether or how, as an acknowledged vital resource for the waging of a war by the military, interpreters, like their soldier counterparts, might assume some responsibility for the ways that wars are conducted.

THE DECISION TO INTERPRET

Interpreters in war zones are also influenced by pragmatic, personal, and political realities that help determine both their decision to work as an interpreter in a particular conflict as well as their approach to a particular interpreting task. Unlike most other interpreting contexts, however, in violent conflict situations interpreters are expected to work exclusively for one side or the other. There is an expectation of allegiance, regardless of whether the motivation for working in a particular conflict is based solely on a desire for financial or material gain or connected to a political or moral cause. Interpreters decide which cause or individual or group they will align themselves with amongst all those involved including the established media, alternative media sources, military institutions, various insurgent groups, and human rights institutions. This decision is often grounded more in ordinary morality given the absence of a role morality attached to any professional status as an interpreter. As Baker notes (M. Baker 2010: 200; and see Rafael 2007):

> On the one hand, each translator or interpreter is ultimately an individual with a personal history, with a potentially complex, shifting and perhaps even ambivalent position in relation to different elements of the public narratives that orient the war, and often with a network of personal relations to different elements on both sides of the war. And yet translators and interpreters, like other members of society, soon find out there is no place in war for fluid, shifting identities, for split or even strained identities, nor for negotiated narratives of any kind.

As a conflict unfolds, social, political, and military conditions on the ground can change rapidly, requiring interpreters to continually consider disparate sets of rights and obligations and weigh one ethical obligation against another. In the case of Iraq, the justification for the invasion was from the outset framed in confused and contradictory rhetoric by the U.S. and its allies designed ultimately to support the case to invade. Although the illegality of the war according to international law made it an ‘unjust’ war in the eyes of many Iraqis and members of the international community, the weapons of mass destruction argument was coupled with the objective of freeing the Iraqi people from a brutal dictator in order to convince others, including many Iraqis, of the ‘justness’ of the war. In the days and months following the invasion, competing images evoked contradictory moral feelings and attitudes—images of Iraqi people burying their dead and fleeing their bombed out homes and cities were juxtaposed with Iraqis in the streets celebrating the end of the dictatorship. As the invasion turned into a prolonged occupation, images of prisoner abuse in Abu Ghraib and illegal torture in Guantánamo revealed gross violations of the Geneva Convention by the U.S. military. Each of these events revealed a different truth about the war.

The potentially complex nature of a conflict can make it difficult to assess the significance and implications of one's own engagement in a war, whether from inside or outside the war zone. As an ex-army officer suggests in relation to his own reporting of the wars in Iraq and Afghanistan (Skaskiw 2008: 1–2):

> It's difficult to write about armed conflict, as emotions are high and the details one chooses can bias a story in almost any direction. The problem with war narratives isn't lying. The problem is there's too much truth. Everything you've ever heard about war is likely true: the leisure, the camaraderie, the sudden, violent unpredictable extinguishing of human life, the extravagant consumption of resources, fear, cynicism, stupidity, opportunism, earnestness, courage, sacrifice. In this regard, it's very human. The enterprise is so vast that almost everything is true, and writers can choose whichever truths support a particular thesis.

Interpreters in Iraq embody many of the contradictory feelings and attitudes that have emerged out of the war in Iraq. Like their counterparts in the asylum system, for local and contract interpreters, the choice to work with the U.S. military and their allies, to take jobs as fixers with international journalists or aid agencies, to work for the invasion or against the occupation involve ethical decisions that are embedded within the social, economic, and political conditions created by the war. Additionally, war zone interpreters are more likely to serve openly as gatekeepers, informants, and informed mediators in a given interaction. Local interpreters dress in army fatigues and sometimes carry weapons; the bond that develops between interpreters and their units is equivalent in many cases to the affective bond which develops among the soldiers of a platoon where safety and survival depend on mutual trust. The same can be said for journalists and their fixers (see Palmer 2007; Palmer and Fontan 20077; Goldfarb 2005; Fahmy 2004; Seierstad 2003). This can weaken the contingent nature of interpreting activity with respect to these institutions at the interactional level, temporarily granting interpreters the status of fictive equals—like fictive kin—within their group. On the other hand, the fact that local interpreters are not legitimate members of the media or the military means that they are not afforded the same institutional protections. Under these circumstances the contingent nature of their position becomes once again exposed, for example in their lack of right to protection or asylum once they relinquish the interpreter role.

The Character of the Military Field

Given that the ethical nature of interpreting activity is likely to be informed by the social and institutional contexts in which it occurs, in the context of war, interpreter ethics will be shaped by such factors as: the political or economic motives for the conflict, the military institutions and personnel waging the war on the ground, and any significant cultural gaps that exist between the warring factions. Each of these factors has the potential to directly or indirectly influence both the decision to interpret and the kind of role that interpreters take on within a particular conflict.

Given the absence for most interpreters in war zones of an autonomous professional identity as interpreter, the role morality of the military institutions for which they work can play a significant role in shaping their relationship to the war itself and their role within it, regardless of whether the decision to interpret is motivated by politics, economic necessity, or the pursuit of dangerous adventure. Though the military as a whole does share significant cultural and structural overlaps with civil society (Moskos et al. 1999; Snider 1999; Morgan 2003), combat units in the military possess some of the characteristics of what Erving Goffman called total institutions: "place[s] of residence and work, where a large number of like situated individuals, cut off from the wider society for an appreciable period of time, together lead an enclosed, formally administered round of life" (Goffman 1961: 11). In these enclosed, formally administered spaces, the subtle set of habits and dispositions that characterize the military field is lived out by its members—akin to the field-habitus relationship theorized by Bourdieu.

The specific values and principles upheld by soldiers in combat units—their role morality—both reflect the beliefs of the wider society but also serve to distinguish military professionals from their civilian counterparts (Cook 2008: 58). Important channels for the inculcation of these habits and dispositions include enforced discipline, ceremonial rituals, hierarchical command structures, and the internalization of a professional military ethos (Snider 1999), the latter largely achieved through ethics training of officers (Challans 2007; Robinson 2007; Robinson et al. 2008) who set the basic norms that guide the behavior of individual soldiers deployed in war zones. In war, the official representatives of the military field, in close association with representatives of the political field, reproduce the rules and principles received through ethics education. Training in military ethics influences how members of the military understand the purpose of a particular conflict, their role within it, and their behavior toward their enemies and allies in combat.

For interpreters in war zones, the absence of any official institutional location means that they cannot justify their actions through appeals to organizational rules and principles as can members of the military. They cannot claim to be just following orders. There are no professional codes of duty and service or of neutrality and impartiality to shield them from the consequences of their ethical subjectivity. Interpreters are therefore more likely to adopt at least certain aspects of its role morality, tacitly buying into the military-political rationale for the war. This can be particularly problematic in the shifting conditions of war. In the absence of an autonomous professional identity, interpreters are positioned within the social/institutional frame of the military-political field, where they seek but do not always find full protection and acceptance as legitimate partners. For many interpreters in Iraq the initial motivation to serve as an interpreter was to assist in the effort to remove Saddam and the Baath Party from power, not to support a prolonged and deadly occupation. However, the status of the war itself, or as in the Iraq war, its presumed illegitimacy in the eyes of the international community, is rarely explicitly mentioned in interpreters' accounts of their motives to interpret, and many interpreters cite reasons for working with the military that have little to do directly with Saddam. Instead they mention, for example, the pay they receive, the adventure of working for the armed forces, the opportunity to use or improve their English or to act as a cultural broker for the Iraqi people. Many blame the insurgency rather than the U.S.-led invasion for destroying their livelihoods and diminishing their wealth. The situation is summed up in a blog entry entitled 'Who is the Interpreter?' dated June 23, 2008, written by 'Sam', an Iraqi interpreter blogger in his early twenties:

> here I'm trying to define the interps and who r they and what r they and why they chose this job. I won't talk only about myself here but I'll talk about other terps too.
>
> the terps community is a mixed lot and different classes of ppl, u can find terps from age 18 years old to 65 years and maybe more and from different life classes, like ppl used to be wealthy families or ppl poor and trying to be rich or ppl just want to live good and in peace. u can find doctors, engineers, and ppl still students and also u find ppl they haven't even graduated from high school and ppl cant read or write Arabic or English!! . . .
>
> I've never met an interpreter he really loves this job and he really wants to stay in it forever or something. they all have goals and most of the goals r two: gettin kinda good money, feeling safer at work more than at home cuz at work u know u r a target and u r ready to protect yourself but at home in any sec somebody can come and kill u.
>
> there is another fact, I've never heard a terp says he works to help his country, I mean I heard some of them say it, but I bet them if they really mean it . . . for myself I work for the money, money and revenge from insurgents and nothing else!! I mean I love my country, but to be honest I'm not doing it for my country. Through terps job, the terp help a loooot of ppl, not only by translating but by talking and explaining to Americans things they think wrong about Iraq and Iraqis.

Interpreters who are adopted as 'fictive kin' within the military-political field hope to avoid being on the outside of a social/institutional frame, standing alone, vulnerable to attack by insurgents, on the one hand, or suspected by the U.S. military of working as double agents or spies, on the other. As far as their working environment is concerned, the military provides local interpreters with the only institutional legitimacy available. This suggests the possibility that, like the military personnel with whom they work, interpreters are inclined to exercise ethical judgment with respect to the war within the framework of the military field itself. Sebastian Junger, writing about his time as an embedded journalist in Afghanistan, has commented on the power of the platoon to engage him deeper in the conflict, threatening to compromise his 'journalist' perspective (Junger 2010: 212):

> Because I didn't carry a gun I would always be relegated to a place outside the platoon, but that didn't mean I was unaffected by its gravitational pull. There was a power and a logic to the group that overrode everyone's personal concerns, even mine, and somewhere in that loss of self could be found relief from the terrible worries that could befall you. And it was pretty obvious that if things got bad enough—and there was no reason to believe they wouldn't—the distinction between journalist and soldier would become irrelevant. A scenario where I found myself stuffing Kerlix into a wound or helping to pull someone to safety was entirely plausible, and that forced me to think in ways that only soldiers usually have to.

In a similar way, interpreters embedded in combat units will be inclined to exercise ethical judgment with respect to the war within the framework of the military field itself, that is, like Junger, to "think in ways that only soldiers usually have to".

Interpreting the War in Iraq

There are a number of inter-related issues to consider when evaluating the moral and ethical status of the decision to interpret in a war including the relationship of interpreters and translators to the parties in the conflict, their original motivation for the decision, and the developments that occur on the ground as the conflict unfolds. In the Iraq war, in addition to U.S. military linguists, contract linguists were relied on in significant numbers due to a shortage of trained linguists within the military itself. According to the Congressional Research Service, as of June 2009, there were an estimated 9,128 contract linguists in Iraq who are native speakers of Arabic and Kurdish (Defense Industry Daily 2009). Contract linguists are divided into three different categories (CAT I, II, III). The average pay for a CAT I linguist is $15,000 per year while CAT II and III linguists can earn over $200,000, depending on their level of clearance and location of duty. CAT I linguists are local national hires with security screening but no security clearance. While possessing native proficiency in the target language, their English language abilities can vary considerably. CAT II linguists must be U.S. citizens, have advanced proficiency in English, and have native proficiency in the target language. Linguists in this category are granted 'Secret' level security clearance. CAT III linguists must also be U.S. citizens who are fluent in English. For this level, native proficiency in the target language is preferred, but not required. CAT III linguists are granted 'Top Secret' level security clearance. Only CAT II and II linguists are allowed to work on sensitive intelligence functions (*Statement of Work for Combined/Joint Task Force Operation Enduring Freedom* 2004). Unlike their CAT I counterparts, many higher level contract linguists are Arabic speakers from countries like Jordan, Egypt, or Sudan, making them less familiar with Iraqi Arabic.[1] They are housed on military bases where they are also provided with meals. Like members of the military, they cannot leave the base unless on patrol or on a mission. They are also not allowed to have any contact with friends or relatives and can be prosecuted as traitors if found acting against U.S. interests (Harman 2009).[2]

There are a number of factors that attract Iraqis and other Arabic speakers to interpreting. The majority of contract linguists cite a combination of economic, political, and personal motives. At the start of the conflict, for many interpreters working in Iraq the motivation to serve as an interpreter was to assist in the effort to remove Saddam and the Baath Party from power:

> In Iraq, we were waiting for Godot. So the Americans were Godot. (Iraqi interpreter, Tyson 2004)
>
> I wanted to be an active part of it [the rebuilding of Iraq] with the Americans—to help them, and also to help my people. (Iraqi interpreter, Susman 2007)
>
> I was the first or second translator to work with the coalition forces in my city, the first or second Iraqi to set foot on the American base in Mosul. The Marines paid me $150 a month, which was better than the $2 I was making as a librarian. So I didn't see the weapons in their hands, I saw flowers, and I took them all as friends. I loved what I was doing because I thought it was a good thing for my country. (Iraqi interpreter, Mardan 2006)
>
> I thought Saddam was a criminal. America was going to give us freedom, and I wanted to help with this. (Iraqi interpreter, LaPlante 2009)
>
> When I spoke to my mom, I told [her] I joined the army, she doesn't like it she told me how come you're going to be against your people, against the Muslim, I told her, listen mom, I got to help those people I'm not going to be against them, you know as a translator interpreter. I'm not a killer. (Moroccan-American interpreter, 'Turning Linguists to Soldiers' 2008)

Some indicate a sense of alienation toward their country as a result of the dictatorship:

> Patriotism has been killed in Iraq. Saddam killed my love for this country. I would be lying if I told you I [was] doing this job because I love my country. I am here because this is a job I like doing. (Iraqi interpreter, Basu 2005)

Others blame the insurgents for destroying their livelihoods and diminishing their wealth:

> My family, we used to be a wealthy family, a very wealthy family, we had three houses. And then the insurgents came to our houses and they threatened us and they told us to leave our houses. We lost everything. I told my dad that we need money. There [is] no options for any jobs, only this job, being an interpreter for the U.S. military. (Iraqi interpreter, 'New Voices', July 2009)

The contrasting, motivating feelings expressed in these examples highlight the multifaceted nature of the decision to interpret in war on the side of an invading, occupying army. For these interpreters, their decisions reflect both Iraq's history of dictatorship and internal division, and a pragmatic faith in the means, the U.S. invasion, to an end, the removal of Saddam from power. This does not necessarily indicate blind support for the conflict. Many of the interpreters quoted above also voiced criticism of the American response to the insurgency, the scandals at Abu Ghraib, the medical treatment for interpreters wounded in military action, and the difficulty of obtaining travel visas or permanent asylum in the U.S. The interpreters' comments, however, betray a willing suspension of belief in their ethical responsibility to judge whether the stated ends (the removal of Saddam) justify the means (a pre-emptive strike on their country). This is accomplished in two ways: at an individual level, through their visceral support for the end of a brutal dictatorship and U.S.-led economic sanctions, and at a social level through their incorporation within the U.S. military institution. As the following comments suggest:

> We became like one family, his family and my family. He [a U.S. soldier] is the only guy I trust . . . he was the only one who knew exactly where I lived in Iraq. (Iraqi interpreter, Sullivan 2008)

> It was normal, you know, I just American soldier, American yeah, a native Arabic speaker, but American soldier serving his country. So it was no problem for me, you know, we are 51st TICO[3] and we're speaking tongues. (Egyptian-American interpreter, 'Turning Linguists to Soldiers' 2008)

> I was working on the transitioning of responsibilities from the Coalition and the U.S. to the Iraqi government. I interpreted at high-level

> presentations on national security at joint meetings between the Ministry of Defense and three-star generals. I ended up spending more time with the officers than with my family. (Iraqi interpreter, Sherr 2008: 1)

In many ways, the motivations and rationales given by these interpreters to serve as interpreters in the war—patriotism and pragmatism, selflessness and self-interest—are similar to the reasons individuals give for enlisting in the military: patriotism, pay, a search for adventure, and a means of escape. It is generally recognized that since the Vietnam war era, a shift in motivation for military service has taken place in the U.S., Canada, and Western Europe, characterized by what the military sociologist Charles Moskos described as "the erosion of the institutional format and the ascendancy of the occupational model" (Moskos 1977: 44; and see Segal 1986; Battistelli 1997; Battistelli et al. 1999; Cowen 2005; Eighmey 2006; Woodruff et al. 2006). According to this thesis, there has been a growing divide between the institutional military model made up of soldiers who serve in response to a call to duty and service to one's country and the occupational model comprised of individuals who enlist primarily out of self-interest, in the form of monetary compensation and educational and employment benefits. Others view these not as contrasting models but as different dimensions of military service, what has been referred to as "pragmatic professionalism" (Segal 1986: 358; and see Krebs 2009), meaning that individuals enlist both out of a sense of duty or obligation and for the potential economic benefits. An alternative paradigm has been considered by a number of military sociologists who question whether the military has taken on the characteristics of 'postmodern' society (Booth et al. 2001; Morgan 2003) and the trend of its citizens toward fragmented commitments and instrumental loyalties toward their communities, societies, or nations as a whole. According to this view, motives for enlistment have become more rooted in individual self-fulfillment than in civic responsibility. This includes the imagined adventure of war which remains an attractive reason for many to join, as Skaskiw comments (2008: 4–5):

> In terms of a soldier's motivation, livelihood and adventure usually trump politics and virtue. For surprisingly many soldiers, politics is unimportant. Thucydides observed this in his description of the Athenian mobilization for the decisively disastrous invasion of Sicily. We kid ourselves into thinking it was all glory, God, and country until Vietnam. It's not and never has been. It's livelihood, adventure, reputation and the fact that young men like to fight.

All of these motives are present in soldier accounts of the war in Iraq, with some questioning the war and its consequences (Crawford 2005; Buzzell 2005; Rieckhoff 2006) more than others (Burden 2006; Yon 2008).

The decision to serve as an interpreter in war is arguably very different from the decision to enlist in the military given that a soldier's primary function is to kill. It is nevertheless the case that interpreting in a war and waging a war both serve as a means to the same end—generally speaking, the achievement of 'victory' over an enemy, often by whatever means, by one side or the other. Although both the means and the ends for waging war may be decided by politicians and commanding officers, through their participation, both interpreters and soldiers tacitly approve these decisions. In the case of Iraq, by working for the U.S. military, Iraqi and other Arabic-speaking interpreters provided support for the putative justness of what many in the international community considered an unjust war. For many of the interpreters who signed up at the invasion stage, the end was believed to be the removal of Saddam.[4] When this 'end' created the conditions for civil war and a prolonged U.S. occupation, both interpreters and soldiers—as well as those who may have supported them initially—had to readjust their understanding of their role in view of the changing nature of the conflict.

The Concept of Just War and the Decision to Interpret

With regard to Iraq, the relationship of means to ends in the decision to wage war raises the question of whether Iraqi and other Arab-speaking interpreters had a moral responsibility to refuse to participate in a war that was perceived as unjust by many in the international community—despite the individual or political benefits they stood to gain.

According to Just War theory, a war is just if two sets of principles are satisfied: there is due cause to wage war, *jus ad bellum*, and proper conduct is exercised in war, *jus in bello*. War must be waged only in self-defense or in defense of others. The decision to go to war must be taken as a last resort, by a legitimate authority, and with the aim of promoting a lasting peace. The force used must be proportional, and whenever possible civilians must be spared from violence (Walzer 1977, 2004). In Just War theory, individual combat soldiers are not held responsible for the principle of *jus ad bellum* as the decision to declare war is not theirs. The ad bellum responsibility is that of the political decision makers alone. Soldiers are however responsible for their conduct in war, the principle of *jus in bello*. From a Just War theoretical perspective, the invasion of Iraq was far from just: it violated Iraqi self-determination and international law; diplomatic means had not been exhausted with regard to the question of WMDs; the war was unnecessary for the defense of U.S. national security; and it caused injury and death to hundreds of thousands of Iraqi civilians. Related events in Guantánamo and Abu Ghraib, and the controversy surrounding the extraordinary rendition of prisoners also called into question the principle of *jus in bello*.

Despite widespread international opposition to the war however, the invasion by the U.S. was approved by the U.S. legislature, and the removal of Saddam was initially welcomed by certain Iraqis, particularly in the immediate aftermath of the invasion, and was a motivation behind individual decisions to sign up to interpret. However, the lack of any post-invasion strategy and the continued failure of the reconstruction efforts to provide peace and stability to the population quickly eroded any support that had existed for the purpose and the presence of U.S. troops in Iraq. As early as 2004, one Special Forces veteran in Iraq reported on the lack of support amongst the Iraq population (Ricks 2004: 15):

> We are without allies amongst the Iraqi populace, including those who have benefited from the ouster of Saddam . . . Across Baghdad, Latifiyah, Mahmudiyah, Salman Pak, Baqubah, Balad, Taji, Baiji, Ramadi and just about everywhere else you can name, the people absolutely hate us. The Iraqi people have not bought into what the Americans are selling, and no amount of military activity is going to change this.

The rapid change in status of the U.S. forces was exacerbated by policy decisions and their realization by combat units on the ground during which violations of the principle of *jus in bello* occurred. As Paul Rieckhoff, a First Lieutenant and Infantry Platoon Leader, notes (Rieckhoff 2006: 170–171):

> My Platoon did things right most of the time. Even if my president did not. Sometimes it was easier than others. It wasn't our choice to come here and wage this war, but we chose how we would be remembered. By the end of our time in Iraq, we had made friends and done all we could to fix what we had broken. After our first cordon and search[5] every one of my soldiers "got it." Maybe some folks in Washington should go to Iraq. They could pick up a rifle, kick a door in and see what it's like. Then maybe they'd get it.

These raids, described by Rieckhoff below, came to define the occupation for many Iraqi citizens (*ibid.*: 168–169):

> Boom! Hinges burst and metal groaned. The door bowed, pieces flew, eyes scanned, and feet shuffled forward in one strong and violent motion [. . .]. The family who lived inside was sleeping on the roof—it was much cooler up there—and couldn't get dressed in time to answer the door. They screamed and yelled in Arabic. We screamed and yelled in English—sweat pouring, babies wailing, muzzles swinging, and hearts pounding. We huddled them into the far corner so we could cuff them, control them, and search the house. The women cried

> uncontrollably, the men were angry and proud-always glaring. And the children just watched intently. Often they were surprisingly calm, curious, attentive.

Interpreters typically accompanied raids like these, as well as participating in combat foot patrols, vehicle patrols, ambushes, bomb-clearing, and base security missions. They dressed in army fatigues, wore body armor, traveled in Humvees, and sometimes carried weapons. Given their symbolic identification with the combat units, practices like 'cordon and search' and the shifts in public opinion they contributed to affected interpreters as hostility toward them increased. Some interpreters responded by re-iterating the belief that the war was an alignment between Iraqi interests and those of the U.S., as the following account reveals (Basu 2005):

> Sammy conceals his face with a mask and dark glasses to hide his identity. But through the dark lenses he can see the resentment in people's eyes when he asks them tough questions for the Americans." They hate us for what we are doing," said Sammy, 51, who interprets for soldiers in the 121st Infantry Regiment's 2nd Battalion. But Sammy is undeterred. One day soon, he is convinced, Iraq will be at peace. "Mr. Bush saved 25 million people in my country," he said. "I put a picture of him up in my home."

Others experienced permanent or temporary ruptures between their own participation, the changing attitudes of Iraqis to the occupation, and the inevitable truths about the war as it unfolded, as Tyson reports (2004):

> Yet Ahmed has also seen ugly sides of the U.S. military. On a handful of raids when 101st soldiers beat Iraqis without justification, he objected and refused to interpret. Earlier this year, when news broke of the prisoner abuse at Abu Ghraib, Ahmed and the other interpreters with his Stryker unit threatened to resign en masse. "When I saw that on TV, I was very upset. All the interpreters were angry," he says, especially over images that play into Iraqi stereotypes of Americans as infidels corrupted by alcohol and pornography. "So I went to the Sergeant Major and said I will give you 30 minutes to apologize or we are leaving," he said. That won an immediate apology, along with a pledge from the military that no such abuses were happening in Mosul. Ahmed stayed.

The intimate involvement of interpreters in war raises the question of how their decision to participate in a particular conflict should be judged, both initially and once the conflict unfolds. In the case of combatants, it is considered morally justifiable for combatants to fight in any war in which they're commanded to fight, even when a war is considered unjust. Their institutional subordination to military and political authority has traditionally excused them from moral judgment regarding the justness of a war (Ceulemans 2007/8; McMahan 2006). Any moral reason they may have not to fight is overridden with their moral need to fulfill their role within the military, in the interest of the institution itself. This does not absolve them of moral responsibility once they are engaged in combat however. Nor does it help them to ignore the multiple conflicting truths that unfold as the war progresses, as in Iraq, for example: discovering that the local population doesn't support their efforts on the ground ('the people absolutely hate us') and their own part in the emergence of insurgencies (see Shadid 2006) or in practices which violate international agreements (see Saar and Novak 2005; Williams 2005; Yee 2005; Lagouranis 2007). The line between these truths is rather blurred—are they questions of *jus in bello* or consequences of an initial violation of the principle *jus ad bellum*? If the latter, then combatants are unavoidably drawn into questions about the justness of a war, not only about what is permissible to do during war but about whether it is right to participate in a war at all. It is at these points that combatants cease to be mere instruments and instead are forced to reflect on the justification of the war itself, despite or because of its complex truths (Marine Infantryman, Tucker 2008: 158):

> In reality, from what I've learned from all my brothers that I've been with, is that we would rank high among antiwar activists. Nobody knows the human cost of combat better than us, no one. Most people who are actually in a war are among the most antiwar people there are, and rightfully so. I'm not saying that war is a needless thing, because at times you must fight—there are things worth fighting for. [. . .] But I don't think that war as it used to be will ever happen again—for instance, World-War II type-conflict. It will never be that way again, where clear lines are drawn where you always know your frontlines.

For Muslim soldiers and interpreters the Qur'an serves as an additional source of guidance regarding the justification of war, whether in Iraq or elsewhere. Islamic theology provides a theory of just war that espouses similar principles to those outlined in Western tradition regarding, for example, proportionality, the protection of innocent civilians, prisoner rights, and the legitimacy of the aims of the war declared (Abou El Fadl 2002: 19; Kelsay 1993: 5). According to religious studies scholar John Kelsay, though any distinctions and overlaps between Western and Islamic-based Just War theories are complex and require a careful historical and political understanding of both traditions, they nevertheless share a belief in applying moral criteria to decisions about peace and war (Kelsay 2009).[6] For many U.S.-based and/or U.S. citizen Muslim soldiers, the question of the moral justification of the war in Iraq was refracted through the lens of both faith-based and state-based traditions, as the following comments suggest:

> Today, a [Muslim] brother said to me, 'You know, if we're about peace, why are we fighting another country? And that's valid. But you have to support the country when it's right and when it's wrong. (U.S.-born Muslim soldier, Boorstein 2009)
>
> The war on terror is not about Islam, This is a war against criminals who use religion to say they are good people, but they're no better than the Mafia. They're just common criminals, many with criminal records . . . It was great that I got to use my training against people who tried to kill us and who tried to give a wrong idea about my religion. (Moroccan-born Muslim American soldier, Avlon 2006)
>
> It's kind of like the Civil War, where brothers fought each other across the Mason-Dixon line. I don't want to stain my faith, I don't want to stain my fellow Muslims, and I also don't want to stain my country's flag. (U.S.-born Muslim soldier, Elliott 2009)

A similar position has been expressed by both local Iraqi and U.S. citizen Muslim civilian interpreters:

> I want to help the Iraqi people understand what the [American] soldiers are there for. To show them there's someone from their culture, who's also from the U.S., who understands them and wants to help. (Egyptian-born Muslim American interpreter, Marks 2007).
>
> I've eased explosive situations at checkpoints when we've stopped cars containing men's sisters and wives. When we search neighborhoods for weapons, I've helped keep tensions low between my guys and local residents . . . I like danger and I fear only two things: failing my guys and Allah. (Iraqi interpreter, Vincent 2003)

Civilian interpreters in war zones are not commanded by any institution; they are contracted to interpret, motivated by their ties to their nation, by a social or political cause, and/or by economic necessity, things which, by whatever means and despite the absence of 'clear lines', can appear to be 'things worth fighting for'. In war, interpreters, like combatants, thus function simultaneously as free agents and embodied conduits for the political and military institutions that they agree to serve. As such, they become de facto players in a conflict which they may not choose but which they sustain both morally and instrumentally. Given their contractual ties to the military, their personal ties to their colleagues, and the absence of an independent institutional location, it is perhaps not surprising that interpreters come to act according to the same or similar moral and ethical principles as the soldiers with whom they serve. This shared understanding of a conflict which develops between interpreters and combatants is not without significance given the increasingly key role interpreters have begun to play as cultural informants for the military.

KNOWING THE ENEMY: INTERPRETERS AS CULTURAL BROKERS

As the occupation of Iraq took hold, cultural information and understanding came to be viewed as central to military operations as a means to counter the ensuing insurgency. A consensus began to emerge that the U.S. administration and the military had failed to grasp the kind of war they were waging. The assumption that victory would be achieved through the defeat of an armed enemy through superior military technology had proven false (Hashim 2003; Betz 2008; Porter 2007). It became clear that the support of the Iraqi people against the insurgency would be won or lost, not through fire power, but through increased information (Kilcullen 2007). What was needed was human judgment and knowledge of Iraqi custom, collective memory, institutions, and traditions.[7] According to reports from the military field, U.S. forces and their allies required the information necessary to "recognize and exploit the underlying tribal structure of the country; the power wielded by traditional authority figures; the use of Islam as a political ideology; the competing interests amongst the Shia, the Sunni and the Kurds; the psychological effects of totalitarianism; and the divide between urban and rural, among other things" (McFate 2005: 37). Maj. Gen. Robert Scales reported in 2007 to the U.S. Senate Armed Services Committee on Emerging Threats & Capabilities on the subject, 'Efforts to Improve the Department of Defense's Language and Cultural Awareness Capabilities':

> In Iraq, a curtain of cultural ignorance continues to separate the good intentions of the American soldier from Iraqis of good will. Inability to speak the language and insensitive conduct become real combat vulnerabilities that the enemy has exploited to his advantage. The military of the future must be able to go to war with enough cultural knowledge to thrive in an alien environment. Empathy will become a weapon. Soldiers must gain the ability to move comfortably among alien cultures, to establish trust and cement relationships that can be exploited in battle.

In his testimony, Scales also notes that graduates of the Defense Language Institute (DLI), where language training for military linguists takes place, were unprepared for this task:

> Generally their knowledge is very basic. I had a lot of experience with DLI graduates in Korea when I was assistant division commander and

> we relied on them to do a lot of the decryption and interpretation. I found them great linear translators. In other words, to use Andre's point about meaning and the subtleties of the language, they didn't have it, so generally we had to rely on native born Korean speakers to be able to provide us those subtleties that you need when you're trying to determine second- and third-order meaning out of things.

The military was also slow to recognize the potential for 'cultural stress'—similar to civilian 'culture shock'—amongst the military personnel interacting with local populations (Azari et al. 2010) which, in combat situations, is understood to be caused by role confusion due to "a lack of clear guidelines or managed expectations of what troops will encounter" and the absence of a clear sense of purpose over the "worthwhileness of their efforts" (*ibid.*: 594). Given the dearth of foreign language skills and regional and cultural expertise within the military itself, specific strategies for a type of 'culture-centric' warfare began to emerge. A major publication was issued at the end of 2006, the *Counterinsurgency Field Manual 3–2*, described by Bing West, a marine veteran of the Vietnam war and assistant secretary of defense in the Reagan administration, as "part sociology, part catechism" and one of the most academically influential field manuals in military history (West 2008: 121). The field manual, which Thomas Ricks wrote "can be read as a scathing critique of the conduct of the war over its first four years" (Ricks 2009a), stressed the importance in counterinsurgency operations of gaining the trust and support of the local people through the provision of security, employment, government services, and respect (West 2008: 120).

In addition to the field operations guide designed for military personnel, the Pentagon also created a controversial project, known as the Human Terrain System (HTS) project, which was designed to recruit social scientists, including anthropologists, to serve as cultural advisors embedded with combat troops. The idea was to accumulate and apply anthropological expertise to the social, ethnographic, cultural, economic, and political terrain of the battlefield in order to develop better strategies and tactics in the war against the insurgents (Stier 2007; Rohde 2007; Stamets 2008; Shay 2009).[8]

Two of the main proponents of this approach, David Kilcullen, an Australian infantry officer turned U.S. State Department advisor, and Montgomery McFate, cultural anthropologist and advisor to the HTS program, were also contributing authors of the *Counterinsurgency Field Manual 3–2*. They argue that anthropological knowledge can contribute to more humane military operations thus better safeguarding civilian populations, as Kilcullen explains (Kilcullen 2007: 20; and see McFate 2007: 21):

> For example, early in the Iraq war, some coalition units alienated friendly communities by failing to understand the social networks through which local, religious, and political threads of identity are

> modulated in Iraqi society. Others arrested innocent bystanders through failure to understand the culture of weapons possession among Iraqi families. Units unnecessarily detained hundreds because they did not understand kinship systems, and lost track of detainees through misunderstanding Arab naming conventions. Some leaders misapplied etic identity categories, or worked on the assumption that constructs like 'democracy', 'human rights' and 'rule of law' apply universally in isolation from a cultural meta-context.

While some anthropologists have signed up for the task, others have been vocal in their opposition to any professional involvement in this call to intellectual arms, viewing it as a violation of their role morality as defined through a code of ethics in which anthropologists vow to do no harm in conducting research.[9] For many anthropologists, the U.S. military's use of operationally relevant cultural knowledge in its counterinsurgency operations in Iraq is no different than its previous attempts to co-opt individuals and governments as native power brokers for colonial and imperialist agendas. In the particular case of Iraq, the military's strategy of using cultural knowledge as a tactical weapon leaves aside questions regarding the justness of the war, the legitimacy of the insurgents' grievances, as well as the unethical practice of using anthropological knowledge to serve the interests of military and intelligence agencies (González 2007; Robben 2009). Anthropologists who have campaigned against this have appealed to their colleagues to refuse "work that is covert, work that breaches relations of openness and trust with studied populations, and work that enables the occupation of one country by another" (Network of Concerned Anthropologists 2007) on the grounds that it violates professional standards.

Consultant anthropologists who have signed on to work with the military possess some of the same attributes and skills as interpreters, for example, knowledge of local geography and politics and cultural and linguistic understanding. In their attempt to work simultaneously for the military and on behalf of Iraqi citizens, they also experience some of the same moral and ethical dilemmas. As one civilian anthropologist working within the military told a *Time* magazine reporter, "You are trying to be loyal to two communities—your subjects, and to the brigade you are attached to. It puts you in an impossible situation" (Stier 2007). This same sentiment is frequently expressed by interpreters, not only in relation to Iraq, but in all conflict situations. There are important differences between them however. Though their decision to serve as informants can be professionally and physically risky (there have been fatalities), anthropologists who work for the military remain strongly situated in their professional role morality, based in an autonomous field of knowledge and power from which they both observe and objectify their task as cultural informants and, as one put it, "the rational analysis that anthropology brings" (Shay 2009: 2). Interpreters, on the other hand, perform their task on the knife edge of cultural, linguistic, and political borders. In war zones, the existential conditions at these borders are shaped by the cross-cultural tensions and turbulence of the limit situation in which interpreters negotiate the ethical for themselves in the face to face of an encounter without their own institutionally defined moral compass.[10]

Interpreters in Culture-Centric Warfare

As the campaigns for and against the engagement of anthropologists as cultural informants develop, interpreters have continued to serve as valuable cultural brokers in Iraq. The military has become increasingly attuned to the position that interpreters can and do occupy as liaisons between the U.S. forces and Iraqi officials and the local population, as the following comments suggest:

> The number one advice I have for people coming to Iraq is become very good friends with your interpreter. They will help you out a lot here. Learn as much as you can from them. They know this place better than anybody else, they have their ears to the streets, they will tell you where the dangerous neighborhoods are, what to look out for, what to do and what not to do. Listen to them. (Infantryman blogger, Buzzell 2005: 191)

> There is nothing more important than communicating with our Iraqi partners. Having someone who gets the nuanced meanings correct, it's so important because you can't underestimate the price of misunderstanding, especially in a combat environment. (Navy captain, Druzin 2008/9: 1)

> What I have come to understand since patrolling the streets of Baghdad day after day is that Joe is one of our most valuable assets for bringing peace to Iraq. He understands the mindset of citizens with which we interact on a daily basis. He lends his support well beyond that of just translation by providing recommendations on projects that are sustainable based on the framework of local government and the precarious rule of law in the city. (Army platoon leader, Bodor 2008)

The references above to linguistic, psychological, economic, and political knowledge indicate the range of expertise that interpreters are understood to possess (at the same time criticisms continue to circulate regarding problems with interpreters' language abilities in English or local dialects and the ever present question of trust). Accounts of the war, written by officers recalling meetings with influential Iraqi government officials or tribal leaders (West and Smith 2003; West 2008; Robinson 2008; Fury 2008; Mansoor 2008) or combatants describing raids and battles (Buzzell 2005;

Rieckhoff 2006; Yon 2008), refer repeatedly to interpreters acting in the capacity of informants or brokers. Some of these interpreters remain nameless or are referred to only by the pseudonyms they adopted; those who are named usually have become influential players in the war and beyond.

One such interpreter is Sadi Othman, a Palestinian born in Brazil, raised in Jordan, and educated by Mennonites, a Christian order which actively promotes pacifism and social justice. Othman, a U.S. citizen and self-proclaimed pacifist, signed up as a contract linguist in Iraq at the start of the war. His linguistic and cultural skills soon called him to the attention of senior military officials, and he eventually became senior advisor to General Petraeus. Some of the details of Othman's biography and service to the U.S. military are highlighted in Ricks' *The Gamble* (2009b), in L. Robinson's *Tell Me How This Ends* (2008), and in military and Mennonite publications (Jeffers 2005; Osborne 2009). In these reports, both high-ranking U.S. military and Iraqi government officials refer to him as a unique and indispensable resource in securing political and diplomatic reconciliation during his time as an interpreter and advisor. As Robinson reports (2008: 175–176):

> When Maliki became prime minister, he told Othman he'd heard good things about him from his predecessor. The gaunt, white-haired man gained a reputation among Iraqi officials as a reliable channel who would transmit their message without prejudice—and deliver an answer. "They know I don't side with one over the other," he said. "The top leaders trust him, and a lot of military guys get their credibility with the Iraqis from Sadi," said Maj. Gen. Frank Helmick, who had been Petraeus' deputy in Mosul. The Iraqis knew that when Othman called, Petraeus was calling, but they were also more willing to respond because "the big Sad" was their friend, and a friend of Iraq.

In this and other accounts of Othman's participation in the war, what is foregrounded, beside his linguistic and cultural knowledge, is his trustworthiness, his courage, and his commitment to peace and brotherhood. There is no suggestion of any conflict between his Arab and American ties or between his pacifist beliefs and his direct involvement in the war as advisor to General Petraeus. Othman was motivated to sign up as a linguist in Iraq following the attacks on the World Trade Center in New York where he lived and worked as a taxi driver. He is quoted as saying that as an Arab-American from a Muslim tradition, he felt humiliated that the attackers were Muslim and he wanted to do something about it (*ibid.*: 175). Like other contract interpreters and local Iraqi interpreters, and like cultural brokers throughout history, his decision to interpret originated in his personal biography and social history. The trust and respect which Othman receives from Iraqi and U.S. officials alike originates in their shared belief in his compliance with one of the principle tenets of the interpreting code of ethics: impartiality—as he states, "they know I don't side with one over the other". His presumed impartiality also seems to shield Othman, an avowed pacifist, from any moral responsibility for his direct participation in a war which has caused the deaths of thousands of innocent civilians and which, for many, was without just cause.

What is striking in the stories of Sadi Othman is the absence of any suggestion of the complex, paradoxical moral and social spaces that interpreters occupy in war, and that appears in many interpreters' accounts of their experience. There is no mention of the risk of symbolic violence to himself or to others which the decision to interpret carries with it. In these accounts, this risk is masked by an implicit appeal to a universalizing ethics which grounds the moral ambiguities of moral practice in impartiality rather than personal responsibility. The descriptions of Othman's role in the conflict appeal implicitly to the type of discourse ethics advocated by Habermas and others that sets out to establish the necessary conditions for mutually effective dialogue amongst conversational partners. As an impartial mediator Othman is seen to demonstrate how communicative reason and reciprocal recognition can work together to achieve consensus through mutually respectful exchanges of perspectives amongst parties in conflict. The assumption is that the parties with whom Othman works share a belief and a desire for a common framework to emerge. His cultural knowledge and communication skills earn him social, political, and legal legitimacy on both sides of the conflict. What fades into the background of this optimistic picture of 'concrete universalism' however is the backdrop of the occupation itself. Though it may be strategically beneficial for both General Petraeus and the Iraqi officials to give this wider context minimal significance in their interactions with one another, their respective unequal roles of occupier and occupied cannot be denied. It is the occupier, not the occupied, who determines when and under what terms the occupation ends. The reciprocal recognition which Othman's presence as neutral arbiter is said to ensure is contingent on this political reality.

In these accounts, Othman's impartiality is presented as a characteristic that guarantees objectively good ethical judgment and moral responsibility.[11] What is never called into question is the ethical subjectivity involved in his decision to interpret for the U.S. military in the Iraq war as a response to events in New York, a decision that no appeal to impartiality can neutralize. In most other accounts of interpreting in war, impartiality is not what is at issue; interpreters know that they have chosen sides and are clear about the risk of violence, both symbolic and physical, that this implies. The trust and camaraderie that develops between them and combat troops is a product of the social, moral, and ethical fissures that war produces, not of any stated or assumed neutrality. Indeed, what makes war an important context for the investigation of interpreting ethics is that codes of neutrality and impartiality largely lose their significance and their power to conceal the undeniability of interpreter agency. The personal histories and ethical issues that inform the decision to interpret are complex. What seem like moral certainties at the outset of a war can be shattered by the shifting and indefinite shape that it takes over time.

INTERPRETING ETHICS IN WAR

Local and contract interpreters recruited from within conflict zones or contracted by the military are by definition non-professional, and their decision to interpret in a specific war frequently involves factors that differ significantly from their professional counterparts. For these interpreters, the ethical demand frequently involves the personal and more immediate consequences of the political and social realties associated with violent conflict, offering them little time and space for moral reflection or rationalization. They operate without the guidance of external moral laws or authority, relying both on ordinary morality to decide on the right course of action under the circumstances and on the role morality of their military counterparts. Interpreters are, like combat soldiers, simultaneously active agents in military action and embodied conduits for political decisions over which they have little influence. And both can appeal to role morality in order to justify their adoption of actions which would be presumed to be morally dubious if undertaken outside their role. Even unprofessional interpreters can be shielded by the myth of neutrality some of the time.

Role Morality in the Military: Duty, Virtue, and Reasoned Reflection

Though the U.S. military is an evolving, increasingly heterogeneous institution, and is influenced by attitudes and expectations to do with gender, race, sexual preference, etc. both within its own and outside its own ranks (Miller and Moskos 1995), it nevertheless relies on a stable set of moral norms to guide the behavior of individual soldiers deployed in war zones. Traditionally the aim of the military with regards to ethics training has been to inculcate, through its officers, a homogeneous set of beliefs and values to guide soldiers in understanding the purpose of a particular conflict, their role within it, and their behavior toward their enemies and allies in combat.

Role morality in the U.S. military and in most armed forces in the past several decades has been influenced by two main ethical approaches. One is based in Aristotelian 'virtue ethics' which seeks to ensure moral behavior by inculcating certain virtues—understood to establish balance and equanimity between extreme forms of behavior—in members of the military in order to create good character (P. Robinson 2007). Typically these virtues include: duty, respect, loyalty, selfless service, honor, integrity, and personal courage. In the military context, virtue ethics presumes to instill 'virtue' in individual officers and soldiers, thus ensuring their moral character. There is an inherent assumption in this approach that right actions are defined according to those who perform them, and if those who perform them (members of the military) can be deemed virtuous (based on their military training), then their actions can be defined as 'right' because they are carried out by individuals possessing good moral character.

There are a number of problems increasingly recognized by military scholars themselves with placing the sole emphasis of ethics training on the cultivation of virtuous character. According to Martin Cook, a philosophy professor at the U.S. Naval War College, the inculcation of values such as duty and loyalty tends to be accomplished through rote learning and uncritical sloganeering, with little space for the development of critical thinking regarding the meaning of these values or any conflict that may exist between them in a particular situation (Cook 2008: 65). Cook has also noted that an important aspect of virtue ethics largely ignored in ethics training is the Aristotelian concept of *phronesis*, or practical wisdom, the ability to reflect on one's actions in a specific situation (*ibid.*: 58). Unfortunately, he suggests, the long-standing view in the military is that such reflection is unnecessary, and a potential distraction when preparing soldiers for action (*ibid.*). Principles like duty and loyalty are thus instilled in recruits without consideration of how they might apply these principles in balance with other factors in specific contexts. Others, however, suggest that the emphasis on the role of individual character and personal values ('What should I do?') risks distancing soldiers from their role identity as soldiers ('What kind of soldier should I be?'), a role that is necessarily grounded in the shared narrative and belief commitments of the military. The feeling is that their role morality shields serve as a useful justification for soldiers "to reinforce themselves and preserve their integrity and identity whilst engaged in the act of killing" (Carrick 2008: 196–197). Another potential weakness of the primary focus on individual character is that it allows certain parties under certain circumstances to omit or ignore the features of military institutions that might lead to unethical behavior, as evident in the aftermath of the Abu Ghraib scandal when the military called into question the behavior of the individuals responsible for torture, while the interrogation policies of the Bush administration were left intact.

A second approach to role morality is grounded in deontological ethics. Applied to the military, this approach encourages members of the military to use their own reasoning to determine universal ethical principles of right and wrong—it allows for greater dialogue between institutionally legitimated reason, based in the constrained norms and interest of the military, and publically legitimated reason, based on a more generalized set of norms established amongst citizens from a range of moral, political, social, etc. backgrounds. Though indoctrination into the rules and principles of the military as institution remains the goal, a deontological approach to ethics training aims to provide soldiers with the tools to reflect on these rules and principles and to come to embrace them because they believe them to be rationally (universally) valid, based on observation and experience, not on blind obedience.

There are a range of objectives behind deontological approaches to ethics training. One is to establish rules within the military regarding the rightness and wrongness of moral actions that will be adhered to voluntarily. Another is to develop better moral intuitions amongst members of the military. More controversial for the military is the use of this approach to challenge the authoritarian character of the military itself. Timothy Challans argues, for example, that current army doctrine is more aimed at manufacturing consent than "employing well-reasoned arguments using standards of evidence and criteria of rationality that admits of public reason" (Challans 2007: 158). Challans calls for a greater understanding of the ethical dimension of conflict and warfare through ethics training that encourages explicit philosophical inquiry into the notion of moral autonomy, in particular, the Kantian idea of morally reflective individuals who live by beliefs based on a rationale they understand, beliefs that are open to correction or abandonment in the presence of good reason (*ibid.*: 24). Whatever the application of a deontological approach in a particular military's ethics training, the overarching aim is to produce individuals who are able to think about ethical problems independently and to produce soldiers who believe that what they think is right is more important than or, at least, as important as merely obeying orders or succumbing to peer pressure.

In actuality, it is not all clear that military training in virtue ethics or deontological ethics willfully sets out to promote the degree of reflection and critical thinking that would make combatants as morally responsible for *jus ad bellum* as they are for *jus in bello*. It is also not clear that the military wishes their employees to view themselves as citizens first (like all others) and soldiers second (Rohall et al. 2006). Given the political and ideological nature of all violent conflicts, ethics training that encourages too much interrogation of state and military policies, as opposed to carefully weighed compliance regarding the rightness or wrongness of the cause of a war, would likely be viewed as undermining the military as an institution. But a conflict of interest between interrogation and compliance can be ethically resolved nonetheless. For it is consistent with both virtue ethics and deontological ethics that the duty to sustain the functioning of the military through unquestioning support for a particular cause, especially one which benefits from a degree of political legitimacy, could override any sense of conflicting duty regarding the moral nature of the conflict itself.[12]

In the end, any approach to ethics training grounded in more abstract ideals may be undermined by the realities of the individual motivations for enlistment in contemporary militaries. As discussed above, the decision to join the military is to a considerable extent based on personal and pragmatic considerations, not political or ideological ones. Although the war in Iraq has produced numerous military blogs and published accounts of daily life and death scenarios written by soldiers, most have little to say about the causes they are fighting for. Critics of the war are mainly concerned with practical issues having to do with tactical operations, leadership, and unit cohesion, though these will sometimes be understood in terms of their effect on 'hearts and minds' and the overall success of the conflict. Combatants appear to derive their ethical behavior from the immediate conditions of the violent conflict in which they participate as both active aggressors and embodied conduits. In combat they rely on a 'self-legislation' informed by a role morality that justifies their actions through a set of moral virtues they are deemed to possess and a set of morally sanctioned rules that are granted rational, universal legitimacy by the particular military whom they serve.

Implications for Just Interpreting

Impartiality and neutrality were not the primary claims or justifications of the majority of the interpreters for their decision to interpret in Iraq however. Most were committed to their respective causes and found an expression for these in the employment of the U.S. military, an institution in which neutrality and impartiality are rarely given as an option, though they did feature in the descriptions in praise of Sadi Othman from high-ranking officials on both sides of the Iraq war. The equating of Othman's moral responsibility with his objectivity was offered as a testament to the impartiality of the interpreter. These accounts of Othman's role are a clear demonstration of the generalized value granted to impartiality as both a virtuous and a rational principle. From a moral point of view, however, the value placed on Othman's impartiality does not make his role in the war any different than that of any other interpreter.

Whatever the professional virtues, personal motivations, or moral intuitions of individual local and contract interpreters, most willingly serve the military institutions to which they have pledged their allegiance. Though in their role as cultural brokers and comrades in arms these interpreters cease to be mere linguistic conduits, consciously or not, like the military personnel with whom they serve, they become conduits for the military. In adopting the 'role morality' of the military, these interpreters, like many professional interpreters, embrace many of the functions of this institution. This does not imply the absence of any moral 'residue' that creates ethical uncertainty for these interpreters. Many contract interpreters in the military share a moral proximity to the individuals for whom they speak based in shared linguistic, cultural, or religious bonds. Though they may sometimes rely on their fictive kinship with the military to shield them from the ethical demands of their role, at other times their lack of a clear professional status will leave them vulnerable to the exigencies of ordinary morality—and war is no place to be existentially unarmed, without a clearly warranted 'impartially justifiable' function.

Considerable overlaps with respect to ethical practice appear to develop amongst combatants and interpreters in situations of violent conflict. Both share a similar motivation for their presence in a conflict, based more in livelihood than patriotism. Both are situated in a battlefield in which there is little time or space to consider meta-ethical issues associated with their actions. Both operate simultaneously as active agents in military action and embodied conduits for political decisions over which they have little influence. And both can appeal to role morality in order to justify their adoption of actions which would be presumed to be morally dubious if undertaken outside their role. Even unprofessional interpreters can hide behind the illusion of neutrality.

With measured optimism, some within the military imagine an "awakening warrior" who is trained to be more ethically aware and morally reflective about the nature of war, its purpose, and its consequences (Challans 2007; see also Cook 2005; French 2003). War, like justice itself, is always accompanied by moral paradoxes. Ethics training aimed at promoting greater reflection can undoubtedly shed valuable light on these paradoxes, helping military personnel to become morally competent to make better judgments. Furthermore, the partnerships that develop between the military and local interpreters, particularly in conflicts involving a significant threat to local civilian populations, could also conceivably contribute to this competence. Although initial caution may be an inevitable condition of any alliance between interpreters and the military, a similar kind of trust to that which develops between lawyers and interpreters may also be possible in the context of war, not for strategic purposes, but for moral reasons aimed at lifting at least some of war's inevitable fog.

6 The Interpreter's Visibility

In recent decades, a number of diverse intellectual influences have helped to shape the critical discourse on translation ethics in both research and professional practice, from modernism, postmodernism, and postcolonialism to more recent perspectives originating in hermeneutics and narrative theory (see Venuti 1995/2008, 1998; Arrojo 1998, 2005; Pym 2001; Koskinen 2000; Fiola 2009; M. Baker 2006; Cronin 2006; Tymockzo 2007; Hermans 2009; Goodwin 2010). An explicit or implicit recognition of the translator's visibility is shared across these different theoretical and practical aims, priorities, and understandings of the task of translation. A focus on visibility and agency is increasingly apparent in research, in publications, and in some training as well, as evidenced in several recent collections that foreground ethics, whether the focus is on theoretical perspectives shaping the literary field (Bermann and Wood 2005), pedagogical approaches (Baker and Maier 2011), or a more 'activist' stance to translation and interpreting in situations of conflict (Boéri and Maier 2010). These volumes respond in different but related ways to the ethical dilemmas that translators and interpreters face in negotiating the tensions between the demands of their tasks, their personal and professional positions, and complex local and global allegiances. They share in common the recognition of the *visible* negotiation and 'creative interpretation' that are involved in different types of translation and interpreting activity.

The recognition of the link between translators' visibility and ethical practice has been slowest to occur in the translation of the spoken language. Despite the important work of Ian Mason (1999) and Cecila Wadensjö (1998) which highlighted the inherent dialogic nature of language and the triadic nature of interpreted encounters, both interpreting theories and interpreting codes of practice have essentially remained committed to a view of language as a system, and of interpreters' invisibility, sustained through their impartial interactive presence, as the means to ensure that interlocutors can speak for themselves. While it is perhaps understandable that the face to face immediacy of spoken encounters has encouraged attention to the cognitive and linguistic demands of the task, the magnitude of the ethical demand which this very immediacy makes on all participants in interpreted encounters has been greatly underestimated in interpreting research and in the field of translation studies as a whole. Historically, translation studies scholarship has been unconcerned with or unaware of the ethical domain of spoken language translation, except perhaps through the identification of interpreters like La Malinche as iconic metaphors for colonialism. This is a topic that merits far more attention than I can provide in this final chapter; nevertheless I would like to briefly consider some possible links between perceptions of interpreting within the field of translation and the quality of attention to its ethical domain.[1]

Franz Pöchhacker traces the distinction between translation and interpreting studies to the early nineteenth century and Schleiermacher's distinction between art and scholarship (literary translation) and commerce (interpreting and technical translation), quoting Schleiermacher's description of interpreting as "a merely mechanical task that can be performed by anyone with a modest proficiency in both languages, and where, so long as obvious errors are avoided, there is little difference between worse and better renditions" (Schleiermacher in Pöchhacker 2004: 53). What is relevant here is not Schleiermacher's description of interpreting, though much could and has been said to dispute this understanding, but his distinction between art and commerce, since this characterization persists within translation studies to this day. Though the idea of interpreting as a 'mechanical task' has been considerably dismantled, its association with 'commerce' remains, maintained by the view of interpreters as a channel between two linguistic systems and by the image of the impartial, invisible interpreter. In contrast, the association of literary translation with art and scholarship set out the potential for a creative and experimental relationship between signifier and signified that was not strictly tied to a representational view of language. And importantly, for the translator, this relationship could also operate as a site of cultural and political transformation, that is, of ethical translation. A similar contrast was noted by Lawrence Venuti, though with respect to technical translation (Venuti 1995/2008: 41):

> As Schleiermacher realized long ago, the choice of whether to domesticate or foreignize a foreign text has been allowed only to translators of literary texts, not to translators of technical materials. Technical translation is fundamentally constrained by the exigencies of communication: during the postwar period, it has supported scientific research, geopolitical negotiation, and economic exchange, especially as multinational corporations seek to expand foreign markets and thus increasingly require fluent, immediately intelligible translations of international treaties, legal contracts, technical information, and instructional manuals [. . .] literary translation remains a discursive practice where the translator can experiment in the choice of foreign texts and in the development of translation methods, constrained primarily by the current situation in the target-language culture.

Venuti's aim here was to challenge literary translators to operate against their own constraints, including the constraint of fluency. He was attempting to initiate Schleiermacher's and others' unrealized (in Venuti's view) descriptions of the translator's potential as a vehicle for dissent aimed at the recognition of less powerful voices and, ultimately, greater social and cultural equality. What he and other translation scholars writing during this period wished to accomplish was to activate the ethical function of literary translation, represented in terms like foreignization, resistance, and abusive fidelity against the norms of fluency, domestication, and ethnocentric violence. The aesthetic function of literary translation, including its norms and values, was treated as primarily social and historical, not moral and transcendental. Literary translation was not viewed as functioning toward the revelation of universal moral truths, but as providing a means for understanding the present, in dialogue with the past and with other cultures. Similarly, the emphasis in postcolonial theories on contact zones, asymmetrical power relations, and the ideological over the aesthetic revealed translation as an activity involving far more than contact between languages (Bassnett and Trivedi 1999)

Writing in 2002, Michael Cronin (2002) argued that interpreting studies had remained "largely unaffected by the exciting theoretical developments" of this 'cultural turn' in translation studies. This remains mostly true, though its explanation, I would suggest, lies as much in the interpreting field and its predominantly linguistic orientation to research as in the lack of any substantive dialogue between the interpreting field and the field of translation, in particular, literary translation which, as Venuti suggested more than fifteen years ago, "has traditionally been the field where innovative theories and practices emerge" (Venuti 1995/2008: 41). Just as interpreting scholars and practitioners may not have found any immediate relevance to their research in the 'cultural turn' in translation studies, there is little evidence to suggest that translation scholars and practitioners have perceived any commonality between the texts interpreters translate—for example, oral narratives of trauma, illness, poverty, victimization or guilt, conditions in war zones, or oral deliveries of corporate or academic discourses—with the fictional or nonfictional works they translate despite the plots, themes, and characters common to both. They have also not registered the shared social, institutional, and historical situatedness of the two kinds of texts. Furthermore, they have not recognized any similarity between 'the play of signifiers' in the translations performed on literary texts and 'the signifiers in play' in interpreting contexts. In both cases, semantic uncertainty is involved as are strategic manipulations, webs of interlocution, cultural and textual grids, and overt or covert political agendas. With the theorization of language outlined in chapter 1, the approach to meaning so fundamental to situated acts of interpreting is, paradoxically, more open to variation and ludic experimentation than any literary 'play of signifiers', dependent as that ultimately is—despite its putative refusal—on Saussurean notions of structure. A good deal of interpretive 'prospecting' may be involved in the reading of a written text, but it is even more essential in reading spoken utterances given the little time and space available to make a reasonable judgment about what an utterance may mean based on its use. Meaning is determined in both types of text against a background of prior uses, against present communicative objectives, and against a spectrum of accumulated beliefs about who the interlocutors are, and what their behavior signifies. The demand on interpreters of spoken texts to be impartial and objective can therefore be no more appropriate than it would be for translators of fictional texts—for both there is a presumption of faithful practice, and even 'abusive fidelity' does not imply that any interpretation can count as valid or appropriate.

There are, without a doubt, important differences in the ethical relationships interpreters and translators develop due to the distinct environments in which these are shaped. A key motivating force behind the emergence of ethical theories of literary translation in the late twentieth century was the growing critique of colonialism, imperialism, and gender inequality from within the literary field. Literary translation was perceived by some as a means to challenge the existing norms regarding which texts and languages had a greater cultural and economic translation value, and the tendency toward assimilative or ethnocentric strategies designed to shield target, mainly Western, readers from the cultural and linguistic otherness of the source text. Literary translation ethics sought to foreground the cultural and linguistic character of the source text and to emphasize a more hybridized middle ground between source and target texts. It combined a commitment to the aesthetic function of a text with an explicitly ideological and political agenda. The ethical relationship that was formed in the translation of literary texts emerged between translator and text and between source and target text; neither the author of the source text nor the imagined reader needed to be directly engaged. Two important aims of a translation ethics were to invest translators with greater agency and to instigate a shift in the relative status of the source and target language and culture. The translated text itself became the site where both translator and cultural other achieved greater visibility.

The equivalent of the translated text in interpreting situations is the interpreting environment itself where plots, themes, and characters come together to create the interpreted text. Yet, despite a similar propensity toward ethnocentric violence and assimilative tendencies in many interpreted interactions, there has been little effort to develop an interpreting ethics aimed at advancing a more visible interactional role for interpreters. Theorizations of language in interpreting theory and practice have privileged aspects of formal discourse at the expense of more productive understandings of the immediate interpretive aspect of communication, its capacity to transform cognitive interpretations and permit individuals to develop new perspectives, drawing from their conventionalized modes of thought. Reported manifestations of interpreter agency within present theorizations are viewed at best with caution, even where they have involved undeniably morally and ethically sound judgments.

The ethical demand which interpreters face normally occurs within fields in which they have no official status: this has traditionally created an additional obstacle to a more visible role. The contingent relationship interpreters occupy in relation to official members of different fields, whether lawyers, doctors, judges, or soldiers, normally obliges interpreters to expect to comply with the decisions of other professionals (who may not possess the implicit knowledge that interpreters do about their interlocutors) about how far to engage in direct dialogue with interlocutors, how or whether to interrupt proceedings to clarify or request clarification of a question or exchange, and also regarding the value of their input on a particular topic, action, or outcome. The degree to which interpreters are accepted as 'fictive' kin is mostly in the hands of others with more social and interactional authority. At the same time, however, interpreted events bring such social and interactional hierarchies to consciousness for all participants, any one of whom can be advantaged or disadvantaged in the newly constituted space. Official members of fields can be equally dependent on interpreters, whether in a controlled institutional environment or in the chaos of a war zone, for information and advice about cultural or linguistic matters or geographical or historical details related to a community, a region, or the particular immediate needs of an individual or group of individuals. And in certain cases, interpreters may be the only participants willing to speak out against an injustice committed within an official field, either because less powerful interlocutors will not out of fear, or because official members of a field determine that their role morality dictates otherwise. Additionally, interpreters are often visibly and audibly co-present as 'non-fictive' kin to less powerful interlocutors through their connection to their culture or their language, though the degree of connection can vary considerably, especially in geo-political regions where ethnic, regional, linguistic, and religious ties are strongly delineated. Interpreters are usually located on more of a cultural continuum between the source and target cultures, depending on their individual histories. This can make for a good deal of implicit understanding of at least one, but often more than one interlocutor in an interpreted encounter.

The complex and nuanced relationship between interpreters, their interlocutors, and the text they create provides an important starting point for a transformed ethics of interpreting that is similar to and yet differs from an ethics of translation as currently constituted. An ethics of interpreting can share the commitment of translation ethics to invest interpreters with greater agency and to instigate a shift in the relative status of source and target languages and cultures in the relevant social and institutional contexts. It must differ, however, in that it cannot be grounded in the idea of interpreters making independent judgments regarding the meaning of utterances, detached from the producers of those utterances. In interpreted interactions, unlike in written translation, the authors of texts, the speakers, and the readers of texts, the hearers, can be directly consulted by interpreters in determining their communicative objectives. This is an ethical advantage that interpreters have over translators which has not been fully exploited in practice or sufficiently acknowledged in the translation field. The significance of the spoken word, as powerfully noted in the following passage from Plato's *Phaedrus* in the form of a dialogue between Phaedrus and Socrates, is its immediacy, its status as a living organism, its connection to its communicants (Plato 1973: 97):

> The fact is, Phaedrus, that writing involves a similar disadvantage to painting. The productions of painting look like living beings, but if you ask them a question they maintain a solemn silence. The same holds true of written words; you might suppose that they understand what they are saying, but if you ask them what they mean by anything they simply return the same answer over and over again. Besides, once a thing is committed to writing it circulates equally amongst those who understand the subject and those who have no business with it; a writing cannot distinguish between suitable and unsuitable readers. And if it is ill-treated or unfairly abused it always needs its parent to come to its rescue; it is quite incapable of defending or helping itself.

The presence of interpreters in interactions is rather like the parents coming to the rescue of Plato's defenseless writing—though without the paternalism this relationship suggests—for without the assistance of an interactive presence who understands *all* its subjects, no public deliberative dialogue can occur: both the subjects and the bureaucratic systems which bring them together would be reduced to silence, all equally incapable of expressing themselves. However, only once the pretense is lifted that these subjects speak and listen to one another with the interpreter not really there can an interpreting ethics emerge that does not require the principles of impartiality or neutrality. These principles are dependent on the contrived invisibility of interpreters to appear salient. Fully visible and engaged interpreters are as accountable as any other interlocutor for the utterances they speak, whether these originate in the interlocutors who are present, or are claimed as their own. In both cases, they represent an augmented contribution to the pursuit of mutual understanding. The presumption of integrity applies to interpreters to the same degree as it does to any individual. Interpreters' situated evaluations of others' communicative objectives will inevitably be a product of their prior experiences as well as present understandings. The most effective verification of the reliability of these evaluations is open, transparent dialogue with others, not the suppression of interpreter autonomy and ethical subjectivity.

Interpreting contexts represent language and, therefore, translation, in action. The process of translating spoken texts provides a firsthand unmediated glimpse into what all translation is, in whatever form: an instrument to reveal and represent the 'living dialogue' that contributes to the formation of worldviews, opinions, values, and beliefs that are formed and transformed by human interaction and the intervention of different environments. As the American poet Charles Olson has noted:

> For the habits of thought are the habits of action, and here, too, particularism has to be fought for anew. In fact, by the very law of identity of definition and discovery, who can extricate language from action? (Though it is one of the first false faces of the law which I shall want to strike away, it is quite understandable—in the light of identity—that the Greeks went on to declare all speculation as enclosed in the "UNIVERSE of discourse". It is their word, and the word of all metaphysicians since—as though language, too, was an absolute, instead of (as even man is) instrument, and not to be extended, however much the urge, to cover what each, man and language, is in the hands of: what we share, and which is enough of power and beauty, not to need an exaggeration of words, especially that spreading one "universe".
>
> [. . .]
>
> If there is any absolute, it is never more than this one, you, this instant, in action. (Olson 1967: 4–5)

Olson's comments, taken from his essay, 'Human Universe', echo the approach to language, meaning and interaction undertaken in this book. It is a call to reject the urge to link shared human discourse with abstract universal principles and, instead, to embrace language as an instrument for the kind of mutual understanding that individuals attempt from one situation to the next, from one moment to the next, with whatever props and assets are at hand, one person to another, in space and time. Language is not an absolute, it is a tool which individuals use to engage in a process of communication, normally with the understanding that satisfactory outcomes cannot always be guaranteed. In communication with others, values and beliefs can be confirmed, challenged, rejected and accepted. These actions of and through language do not require any metalinguistic approval or 'exaggeration of words' where language overreaches its human universe. They are human actions, integral to their contexts - and interpreters are as human as the rest.

Notes

NOTES TO CHAPTER 1

1. There is a substantial body of literature in the field of interpreting that draws directly or indirectly on these disciplinary traditions. More recent influential works include: Angelelli 2004a, 2004b; Berk-Seligson 1990; B. Davidson 2000; Diriker 2004; Hale 2004; Martin and Valero Garcés 2008; Mason 1999; Mikkelson 1998, 2008; Morris 1995, 1999, 2010; Niska 1995; Pöchhacker and Shlesinger 2002; Roy 2000; Shlesinger and Pöchhacker 2010; Turner 2007; and Wadensjö 1998). A consistently valuable source for understanding the evolution of thinking amongst researchers and practitioners about the role of the interpreter are the collections of papers from the Critical Link conferences (volumes 1–5) published by John Benjamins since 1997.
2. This image of humans as passive and constrained spectators was rejected during this same period through several alternative ideas about language which emerged from German thinkers like Hamann, Herder, and von Humboldt who in different ways challenged the idea of language as a medium intervening between self and reality. They refused to embrace Kant's idea of reason as an innate and independent activity and insisted on a view of reason as creative energy, evolving out of human relationships, in relationship to God, and most importantly, structured in and by language. Against Kant's attempt at a synthesis of experience and the understanding within the mind, foreshadowing Wittgenstein's later ideas, they insisted on a unity within language of the perceptive and reflective processes of the mind. (For an account of the relevance of their writings for models of inter-subjectivity that do not rely on a representational view of communication, see Inghilleri 2000).
3. James describes this process as one in which an individual's stock of old opinions meets a new experience that puts them under strain. Importantly, James suggests, "The new contents themselves are not true, they simply *come* and *are*. Truth is *what we say about* them, and when we say that they have come, truth is satisfied by the plain additive formula" (James 1975/1907: 36, original italics).
4. There are unresolved differences between Putnam and Rorty, however, which return us to the objectivism-relativism question. Putnam wants Rorty to acknowledge the validity of a normative notion of rationality, an 'idealized rational acceptability' (a form of 'moral objectivity') in relation to the rightness or wrongness of a set of norms and standards (Putnam 1990: 41). Putnam is sympathetic to Habermas' notion of 'universal validity claims' and would likely support Umberto Eco's assertion that "[l] anguage does not construct being *ex novo*: it questions it, in some way always finding something already given (even though being *already given*

does not mean already finished and completed). Even if being were moth-eaten, there would always be a fabric whose warp and web, confused by the infinite holes that have eaten into it, still subsist in some stubborn way" (Eco 1999: 54, original italics). Rorty wants to be able to talk about revising norms and standards that have ceased to be considered acceptable or useful without resorting to 'already given' lines of resistance. He insists that rightness or wrongness is always local and transient, not in a relativist sense, but in the sense that whether or not an assertion is warranted is more a sociological matter, dependent on whether the majority of one's cultural peers would accept it as such (Rorty 1998: 43–62).

5. For Davidson, the possibility of agreement or disagreement is secondary to inter-subjective understanding, which for him is the root of thought itself. The crucial issue is whether human beings succeed in talking and thinking together; whether they agree or disagree is another matter. This implies that relativists deny others the ability to speak or to think, and that the question of 'universal validity claims', for example, is a political matter that is relevant at a later stage where consensus, not communication as such, is the objective (see Borradori 1994: 40–54). See chapter 2 for a critical discussion of discourse ethics and its presumptions about universal validity claims and the workings of discourse, inter-subjectivity, and an open and democratic public sphere.
6. The interviews in this and subsequent chapters in the book form part of the data collected from interviews with immigration officials, judges, attorneys, and asylum applicants, observations of asylum hearings, and documentary evidence during the ethnographic study I conducted of key contexts in the U.K. asylum system from 2002 to 2007 funded by the ESRC. The final reports for these projects can be accessed at the ESRC research website: www.regard.ac.uk.
7. Saar's reflections share something in common with the process undertaken by whistleblowers. In an insightful article on the ethics of whistleblowers which owes much to the writings of Hannah Arendt, C. Fred Alford describes the thoughts of whistleblowers as "introspection that is willing to be molested by reality, indeed to engage in internal dialogue with the assailant" (Alford 2001: 413).

NOTES TO CHAPTER 2

1. Though some community interpreters or bilingual advocates are trained to act as advocates in cases of discrimination, it is not always clear in the event what constitutes a discriminatory practice or utterance, and not all interpreters trained as advocates feel able to challenge individuals whose social and institutional positions grant them explicit or implicit warrant.
2. Repeating the client's words verbatim does not necessarily rule out the possibility that the interpreter's personal feelings toward this individual might register in paralinguistic cues like facial expression or body posture, for example.
3. There is an affinity here with the view attributed to Davidson in the previous chapter—that if the languages and experiences of different individuals or communities had nothing in common, it would no longer be intelligible even to speak of understanding. It is also closely linked to Gadamer's hermeneutics, specifically, his notion of a 'fusion of horizons'—the view that individuals belong to traditions, histories, and languages and that it is only in attempting to understand themselves in dialogue with others that they

become reflexively aware of their own contingency (Gadamer 1975: 272). From a pragmatist perspective, Rorty has also argued that individuals 'privilege' the interpretive horizon of their own linguistic communities, that they must "grasp the ethnocentric horn" in the face of pretending an endless tolerance of all others, "even though there can be no noncircular justification for doing so" (Rorty 1991a: 29). Here Rorty appears to treat ethnocentrism in much the same way as Gadamer does the notion of prejudice. He attempts to rehabilitate it from its strictly negative sense and allow it to mean simply the beliefs proposed by one culture that must be tested by trying to weave them together with the beliefs of another. Rorty, though, would refute the question of whether "justifiability to the community with whom we identify entails truth" (1991b: 177).

NOTES TO CHAPTER 3

1. Refusing a role in a particular case for moral reasons is sometimes given as an option for some professionals. For interpreters, many of whom work freelance, this is frequently cited in codes of ethics as the choice to make where an ethical conflict arises. Where overt prejudices have absolute moral force over individuals to the extent that they jeopardize their ability to act professionally in 'good faith', the refusal to participate is viewed as morally and ethically justified. In the interpreting profession, this might be the case, for example, where interpreters and clients are members of opposing ethnic or national groups or interpreters' religious or cultural beliefs make it problematic or impossible to participate in discussions of certain topics. The option to refuse to interpret in a particular context or for a particular individual or category of individuals underscores the principles of neutrality and impartiality central to the interpreting profession and the accompanying assumption that an individual's personal moral code has no place in his or her professional life.
2. Though many within the profession would characterize the depiction of the lawyer's role as a mere mouthpiece as extreme and unfounded, Markovits uses this language to argue that the weakening of boundaries between role morality and ordinary morality has pressured lawyers to abandon their unselfconscious commitment to the norm of zealous advocacy. In order to rescue their personal integrity from the effects of outside scrutiny, Markovits suggests lawyers have been forced into mere "mimicry" of zealous advocacy, once considered an impartially justifiable function of their role. Though Markovits acknowledges the political and egalitarian reasons for "undercutting the lawyer's traditional insular role" (Markovits 2004: 293), he perceives lawyers as victims of ordinary morality—unable to inhabit their role as before *and* unable to "preserve their integrity in the face of the charges that they lie, cheat and abuse" to support their clients' interests (*ibid.*: 292).
3. The discussion is confined to the central ideas of each point of view and their relevance to interpreters and the task of interpreting. It should be clear that the different perspectives are overlapping in many respects in relation to one another.
4. This distinction between formal and substantive compliance is a core issue within legal ethics and is interpreted somewhat differently in each of the perspectives summarized in this chapter. A key issue in analytical jurisprudence is how lawyers balance their role obligation of fidelity to the law with more substantive principles associated with morality and justice, particularly in 'hard' cases where the law may deviate from ordinary, i.e., societal, views

of morality in significant ways. At the heart of this dilemma lies one of the central questions for legal ethics—whether the function of law is to represent society's conceptions of justice, fairness, and due process (see Dworkin 1986) or to function as a set of established rules and procedures or 'social facts', that are reasonably applied without explicit regard for questions of morality (see Hart 1961).

5. As Bourdieu notes in relation to the juridical field, "Within this field there occurs a confrontation among actors possessing a technical competence which is inevitably social and which consists essentially in the socially recognized capacity to *interpret* a corpus of texts sanctifying a correct or legitimized vision of the social world.[. . .]Competition for control of access to the legal resources inherited from the past contributes to establishing a social division between lay people and professionals by fostering a continual process of rationalization. Such a process is ideal for constantly increasing the separation between judgments based upon the law and naïve intuitions of fairness" (Bourdieu 1987: 817, original italics).
6. Amongst the legal options some of these workers may have been eligible to pursue with regard to their immigration status were: applying for legal permanent residence status based on their marriage to or being a parent of a U.S. citizen or legal permanent resident; applying for suspension of deportation based on the length of time they had resided in the U.S. and the exceptional hardship their deportation might cause their U.S. citizen or legal permanent resident children; or applying for political asylum if they had fled their country of origin from fear of persecution.
7. Although the detainees had a constitutional right to a criminal defense attorney, they did not have the same right to an immigration attorney because they had not been charged with an immigration offense. AILA's argument was that due process however required that the defendants be fully informed of the immigration consequences of the specific charges before accepting any deal.
8. At the time of the Postville raids, there was a significant split in the courts regarding the interpretation of the federal aggravated-identity-theft statute the workers were threatened with. The statute states: "Whoever, during and in relation to any felony violation enumerated in subsection (c), *knowingly transfers, possesses or uses, without lawful authority, a means of identification of another person*, shall in addition to the punishment provided for such felony, be sentenced to a term of imprisonment of 2 years" (my emphasis). Three district courts held that 'knowingly' modified only 'transfers, possesses or uses'. Another three held that it included the object 'a means of identification of another person'. In the Postville prosecution, if the latter phrase was excluded, the prosecutors could convict the workers for 'knowingly possessing' false papers without having to prove beyond a reasonable doubt that they 'knowingly' possessed the papers *of another person* (that is, someone they *knew* to be an actual living person). A year later, the U.S. Supreme Court decided in relation to a similar case that the adverb 'knowingly' did indeed apply to *a means of identification of another person*, making the charge a "substantially less powerful bargaining chip" in future prosecutions (Peterson 2009: 338–340). Claiming that the federal prosecutors "had used the law as a hammer to coerce the workers" in Postville a year earlier, a day after the Supreme Court's decision, David Leopold called on Eric Holder, Attorney General in the Obama administration, to dismiss all charges in the Postville cases where the threat of prosecution under the statute 'was a miscarriage of justice' (Preston 2009).

9. It was later alleged that the supervisor at the plant told employees "to give him $220 and a personal photo, for which the employee later received a 'green card'" (Peterson 2009: 340).

NOTES TO CHAPTER 4

1. Despite international support and attachment to universal human rights principles and organizations such as the 1948 Universal Declaration of Human Rights, the 1949 Geneva Convention and its Protocols, and the 1951 United High Commission on Refugees (UNHCR), individual states continue to demonstrate ambivalence regarding any connection between global interdependence and the universal right to hospitality. The UNHCR was created as a small international agency that "would pose no threat to state interests or national sovereignty, that imposed no financial obligation of states, and provided no open-ended commitment to refugees" (Loescher 1999: 237). And recent stricter interpretations by nation states of the 1949 Geneva Convention's criteria for what constitutes a refugee have resulted in more and more asylum seekers failing to obtain formal refugee status.
2. The relationship between subjective and objective evidence is constructed in very specific ways in the asylum context. Anthony Good, an anthropologist who serves regularly as an expert witness in asylum appeals, has observed, for example, that credibility is used as "a term of art, denoting a judgment which only the court is entitled to make" (Good 2003: 7). He notes that, whereas in an academic context the terms 'consistency', 'plausibility', and 'credibility' tend to be used interchangeably, in the asylum system, stating that an account is plausible or consistent with objective evidence is not the same as judging it to be credible. In the judicial system, evaluative reports from anthropologists that attempt to link the assessment of a claimant's case to that individual's credibility are considered outside their remit and are routinely devalued or dismissed by the courts (*ibid.*; see also Good 2004).
3. In their report on an ethnographic study they conducted on NGOs providing medical and social assistance to foreigners and asylum seekers in France, Fassin and d'Halluin discuss how the verification of trauma plays out in an application for refugee status. They note the role of two collective histories: the first is based in the legitimization of trauma as a category for understanding hardship within the field of psychiatry and more generally, and the second is rooted in the delegitimization of asylum as a category justifying the protection of the international community largely due to an increased xenophobia toward migrants in France and elsewhere (Fassin and d'Halluin 2007: 306).
4. In asylum interviews, narratives of flight from actual or potential persecution and imprisonment are the norm. The credibility of applicants' accounts, due to the absence of any corroborating documentary evidence, relies on the clear and consistent presentation of dates, times, political or familial affiliations, etc. This is generally accomplished through the use of open questions to guide applicants to tell their stories and elaborate in detail the circumstances of their persecution. In contrast, at the immigration interview, both open and closed questions can be used depending on the stage of the interview and depending on the nationality of the applicant. In an interview I conducted with a group of U.K. Home Office officials, one mentioned that Turkish applicants were notorious for taking seven hours over an interview, so in those cases and in other cases where there was a "tendency to

over elaborate", more closed questions were used. Many interpreters have reported this occurrence and their struggle to help the applicant say *enough* to present an accurate account of their flight despite the pressure to say *less*.

5. With some variation from case to case and country to country, the first points of communication for asylum seekers entering by land, air, or sea is with an immigration official. Although officials at ports of entry do not make decisions on asylum applications, they are the first to assess the legal validity and credibility of a request for asylum and have the authority to refuse, detain, or grant an individual admission in order to make a formal asylum application (Human Rights First 2004: 10–11). Additional categories of asylum seekers include: illegal entrants, overstayers, and individuals with legal permission to be in the receiving country but who due to ongoing or changing political conditions in their country of origin seek extended leave to remain or permanent asylum. These individuals may apply for asylum as a result of a detention or arrest or may apply proactively with the immigration services.
6. In interpreting contexts, the absence of any observable negotiations over utterances helps to reinforce the illusion of the transparency of the message and may also lead in some cases to the false assumption that the meanings expressed in a particular exchange are unproblematic. As discussed in chapter 1 following Fabian's observations, violations of communicative competence in attempting understanding in inter-cultural communicative contexts can be valuable and significant, ethnographically speaking. This point has been insufficiently acknowledged or theorized in much of the interpreting research that draws its models from discourse analysis and sociolinguistics.

NOTES TO CHAPTER 5

1. Iraqi CAT I interpreters recruited in Iraq have noted with frustration that these interpreters, though paid ten times as much as they are, tend not to be familiar with Iraqi culture or the nuances of Iraqi Arabic, causing misunderstandings to occur. As one suggested, "The defense and intelligence communities often value irrelevant issues of security over competence" (Sherr 2008: 1).
2. The army has also begun to pay Arabic-speaking soldiers retention bonuses of up to $150,000 in recognition of the importance of their language proficiency and cultural knowledge. These soldiers, known as '09 Limas', come from Morocco, Sudan, and Egypt and are recruited by the army from communities in the U.S. with large Arab-American populations and fast tracked to U.S. citizenship (Lubold 2008).
3. TICO refers to the Translator Interpreting Company, a U.S. military program which trains 'native' and 'heritage' speakers to provide translation, interpreting, and cultural advice to the army.
4. There were of course multiple ends used to justify the invasion of Iraq by the Bush administration which amounted to a "cat's cradle of ideals and justifications, procedures and outcomes" (Brenkman 2007: 110) including the search for WMDs, protection of oil supplies, regime change, and victory in the all encompassing 'war on terror'.
5. 'Cordon and search' refers to the practice of surrounding a neighborhood with tanks and armed units and bursting down the doors of Iraqi households in search of weapons or suspected insurgents, often the result of faulty intelligence.
6. In response to the Bush administration's decision to retaliate for the September 11 bombings, a *fatwa* delivered by the American Muslim Council in

October 2011 stated, "All Muslims ought to be united against all those who terrorize the innocents, and those who permit the killing of non-combatants without a justifiable reason. The Muslim soldier must perform his duty in this fight despite the feeling of uneasiness of 'fighting without discriminating.' His intention must be to fight for enjoining of the truth and defeating falsehood. It's to prevent aggression on the innocents, or to apprehend the perpetrators and bring them to justice. It's not his concern what other consequences of the fighting that might result in his personal discomfort, since he alone can neither control it nor prevent it. Furthermore, all deeds are accounted (by God) according to the intentions. To sum up, it's acceptable—God willing—for the Muslim American military personnel to partake in the fighting in the upcoming battles, against whomever their country decides has perpetrated terrorism against them. Keeping in mind to have the proper intention, as explained earlier, so no doubts would be cast about their loyalty to their country, or to prevent harm to befall them as might be expected. This is in accordance with the Islamic jurisprudence rules, which state that necessities dictate exceptions, as well as the rule that says one may endure a small harm to avoid a much greater harm. And God the Most High is Most Knowledgeable and Most Wise" (American Muslim Council 2001).

7. As Richard Collin (2009: 254) points out, it was not so much that this knowledge was unavailable to the Bush administration as it was its failure to consider its relevance. As a result, it undertook the invasion of Iraq "ignorant of information available to anyone with a library card" and "significantly underequipped linguistically" both in terms of the number of officers and soldiers who spoke Arabic and also in their lack of awareness of the distinct languages, dialects, and vernaculars spoken throughout the region.
8. It has been reported that the government is developing training programs for anthropologists who seek work in the military "before they develop any of their professional qualms" (Stier 2007: 3). This suggests a move to co-opt rather than adopt their expertise and position them more like embodied conduits that serve a military agenda rather than an anthropological one. Others dispute such a view and underscore the value to the military of academics as "objective, observant outsiders" (Miller 2010: 709).
9. A Pledge of Non-participation in Counterinsurgency was circulated by the Network of Concerned Anthropologists, and both the Network and the executive board of the American Anthropological Association have strongly criticized the HTS project and its aims (see Network of Concerned Anthropologists 2007).
10. This is the same position interpreters have occupied throughout the history of conflict and conquest: from the dragomans of the Ottoman Empire (see Lewis 2004: 21–39) to the native people of the Americas (Hagedorn 1988; Szasz 1994; Lepore 1998: 21–47), World War II (Tobia 2010; Takeda 2009, 2010), the Balkans (Stahuljak 2000, 2009, 2010), in recent international peacekeeping and relief efforts (Bos and Soeters 2006; Van Dijk and Soeters 2008), in Iraq and Afghanistan (Rafael 2007; C. Baker 2010; M. Baker 2010; Inghilleri 2008, 2009, 2010); and see Hajjar (2000) for an account of Arabic-speaking Druze Israel interpreters in the West Bank and Gaza. Evident in each of these cases is the precarious nature of the political and cultural role of interpreters and translators in conflict situations (see Inghilleri and Harding 2010).
11. In many respects, a kind of 'mediating role' for the principle of impartiality is claimed here that is similar in kind to the role claimed for law in the legal field and for universal pragmatics in discourse ethics. In each case, a universalizing legitimating role is given to the mediating device which acquires

rationality and validity that transcend the subjectivities of the individuals or the particularities of their situations, whether morally good or morally questionable.

12. Though, as Challans points out, the idea of political legitimacy as a rationale for the just nature of a war is another example of the vagaries of moral authority: "are there any cases of a state ever going to war believing that their cause was not just?" (Challans 2007: 153).

NOTES TO CHAPTER 6

1. Nadja Grbić makes the important point in her discussion of the professionalization process with regard to sign language interpreters in Austria, that classifications and categorizations within or between professional practices involve politically and ideologically informed decisions to do with boundary maintenance (Grbić 2010: 112–113). The boundaries that have operated with regard to the domains of translation and interpreting include: the literary and the non-literary, the written and the oral, art and science, highbrow and lowbrow culture, and native and non-native, to name a few.

Bibliography

Abou El Fadl, Khaled (2002) 'The Place of Tolerance in Islam', in Joshua Cohen and Ian Lague (eds) *The Place of Tolerance in Islam*, Boston MA: Beacon Press, 3-26.

Ahmad, Muneer I. (2007) 'Interpreting Communities: Lawyering across Language Difference', *UCLA Law Review* 54: 999–1086.

Alford, C. Fred (2001) 'Whistleblowers and Ethics', *Journal of Social Philosophy* 32 (3): 402–418.

American Civil Liberties Union (2008a) 'Written Statement for a Hearing on Immigration Raids: Postville and Beyond', http://www.aclu.org/files/images/asset_upload_file428_36231.pdf: 1–8. (accessed March 2011)

———(2008b) 'ACLU Obtains Government Manual for Prepackaged Guilty Pleas for Prosecution of Immigrant Workers in Postville, Iowa', http://www.aclu.org/immigrants-rights/government-manual-distributed-iowa-defense-lawyers (accessed March 2011)

American Muslim Council (2001) 'American Muslim Military Participation in the War Clarified by American Muslim Scholars', *The Islamic Center of Greater Toledo*, 11 October. Available at http://www.icgt.org/SpecialArticles/MuslimsInMilitary.htm (accessed July 2010)

Angelelli, Claudia (2004a) *Revisiting the Interpreter's Role: A Study of Conference, Court, and Medical Interpreters in Canada, Mexico and United States*. Amsterdam and Philadelphia: John Benjamins.

———(2004b) *Medical Interpreting and Crosscultural Communication*. Cambridge: Cambridge University Press.

Anker, Deborah (1991) 'Determining Asylum Claims in the United States: Executive Summary of an Empirical Study of the Adjudication of Asylum Claims before the Immigration Court', in H. Adelman (ed) *Refugee Policy: Canada and the United States*. Toronto: York Lanes Press, 268–281.

Apel, Karl-Otto (1977) 'The A Priori of Communication and the Foundation of the Humanities', in F. Dallmayr and T. McCarthy (eds), *Understanding and Social Inquiry*. Notre Dame, IN: University of Notre Dame Press, 292–315.

Applbaum, Arthur Isak (1999) *Ethics for Adversaries*. Princeton: Princeton University Press.

Arrojo, Rosemary (1998) 'The Revision of the Traditional Gap between Theory and Practice and the Empowerment of Translation in Postmodern Times', *The Translator* 4 (1): 25–48.

———(2005) 'The Ethics of Translation in Contemporary Approaches to Translation', in Martha Tennant (ed.) *Training for the New Millennium—Pedagogies for Translation and Interpreting*. Amsterdam and Philadelphia: John Benjamins, 225–245.

Asylum Aid (1999) *Still No Reason at All; Home Office Decisions on Asylum Claims*. London: Asylum Aid.

Avlon, John P. (2006) 'Muslims in the Military', *New York Sun*, April 21, http://www.nysun.com/opinion/muslims-in-the-military/31393 (consulted July 2010).

Azari, Jaz, Christopher Dendeker and Neil Greenberg (2010) 'Cultural Stress: How Interactions with and among Foreign Populations Affect Military Personnel', *Armed Forces & Society* 36: 585–603.

Baker, Catherine (2010) '"It's Not Their Job to Soldier": Distinguishing Civilian and Military in Soldiers' and Interpreters' Accounts of Peacekeeping in 1990s Bosnia-Herzegovina', *Journal of War and Culture Studies* 3 (1): 37–50.

Baker, Mona (2006) *Translation and Conflict*. London: Routledge.

———(2010) 'Interpreters and Translators in the War Zone', *The Translator* 16 (2): 197–222.

Baker, Mona and Carol Maier (eds) (2011) 'Ethics and the Curriculum: Critical Perspectives', Special Issue of *The Translator and Interpreter Trainer* 5 (1).

Barsky, Robert F. (1996) 'The Interpreter as Intercultural Agent in Convention Refugee Hearings', *The Translator* 1 (2): 45–64.

Bassnett, Susan and Harish Trivedi (eds) (1999) *Postcolonial Translation*. London: Routledge.

Basu, Moni (2005) 'Iraqi Interpreters Risk Their Lives to aid GIs', *Cox News Service*, November 3, http://www.oxfordpress.com/hp/content/shared/news/nation/stories/11/1103_COXIRAQ_TRANSLATE.html (consulted December 2009).

Battistelli, Fabrizio (1997) 'Peacekeeping and the Postmodern Soldier', *Armed Forces & Society* 23 (3): 467–484.

Battistelli, Fabrizio, Teresa Ammendola and Maria Grazia Galantino (1999) 'The Fuzzy Environment and Postmodern Soldiers: The Motivations of the Italian Contingent in Bosnia', *Small Wars and Insurgencies* 10 (2): 138–160.

Bauman, Zygmunt (1993) *Postmodern Ethics*. London: Blackwell.

Benhabib, Seyla (1992) *Situating the Self*. Cambridge: Polity Press.

———(2002) *The Claims of Culture*. Princeton: Princeton University Press.

———(2004) *The Rights of Others: Aliens, Residents and Citizens*. Cambridge: Cambridge University Press.

———(2008) *Another Cosmopolitanism* (The Berkeley Tanner Lectures), Robert Post (ed). Oxford: Oxford University Press.

Berk-Seligson, Susan (1990). *The Bilingual Courtroom: Court Interpreters in the Judicial Process*. Chicago: University of Chicago Press.

Bermann, Sandra and Michael Wood (eds) (2005) *Nation, Language and the Ethics of Translation*. Princeton: Princeton University Press.

Betz, David (2008) 'The Virtual Dimension of Contemporary Insurgency and Counterinsurgency', *Small Wars & Insurgencies* 19 (4): 510–540.

Blake, Charles (2001) 'Judging Asylum and Immigration Claims', *Public Money and Management* July–September: 25–28.

Blommaert, Jan (2009) 'Language, Asylum and the National Order', *Current Anthropology* 50 (4): 415–425.

Bodor, Brandon (2008) 'The Iraqi Interpreter: An Unrecognized Hero Who Was Also Missing His Family This Holiday Season', *OpEd News*, January 9, http://www.opednews.com/articles/opedne_first_li_080109_the_iraqi_interprete.htm (consulted December 2009).

Boéri, Julie and Carol Maier (eds) (2010) *Translation and Social Activism*. Granada: ECOS.

Bohman, James and Matthias Lutz-Bachman (eds) (1997) *Perpetual Peace: Essays on Kant's Cosmopolitan Ideal*. Cambridge: MIT Press.

Boorstein, Michelle (2009) 'Muslims in Military Seek a Bridge between Worlds', *The Washington Post*, 11 November.

Booth, Bradford, Meyer Kestenbaum and David R. Segal (2001) 'Are Post Cold War Militaries Postmodern?', *Armed Forces & Society* 27 (3): 312–342.

Borradori, Giovanna (1994) *The American Philosopher*. Trans. Rosanna Crocitto. Chicago: University of Chicago Press.

Bos, Geesje and Joseph Soeters (2006) 'Interpreters at Work: Experiences from Dutch and Belgian Peace Operations', *International Peacekeeping* 13 (2): 261–268.

Bourdieu, Pierre (1987) 'The Force of Law: Toward a Sociology of the Juridical Field', Translation and Introduction, Richard Terdiman, *The Hastings Law Journal* 38: 805–853.

———(1991) *Language and Symbolic Power*. Trans. Gino Raymond and Matthew Adamson. Cambridge: Polity Press.

Bowie, Norman (1982) *Business Ethics*. Englewood Cliffs, NJ: Prentice-Hall.

Brenkman, John (2007) *The Cultural Contradictions of Democracy: Political Thought since September 11*. Princeton: Princeton University Press.

Burden, Matthew Currier (2006) *The Blog of War*. New York: Simon and Schuster.

Buzzell, Colby (2005) *My War: Killing Time in Iraq*. New York: Berkeley.

Camayd-Freixas, Eric (2008a) 'Interpreting After the Largest ICE Raid in US History: A Personal Account', June 13, http://graphics8.nytimes.com/images/2008/07/14/opinion/14ed-camayd.pdf (consulted May 2011).

———(2008b) 'Statement to the Profession', *Proteus* (Fall): 5–8.

Carrick, Don (2008) 'The Future of Ethics Education in the Military: A Comparative Analysis', in Paul Robinson, Nigel De Lee, and Don Carrick (eds), *Ethics Education in the Military*. Aldershot: Ashgate, 187–197.

Ceulemans, Carl (2007/8) 'The Moral Equality of Combatants', *Parameters* (Winter): 99–109.

Challans, Timothy L. (2007) *Awakening Warrior: Revolution in the Ethics of Warfare*. Albany: SUNY Press.

Cole, Rockne (2008) 'Written Statement for July 24, 2008, House Judiciary Committee Hearing on Immigration Raids', http://graphics8.nytimes.com/packages/pdf/national/ColeLetter.pdf (consulted May 2011).

Collin, Richard Oliver (2009) 'Words of War: The Iraqi Tower of Babel', *International Studies Perspective* 10: 245–264.

Connell Szasz, Margaret (ed) (1994) *Between Indians and White Worlds: The Cultural Broker*. Norman: University of Oklahoma Press.

Cook, Martin L. (2005) *The Moral Warrior*. Albany: SUNY Press.

———(2008) 'Ethics Education, Ethics Training, and Character Development: Who "Owns" Ethics Education in the US Air Force Academy?', in Paul Robinson, Nigel De Lee, and Don Carrick (eds) , *Ethics Education in the Military*. Aldershot: Ashgate, 57–65.

Coutin, Susan Bibler (2001) 'The Oppressed, the Suspect and the Citizen: Subjectivity in Competing Accounts of Political Violence', *Law and Social Inquiry* 26 (1): 63–94.

Cowen, Deborah (2005) 'Welfare Warriors: Towards a Genealogy of the Soldier-Citizen in Canada', *Antipode: A Radical Journal of Geography* 37: 654–678.

Crawford, John (2005) *The Last True Story I'll Ever Tell*. New York: Riverhead Books.

Crisp, Jeff (2003) 'Refugees and the Global Politics of Asylum', in Sarah Spencer (ed) *The Politics of Migration*. Oxford: Blackwell, 75–87.

Cronin, Michael (2002) 'The Empire Talks Back: Orality, Heteronomy and the Cultural Turn in Intepreting Studies', in Franz Pöchhacker and Miriam Shlesinger (eds) *The Interpreting Studies Reader*. London: Routledge, 387–397.

———(2006) *Translation and Identity*. London: Routledge.

Dare, Tim (2004) 'Mere-Zeal, Hyper-Zeal and the Ethical Obligations of Lawyers', *Legal Ethics* 7 (1): 24–38.

———(2010) 'Detachment, Distance and Integrity' in Tim Dare and W. Bradley Wendel (eds), *Professional Ethics and Personal Integrity*. Newcastle-upon Tyne: Cambridge Scholars, 100–124.

Das, Veena (2007) 'Commentary: Trauma and Testimony: Between Law and Discipline', *ETHOS* 3: 330–335.

Davidson, Brad (2000) The Interpreter as Institutional Gatekeeper: The Social-Linguistic Role of Interpreters in Spanish-English Medical Discourse', *Journal of Sociolinguistics* 4 (3): 379–405.

Davidson, Donald (1984) 'On the Very Idea of a Conceptual Scheme', in *Inquiries into Truth and Interpretation*. Oxford: Clarendon Press, 183–198.

———(1986) 'A Nice Derangement of Epitaphs', in Ernest Lepore (ed) *Truth and Interpretation: Perspectives on the Philosophy of Donald*. Oxford: Blackwell, 433–446.

———(1990) 'A Coherence Theory of Truth and Knowledge', in Alan Malachowski (ed), *Reading Rorty*. London: Basil Blackwell, 120–138.

———(2001) *Subjective, Intersubjective, Objective*. Oxford: Clarendon Press.

Dawes, James (2007) *That the World May Know: Bearing Witness to Atrocity*. Cambridge: Harvard University Press.

Defense Industry Daily (2009) 'Lend Me Your Ears: US Military Turns to Contractor Linguists', http://www.defenseindustrydaily.com/Lend-Me-Your-Ears-US-Military-Turns-to-Contractor-Linguists-05934/ (consulted December 2009).

Derrida, Jacques (2000) *Of Hospitality*. Trans. Rachel Bowlby. Stanford: Stanford University Press.

Diriker, Ebru (2004) *De-/Re-Contextualising Conference Interpreting*. Amsterdam and Philadelphia: John Benjamins.

Donagan, Alan (1983) 'Justifying Legal Practice in the Adversary System', in David Luban (ed) *The Good Lawyer: Lawyers' Roles and Lawyers' Ethics*. Totowa, NJ: Rowman and Allenheld, 123–149.

Druzin, Heath (2008/9) 'Lost in Translation: Interpreters' Role Can Make or Break U.S. Effort in Iraq', *Stars and Stripes*, March 31, 2009, http://www.stripes.com/articleprint.asp?section=104&article=59222 (consulted April 2009).

Dunnigan, Timothy and Bruce T. Downing (1995) 'Legal Interpreting on Trial: A Case Study', in Marshall Morris (ed) *Translation and the Law*. Amsterdam and Philadelphia: John Benjamins, 93–113.

Dworkin, Ronald (1986) *Law's Empire*. Cambridge: Harvard University Press.

Eco, Umberto (1999) *Kant and the Platypus: Essays on Language and Cognition*. Trans. Alastair McEwen. New York: Harcourt.

Eighmey, John (2006) 'Why Do Youth Enlist?: Identification of Underlying Themes', *Armed Forces & Society* 32 (2): 307–328.

Elliott, Andrea (2009) 'Complications Grow for Muslims Serving in U.S. Military', *The New York Times*, November 9, http://www.nytimes.com/2009/11/09/us/09muslimhtml?_r=1&pagewanted=print (consulted July 2010).

Fabian, Johannes (1979) 'Rules and Process: Thoughts on Ethnography as Communication', *Philosophy of the Social Sciences* 9: 1–26.

———(2001) *Anthropology with an Attitude*. Stanford: Stanford University Press.

Fahmy, Mohamed Fadel (2004) *Baghdad Bound: An Interpreter's Chronicles of the Iraq War*. Victoria: Trafford.

Fassin, Didier and Estelle d'Halluin (2007) 'Critical Evidence: The Politics of Trauma in French Asylum Policies', *ETHOS* 35 (3): 300–329.

Fiola, Marco A. (ed) (2004) 'Translation, Ethics and Society', Special Issue of *TTR* 17 (2).

Fraser, Nancy and Axel Honneth (2003) *Redistribution or Recognition?: A Political-Philosophical Exchange*. Trans. Joel Golb, James Ingram, and Christiane Wilke. London: Verso.

Freedman, Monroe (1966) 'Professional Responsibility of the Criminal Defense Lawyer: The Three Hardest Questions', *Michigan Law Review* 64: 1469–1484.

———(1992) 'Professionalism in the American Adversary System', *Emory Law Journal* 41: 467–472.

French, Shannon (2003) *The Code of the Warrior*. New York: Rowman & Littlefield.

Fury, Dalton (2008) *Kill Bin Laden*. New York: St. Martin's Press.

Gadamer, Hans-Georg (1975) *Truth and Method*. London: Sheed and Ward.

Gert, Bernard and C. M. Culver (1982) *Philosophy in Medicine: Conceptual and Ethical Issues in Medicine and Psychiatry*. New York: Oxford University Press.

Gibson, Kevin (2003) 'Contrasting Role Morality and Professional Morality: Implications for Practice', *Journal of Applied Philosophy* 20 (1): 17–29.

Giglioli, Pier P. (ed) (1972) *Language and Social Context*. Harmondsworth: Penguin Books.

Goffman, Erving (1961) *Asylums*. Harmondsworth: Penguin Books.

Goldfarb, Michael (2005) *Ahmad's War, Ahmad's Peace*. New York: Carroll & Graf.

Goldman, Alan H. (1980) *The Moral Foundation of Professional Ethics*. Totowa, NJ: Rowman & Littlefield.

———(1998) 'Roles and Role Morality', in Cary L. Cooper and Chris Argyris (eds), *The Concise Blackwell Encyclopedia of Management*. Oxford: Blackwell, 576–579.

González, Roberto J. (2007) 'Towards Mercenary Anthropology?', *Anthropology Today*, 23 (3): 14–19.

Good, Anthony (2003) 'Anthropologists as Experts: Asylum Appeals in British Courts', *Anthropology Today* 19 (5): 3–7.

———(2004) '"Undoubtedly and Expert'?: Anthropologists in British Asylum Courts', *Journal of the Royal Anthropological Institute* 10: 113–133.

Goodenough, Ward (1964) 'Cultural Anthropology and Linguistics', in Dell Hymes (ed), *Language in Culture and Society*. New York: Harper and Row, 36–39.

Goodman, Russell B. (1998) 'Wittgenstein and Pragmatism', *parallax* 4 (4): 91–105

Goodwin, Phil (2010) 'Ethical Problems in Translation: Why We Might Need Steiner After All', *The Translator* 16 (1): 19–42.

Grbić, Nadja (2010) '"Boundary Work" as a Concept for Studying Professionalization Processes in the Interpreting Field', *Translation and Interpreting Studies* 5 (1):109–123.

Gumperz, John (1982) *Discourse Strategies*. Cambridge: Cambridge University Press.

Gumperz, John and Dell Hymes (eds) (1972) *Directions in Sociolinguistics*. New York: Holt, Rhinehart and Winston.

Habermas, Jürgen (1977) 'A Review of Gadamer's Truth and Method', in Fred Dallmayr and Thomas McCarthy (eds), *Understanding and Social Inquiry*. Notre Dame: University of Notre Dame Press, 335–363.

———(1990) *Moral Consciousness and Communicative Action*. Trans. Christian Lenhardt and Shierry Weber Nicholsen. Cambridge: MIT Press.

———(1992) 'The Unity of Reason in the Diversity of Its Voices', in *Postmetaphysical Thinking*. Cambridge: Polity Press, 115–148.

Hagedorn, Nancy L. (1988) ' "A Friend to Go between Them": The Interpreter as Cultural Broker during Anglo-Iroquois Councils 1740–70', *Ethnohistory*, 35 (1) (Winter): 60–80.

Hajjar, Lisa (2000) 'Speaking the Conflict, or How the Druze Became Bilingual: A Study of Druze Translators in the Israeli Military Courts in the West Bank and Gaza', *Ethnic and Racial Studies* 23 (2): 299–328.

Hale, Sandra (2004) *The Discourse of Court Interpreting: Discourse Practices and the Law, the Witness and the Interpreter.* Amsterdam: John Benjamins.

Harman, Danna (2009) 'Trading a Life in Vegas to Speak for Troops in Afghanistan', *The Christian Science Monitor Online*, January 9, http://www.csmonitor.com/2009/0109/p01s03-wosc.html (consulted December 2009),

Harris, Roy (1981) *The Language Myth.* London: Duckworth.

———(1987) *Reading Saussure: A Critical Commentary on the Cours de linguistique generale.* London: Duckworth.

———(1998) 'Making Sense of Communicative Competence', in Roy Harris and George Wolf (eds), *Integrational Linguistics: A First Reader.* Oxford: Pergamon, 27–45.

Hart, H. L. A. (1961) *The Concept of Law.* London: Clarendon Press.

Hashim, Ahmed S. (2003) 'From Conventional War to Insurgency', *Small Wars and Insurgencies* 14 (3): 1–22.

Hathaway, James C. (1991) *The Law of Refugee Status.* Toronto: Buttersworth.

Hermans, Theo (2009) 'Translation, Ethics and Politics', in Jeremy Munday (ed) *The Routledge Companion to Translation Studies.* Abingdon, Oxon: Routledge, 93–105.

Hollis, Martin and Steven Lukes (eds) (1982) *Rationality and Relativism.* Oxford: Basil Blackwell.

Honneth, Axel (1995) *The Struggle for Recognition.* Trans. Joel Anderson. Cambridge: MIT Press.

Honneth, Axel and Joel Anderson (2005) 'Autonomy, Vulnerability, Recognition, and Justice', in John Christman and Joel Anderson (eds), *Autonomy and the Challenges to Liberalism: New Essays.* Cambridge: Cambridge University Press,127–149.

Human Rights First (2004) *In Liberty's Shadow: U.S. Detention of Asylum Seekers in the Era of Homeland Security*, http://www.humanrightsfirst.org/about_us/events/Chasing_Freedom/asylum_report.htm (consulted February 2009).

Hutchinson, Allan C. (1995) 'Calgary and Everything After: A Post-modern Revision of Lawyering', *Alberta Law Review* XXXIII (4): 768–786.

———(1998) 'Legal Ethics for a Fragmented Society: Between Professional and Personal', *International Journal of the Legal Profession* 5 (2/3): 175–192.

Hymes, Dell (1972) 'On Communicative Competence', in J. B. Pride and Janet Holmes (eds), *Sociolinguistics.* Harmondsworth: Penguin Books, 269–293.

Inghilleri, Moira (2000) 'Intersubjectivity: The Holy Grail of Mutual Understanding?', *Language and Communication* 20: 133–148.

———(2003) 'Habitus, Field and Discourse: Interpreting as a Socially-Situated Activity', *Target: International Journal of Translation Studies* 15 (2): 243–268.

———(2005) 'Mediating Zones of Uncertainty: Interpreter Agency, the Interpreting Habitus and Political Asylum Adjudication', *The Translator* 11(1): 69–85.

———(2007) 'National Sovereignty vs. Universal Rights: Interpreting Justice in a Global Context', Myriam Salama-Carr (ed) 'Translation and Conflict', Special Issue of *Social Semiotics*, 17 (2): 195–212.

———(2008) 'The Ethical Task of the Translator in the Geo-political Arena: From Iraq to Guantánamo Bay', *Translation Studies* 1 (2): 212–223.

———(2009) 'Translators in War Zones: Ethics Under Fire in Iraq', in Esperanca Bielsa and Christopher Hughes (eds) *Globalisation, Political Violence and Translation*. Houndsmills: Palgrave Macmillan, 207–221.

———(2010) '"You Don't Make a War without Knowing Why": The Decision to Interpret in Iraq', *The Translator* 16 (2): 174–195.

Inghilleri, Moira and Sue-Ann Harding (eds) (2010) 'Translation and Violent Conflict', Special Issue of *The Translator* 16 (2).

Ishiguro, Kazuo (1989) *The Remains of the Day*. New York: Vintage Books.

Jacquemet, Marco (2005) 'The Registration Interview: Restricting Refugees' Narrative Performances', in Mike Baynham and Anna De Fina (eds) *Dislocations/Relocations: Narratives of Displacement*. Manchester: St Jerome, 197–220.

James, William (1975/1907) *Pragmatism and the Meaning of Truth*. Cambridge: Harvard University Press.

Jarvis, Catriona (2003) 'The Judge as Juror Revisited', *Immigration Law Digest* (Winter): 7–23.

Jeffers, Tim (2005) 'General's Adviser Is Driven to Make a Difference' *The Advisor* 14, April 2, MNSTC-I, U.S. Department of Defense, http://www.mnstci.iraq.centcom.mil/advisor (consulted January 2010).

Junger, Sebastian (2010) *War*. New York: Twelve.

Juss, Satvinder (1997) *Discretion and Deviation in the Administration of Immigration Control*. London: Sweet and Maxwell.

———(2005) *A Guide to the Asylum and Immigration (Treatment of Claimants, etc.) Act 2004*, London: Cavendish Publishing Ltd.

Kant, Immanuel (1795/1957) *Perpetual Peace*, Lewis White Beck (ed). New York: Bobbs-Merrill.

Kelsay, John (1993) *Islam and War: A Study in Comparative Ethics*. Louisville, KY: Westminster/John Knox Press.

———(2009) *Arguing the Just War in Islam*. Cambridge: Harvard University Press.

Kidane, Won (2006) 'An Injury to the Citizen, a Pleasure to the State: A Peculiar Challenge to the Enforcement of International Refugee Law', *Chi-Kent Journal of International and Comparative Law* 6: 116–181.

Kilcullen, David (2007) 'Ethics, Politics and Non-State Warfare: A Response to González', *Anthropology Today* 23 (3): 20.

Kleingeld, Pauline (1998) 'Kant's Cosmopolitan Law: World Citizenship for a Global Order', *Kantian Review* 2: 72–90.

Koskinen, Kaisa (2000) *Beyond Ambivalence: Postmodernity and the Ethics of Translation*. Tampere: University of Tampere.

Krebs, Ronald R. (2009) 'The Citizen-Soldier Tradition in the United States, *Armed Forces & Society* 20 (10): 1–22.

Lagouranis, Tony (2007) *Fear up Harsh: An Army Interrogator's Dark Journey through Iraq*. New York: New American Library Caliber.

LaPlante, Matthew (2009) 'U.S. Welcome Disappoints Iraqi Interpreter Who Lost His Legs', *The Salt Lake Tribune*, June 12, http://www.sltrib.com/ci_11350493 (consulted December 2009).

Laster, Kathy (1990) 'Legal Interpreters: Conduits to Social Justice?', *Journal of Intercultural Studies* 11: 15–32.

———(1994) *Interpreters and the Legal System*. Sidney: Federation Press.

Legomsky, Stephen H. (2007) 'Learning to Live with Unequal Justice: Asylum and the Limits to Consistency', *Stanford Law Review* 60 (2): 413–474.

Leopold, David (2008) 'Written Statement for July 24, 2008, House Judiciary Committee Hearing on Immigration Raids', http//judiciary.house.gov/hearings/pdf/Leopold080724.pdf (consulted May 2011).

Lepore, Jill (1998) *The Name of War: King Philip's War and the Origins of American Identity.* New York: Vintage Books.
Lewis, Bernard (2004) *From Babel to Dragomans: Interpreting the Middle East.* London: Phoenix.
Loescher, Gil (1999) 'Refugees: A Global Human Rights and Security Crisis', in Tim Dunne and Nicholas J. Wheeler (eds) *Human Rights in Global Politics.* Cambridge: Cambridge University Press, 233–258.
Luban, David (1988) *Lawyers and Justice: An Ethical Study.* Princeton: Princeton University Press.
———(2007) *Legal Ethics and Human Dignity.* Cambridge: Cambridge University Press.
Lubold, Gordon (2008) 'U.S. Army Hopes to Keep Native Arabic Speakers', *The Christian Science Monitor*, August 5, http://www.csmonitor.com/2008/0805/p01s01-usmi.html (consulted December 2009).
MacIntyre, Alistair (1988) *Whose Justice? Whose Virtue?* Notre Dame, IN: University of Notre Dame Press.
———(1999) *Dependent Rational Animals: Why Human Beings Need the Virtues* (The Paul Carus Lecture Series 20). Chicago: Open Court.
Mansoor, Peter R. (2008) *Baghdad at Sunrise.* New Haven: Yale University Press.
Mardan, Basil (2006) 'Lost after Translation' *New York Times*, November 20, http://www.nytimes.com/2006/11/20opinion/20mardan.html?_r=1&pagewanted=print (consulted June 2009).
Marfleet, Philip (2006) *Refugees in a Global Era.* Houndsmills: Palgrave Macmillan.
Markovits, Daniel (2004) 'Legal Ethics from the Lawyer's Point of View', *Faculty Scholarship Series*, Paper 413, http://digitalcommons.yale.edu/fss_papers/413. (accessed March 2011)
Marks, Alexandra (2007) 'One Muslim's Decision to Join the US Army, *The Christian Science Monitor*, March 28, http://www.csmonitor.com/2007/0328/p01s02-usmi.html (consulted July 2010).
Martin, Anne and Carmen Valero Garcés (eds) (2008) *Crossing Borders in Community Interpreting: Definitions and Dilemmas.* Amsterdam and Philadelphia: John Benjamins.
Maryns, Katrijn (2006) *The Asylum Speaker: Language in the Belgian Asylum Procedure.* Manchester: St. Jerome.
Mason, Ian (ed) (1999) *Dialogue Interpreting*, Special Issue of *The Translator* 5 (2).
McCarthy, Thomas (1978) *The Critical Theory of Jürgen Habermas.* Cambridge: MIT Press.
———(1991) *Ideals and Illusions: Reconstruction and Deconstruction in Critical Theory.* Cambridge: MIT Press.
McFate, Montgomery (2005) 'Anthropology and Counterinsurgency: The Strange Story of Their Curious Relationship', *Military Review*, March–April: 24–38.
———(2007) 'Building Bridges or Burning Heretics: A Response to González', *Anthropology Today* 23 (3): 21.
McKinney, Kelly (2007) '"Breaking the Conspiracy of Silence": Testimony, Traumatic Memory, and Psychotherapy with Survivors of Political Violence', *ETHOS* 35 (3): 265–299.
McMahan, Jeff (2006) 'On the Moral Equality of Combatants', *The Journal of Political Philosophy* 14 (4): 377–393.
Mertens, Thomas (1996) 'Cosmopolitanism and Citizenship: Kant against Habermas', *European Journal of Philosophy* 4 (3): 328–347.

Mikkelson, Holly (1998) 'Towards a Redefinition of the Role of Court Interpreters', *Interpreting* 3 (1): 21–45.

———(2008) 'Evolving Views of the Court Interpreter's Role: Between Scylla and Charybdis', in Anne Martin and Carmen Valero Garcés (eds) *Crossing Borders in Community Interpreting: Definitions and Dilemmas.* Amsterdam and Philadelphia: John Benjamins, 81–98.

Miller, Bowman H. (2010) 'Soldiers, Scholars and Spies: Combining Smarts and Secrets', *Armed Forces & Society* 36 (4): 695–715.

Miller, Laura L. and Charles C. Moskos (1995) 'Humanitarians or Warriors: Race, Gender and Combat Status in Operation Restore Hope', *Armed Forces & Society*, 21 (4): 615–637.

Morgan, Matthew J. (2003) 'The Reconstruction of Culture, Citizenship and Military Service', *Armed Forces & Society* 29 (3): 373–391.

Morris, Ruth (1995) 'The Moral Dilemmas of Court Interpreting', *The Translator* 1 (1): 25–46.

———(1999) 'The Gum Shoe Syndrome: Predicaments in Court Interpreting', *Forensic Linguistics* 6 (1): 6–29.

———(2010) 'Images of the Court Interpreter', *Translation and Interpreting Studies* 5 (1): 20–40.

Moskos, Charles C. (1977) 'From Institution to Occupation: Trends in Military Organization',*Armed Forces & Society* 4 (1): 41–50.

Moskos, Charles, John Allen Williams and David Segal (eds) (1999) *The Postmodern Military: Armed Forces after the Cold War.* New York: Oxford University Press.

Network of Concerned Anthropologists (2007) *Pledge of Non-participation in Counter-insurgency*, http://concerned.anthropologists.googlepages.com/ (consulted January 2010).

'New Voices' (2009) *War News Radio*, Swarthmore College, July 31, http://www.warnewsradio.org/2009/07/31/new-voices/ (consulted December 2009).

Niska, Helga (1995) 'Just Interpreting: Role Conflicts and Discourse Types in Court Interpreting', in Marshall Morris (ed) *Translation and the Law.* Amsterdam and Philadelphia: John Benjamins.

Olson, Charles (1967) *Human Universe and other Essays*, Donald Allen (ed). New York: Grove Press.

Osborne, Dave ((2009) 'Sadi Othman Praised by Leaders of Iraq and the U.S.', *Heston College Today* (Spring): 8–9, http://www.hesston.edu/hesstoncollegetoday/09spring/othman.htm (consulted January 2010).

Palmer, Jerry (2007) 'Interpreting and Translation for Western Media in Iraq', in Myriam Salama-Carr (ed) *Translating and Interpreting Conflict.* Amsterdam and New York: Rodopi, 13–28.

Palmer, Jerry and Victoria Fontan (2007) '"Our Ears and Our Eyes": Journalists and Fixers in Iraq', *Journalism* 8 (1): 5–24.

Papademetriou, Demetrios G. (2003) 'Managing Rapid and Deep Change in the Newest Age of Migration', in Sarah Spencer (ed) *The Politics of Migration.* Oxford: Blackwell, 39–58.

Papastergiadis, Nikos (2000) *The Turbulence of Migration.* Cambridge: Polity Press.

Parkert, Cecilia (1995) *Witness.* Trans. Keven Halliwell. London: Oberon Books.

Peterson, Cassie L. (2009) 'An Iowa Immigration Raid Leads to Unprecedented Criminal Consequences: Why ICE Should Rethink the Postville Model', *Iowa Law Review* 95: 323–346.

Plato (1973) *Phaedrus and Letters VII and VIII.* Trans. Walter Hamilton. London: Penguin.

Pöchhacker, Franz (2004) *Introducing Interpreting Studies.* London: Routledge.

Pöchhacker, Franz and Miriam Shlesinger (eds) (2002) *The Interpreting Studies Reader.* London: Routledge.

Pollbauer, Sonja (2004) 'Interpreting in Asylum Hearings: Issues of Role, Responsibility and Power', *Interpreting* 6 (2): 143–180.

Popper, Nathaniel (2009) 'Justices Strike Down Postville Tactic', *The Jewish Daily Forward*, May 6, http://www.forward.com/articles/105676. (accessed March 2011)

Porter, Patrick (2007) 'Good Anthropology, Bad History: The Cultural Turn in Studying War', *Parameters* (Summer): 45–58.

Postema, Gerald J. (1980) 'Moral Responsibility in Professional Ethics', *New York University Law Review* 55: 63–89.

Preston, Julia (2008a) '270 Illegal Immigrants Sent to Prison in Federal Push', *The New York Times*, May 24, http://www.nytimes.com/2008/05/24/us/24immig.html?pagewanted=print (consulted May 2011).

———(2008b) 'An Interpreter Speaking Up for Migrants', *The New York Times*, July 11, http://www.nytimes.com/2008/07/11/us/11immig.html (consulted May 2011).

———(2008c) 'Immigrants' Speedy Trials after Raid Become Issue', *The New York Times*, August 9, http://www.nytimes.com/2008/08/09/us/09immig.html?em=&pagewanted=print (consulted May 2011).

———(2009) 'Dismissal of Guilty Pleas Is Sought for Immigrants', *The New York Times*, May 6, http://www.nytimes.com/2009/05/06/us/06immig.html?pagewanted=print (consulted May 2011).

Putnam, Hilary (1981) *Reason, Truth and History.* Cambridge: Cambridge University Press.

———(1990) *Realism with a Human Face.* Cambridge: Harvard University Press.

———(1995) *Pragmatism: An Open Question.* Oxford: Wiley-Blackwell.

Pym, Anthony (1999) '"Nicole Slapped Michelle": Interpreters and Theories of Interpreting at the O.J. Simpson Trial, *The Translator* (5) 2: 265–283.

———(2001) (ed) 'The Return to Ethics', Special Issue of *The Translator* 7 (2).

Rafael, Vicente (2007) 'Translation in Wartime', *Public Culture* 19 (2): 239–246.

Ramji-Nogales, Jaya, Andrew I. Schoenholtz and Phillip G. Schrag (2007) 'Refugee Roulette: Disparities in Asylum Adjudication', *Stanford Law Review* 60 (2): 295–412.

Rawls, John (1995) *Political Liberalism.* New York: Columbia University Press.

Rhodes, Deborah L. (ed) (2000) *Ethics in Practice: Lawyers' Roles, Responsibilities and Regulation.* Oxford: Oxford University Press.

Ricks, Thomas E. (2004) 'Troops Climbing First Rung of Steep Ladder', *The Washington Post*, November 17, A15.

———(2009a) "Understanding the Surge in Iraq and What's Ahead', *E-Notes, Foreign Policy Research Institute*, May, http://www.fpri.org/enotes/200905.ricks.understandingsurgeiraq.html (consulted September 2009).

———(2009b) *The Gamble.* New York: Penguin Press.

Ricouer, Paul (1965) *History and Truth.* Trans. with an introduction by Charles A. Kelbley. Evanston: Northwestern University Press.

———(2006) *On Translation.* Trans. Eileen Brennan with an introduction by Richard Kearney. London: Routledge.

Rieckhoff, Paul (2006) *Chasing Ghosts: Failures and Facades in Iraq. A Soldier's Perspective.* New York: New American Library

Robben, Antonius (2009) 'Anthropology and the Iraq War: An Uncomfortable Engagement', *Anthropology Today* 25 (1): 1–3.

Robinson, Linda (2008) *Tell Me How This Ends: General Petraeus and the Search for a Way Out of Iraq.* New York: Public Affairs.

Robinson, Paul (2007) 'Ethics Training and Development in the Military', *Parameters* (Spring): 23–36.

Robinson, Paul, Nigel De Lee and Don Carrick (eds) (2008) *Ethics Education in the Military*. Aldershot: Ashgate.
Rohall, David E., Morten G. Ender and Michael D. Matthews (2006) 'The Effects of Military Affiliation, Gender, and Political Ideology on Attitudes toward the Wars in Afghanistan and Iraq', *Armed Forces & Society* 33 (1): 59–77.
Rohde, David (2007) 'Army Enlists Anthropology in War Zones', *The New York Times*, October 5, http://www.nytimes.com/2007/10/05/world/asia/05afghan.html (consulted January 2010).
Rorty, Richard (1989) 'The Contingency of Language', in *Contingency, Irony and Solidarity*. Cambridge: Cambridge University Press, 3–22.
———(1991a) 'Solidarity or Objectivity', in *Objectivity, Relativism and Truth*. Cambridge: Cambridge University Press, 21–45.
———(1991b) 'Priority of Democracy to Philosophy', in *Objectivity, Relativism and Truth*. Cambridge: Cambridge University Press, 175–196.
———(1991c) 'Pragmatism, Davidson and Truth', in *Objectivity, Relativism and Truth*. Cambridge: Cambridge University Press, 126–150.
———(1998) 'Hilary Putnam and the Relativist Menace', in *Truth and Progress*. Cambridge: Cambridge University Press, 43–62.
Roy, Cynthia (2000) *Interpreting as a Discourse Process*. Oxford: Oxford University Press.
Rycroft, Roxanna (2003) *Communicative Barriers in the Asylum Account*. Unpublished MA thesis, London School of Economics, 1–50.
———(2005) 'Communicative Barriers in the Asylum Account', in Prakash Shah (ed), *The Challenge of Asylum to Legal Systems*. London: Cavendish, 223–244.
Saar, Eric and Viveca Novak (2005) *Inside the Wire*. New York: Penguin Press.
Sandel, Michael (1982) *Liberalism and the Limits of Justice*. Cambridge: Cambridge University Press.
Sassen, Saskia (1999) *Guests and Aliens*. New York: New Press.
Scales, Robert H. (2007) 'Statement for the record', Senate Armed Services Committee, April 25, *Colgen LP*, Mico, Texas, http://www.colgen.net/media/SASC_Statement_for_the_Record_April_25_2007.pdf. (consulted October 2009)
Segal, D. R. (1986) 'Measuring the Institutional/Occupational Change Thesis', *Armed Forces & Society* 1 (3): 351–376.
Seierstad, Asne (2003) *A Hundred and One Days*. Trans. Ingrid Christophersen. New York: Basic Books.
Shadid, Anthony (2006) Night Draws Near. New York: Picador.
Shay, Christopher (2009) 'Should Anthropologists Go to War?', Time, December 13, http://www.time.com/time/printout/0,8816,1947095,00.html (consulted January 2010).
Sherr, Daniel (2008) 'An Iraqi Interpreter Stateside', *Proteus* XVII (3): 1, 4.
Shlesinger, Miriam and Franz Pöchhacker (2010) *Doing Justice to Court Interpreting*. Amsterdam/Philadelphia: John Benjamins.
Simon, William H. (1988) 'Ethical Discretion in Lawyering', *Harvard Law Review* 101 (6): 1083–1145.
———(1996/97) 'Should Lawyers Obey the Law', *William and Mary Law Review* 38: 217–253.
———(1999/2000) "Think Like a Lawyer—about Ethics', *Duquesne Law Review* 38 (4): 1015–1057.
Skaskiw, Roman (2008) 'E-mail from Afghanistan', *The Atlantic*, October 21, http//www.theatlantic.com/doc/print/200810u/Afghanistan-soldier (consulted October 2009).
Smith, Barbara Herrnstein (1997) *Belief and Resistance*. Cambridge: Harvard University Press.

Snider, Don M. (1999) 'An Uninformed Debate on Military Culture', *Orbis* 43 (1): 1–16.

Soysal, Yasemin Nuhoglu (1994) *Limits of Citizenship: Migrants and Postnational Membership in Europe*. Chicago: University of Chicago Press.

Spivak, Gaytri (1988) 'Can the Subaltern Speak? Speculations on Widow Sacrifice', in Cary Nelson and Lawrence Grossberg (eds), *Marxism and the Interpretation of Culture*. Urbana: University of Illinois Press, 271–313.

Stahuljak, Zrinka (2000) 'Violent Distortions: Bearing Witness to the Task of Wartime Translators', *TTR* 13 (1): 37–51.

———(2009) 'War, Translation, Transnationalism: Interpreters in and of the War (Croatia, 1991–1992)', in Mona Baker (ed) *Critical Readings in Translation Studies*. London and New York: Routledge, 391–414.

———(2010) 'Minor Empires: Translation, Conflict and Postcolonial Critique', *The Translator* 16 (2): 255–274.

Stamets, Bill (2008) 'Anthropologists at War', *In These Times*, June 19, http://inthesetimes.com/main/print/3749 (consulted January 14, 2010).

Statement Of Work For Combined/Joint Task Force Operation Enduring Freedom (2004). http://www.acq.osd.mil/dpap/pacc/cc/jcchb/Contingency%20Model/Contract%20Actions/SOWs/SOW%2018%20Sep%2004(6%20month%20effort)Linguists.doc

Stier, Ken (2007) 'Anthropologists on the Front Lines', *Time*, December 11, http://www.time.com/time/printout/0,8816,1693592,00.html (consulted January 2010).

Subcommittee on Immigration, Citizenship, Refugees, Border Security and International Law (July 2008) *Immigration Raids: Postville and Beyond*, Serial Number 110–198, http://judiciary.house.gov/hearings/printers/110th/43682.PDF (consulted May 2011).

Sullivan, Julie (2008) 'Salem Native Capt. Jason Faler Founds Non-Profit to Help Settle Iraqi Interpreters in the U.S.', *The Christian Science Monitor*, December 10, http://www.csmonitor.com/2008/0507/p01s05-usgn.htm?print=true (consulted December 2007).

Susman, Tina (2007) 'Iraqi Interpreters Walk the Talk', *LA Times*, October 21, http://fairuse.100webcustomers.com/fairenough/latimesC63.html (consulted December 2007).

Szasz, Margaret Connell (1994) *Between Indian and White Worlds: The Cultural Broker*. Norman: University of Oklahoma Press.

Takeda, Kayoko (2009) 'War and Interpreters', *Across Languages and Cultures* 10 (1): 49–62.

———(2010) *Interpreting the Tokyo War Crimes Tribunal*. Ottawa: University of Ottawa Press.

Tanovich, David (2005) 'Law's Ambition and the Reconstruction of Role Morality in Canada', 28 *Dalhousie L. Rev*. 267-310.

Taylor, Charles (1985) 'Theories of Meaning', in *Philosophy and the Human Sciences, Philosophical Papers*,1. Cambridge: Cambridge University Press, 248–292.

———(1989) *Sources of the Self*. Cambridge: Harvard University Press.

Thomas, Robert (2005) 'Evaluating Tribunal Adjudication: Administrative Justice and Asylum Appeals', *Legal Studies* 25 (3): 462–498.

———(2008) 'Consistency in Asylum Adjudication: Country Guidance and the Asylum Process in the United Kingdom', *International Journal of Refugee Law* 20: 489–532.

Tobia, Simona (2010) 'Crime and Judgement: Interpreters/Translators in British War Crimes Trials, 1945–1949', *The Translator* (16) 2: 275–314.

Tribe, Rachel and Hitesh Raval (eds) (2003) *Working with Interpreters in Mental Health*. New York: Brunner-Routledge.

Tucker, Mike (2008) *Ronin: A Marine Scout-Sniper in Iraq*. Mechanicsburg, PA: Stackpole Books.

Turner, Graham H. (2007) 'Professionalism of Interpreting *with* the Community: Refining the Model', in Cecilia Wadensjö, Birgitta Englund Dimitrova, and Anna-Lena Nilsson (eds), *The Critical Link 4*. Amsterdam and Philadelphia: John Benjamins, 181–192.

'Turning Linguists to Soldiers' (2008) *All Things Considered*, National Public Radio, December 24, 2008, http://nl.newsbank.com/nl-search/we/Archives?p_action=doc&p_docid=1254EO4B5C8E5 (consulted July 2009).

Tymockzo, Maria (2007) *Enlarging Translation, Empowering Translators*. Manchester: St. Jerome.

Tyson, Ann Scott (2004) 'Always in Hiding, an Iraqi Interpreter's Anguished Life', *The Christian Science Monitor*, September 15, http://www.csmonitor.com/2004/0915/p01s04-woiq.html (consulted December 2007).

van Dijk, Andrea and Joseph L. Soeters (2008) 'Language Matters in the Military', in Giuseppe Caforio, Gerhard Kummel, and Bandana Purkayastha (eds), *Armed Forces and Conflict Resolution: Sociological Perspectives*. Bingley, UK: Emerald Group, 303–325.

Venuti, Lawrence (1998) *The Scandals of Translation*. London and New York: Routledge.

———(1995/2008) *The Translator's Invisibility*, 2nd Edition. London and New York: Routledge.

———(2000) 'Translation, Community, Utopia', in Lawrence Venuti (ed) *The Translation Studies Reader*. London: Routledge, 468–488.

Vertovec, Steven and Robin Cohen (eds) (2003) *Conceiving Cosmopolitanism: Theory, Context, and Practice*. Oxford: Oxford University Press.

Vincent, Steven (2003) 'The Translator: Iraqis Making Coalition Work Possible', *National Review Online*, October 16, http://old.nationalreview.com/comment/vincent200310160837.asp (consulted July 2010).

Wadensjö, Cecilia (1998) *Interpreting as Interaction*. London: Longman.

Walzer, Michael (1977) *Just and Unjust Wars: A Moral Argument with Historical Illustrations*. New York: Basic Books.

———(1983) *Spheres of Justice: A Defence of Pluralism and Equality*. New York: Basic Books.

———(1985) 'Interpretation and Social Criticism', *The Tanner Lectures on Human Values*, Harvard University, November 13–14: 1–80, http://www.tannerlectures.utah.edu/lectures/documents/walzer88.pdf (consulted February 2010).

———(2004) *Arguing about War*. New Haven: Yale University Press.

Wendel, W. Bradley (2005) 'Professionalism as Interpretation', *Cornell Law Faculty Publications*, Paper 27, http://scholarship.law.cornell.edu/lsrp_papers/27. (accessed March 2011)

———(2010) 'Personal Integrity and the Conflict between Ordinary and Institutional Values', in Tim Dare and W. Bradley Wendel (eds) *Professional Ethics and Personal Integrity*. Newcastle-upon Tyne: Cambridge Scholars, 238–269.

West, Bing (2008) *The Strongest Tribe*. New York: Random House.

West, Bing and Ray L. Smith (2003) *The March Up: Taking Baghdad with the United States Marines*. New York: Bantam Books.

Williams, Kalya (2005) *Love My Rifle More Than You*. London: Weidenfeld and Nicolson.

Wittgenstein, Ludwig (1963/1953) *Philosophical Investigations*. Oxford: Basil Blackwell.

Woodruff, Todd, Ryan Kelty and David R. Segal (2006) 'Propensity to Serve and Motivation to Enlist among American Combat Soldiers', *Armed Forces & Society* 32 (3): 353–366.
Yee, James (2005) *For God and Country*. New York: Public Affairs.
Yellen, David (1998/99) '"Thinking Like a Lawyer" or Acting Like a Judge: A Response to Professor Simon', *Hofstra Law Review* 27: 13–19.
Yon, Michael (2008) *Moment of Truth in Iraq*. Minneapolis: Richard Vigilante Books.

Index

For Product Safety Concerns and Information please contact our EU representative GPSR@taylorandfrancis.com
Taylor & Francis Verlag GmbH, Kaufingerstraße 24, 80331 München, Germany

www.ingramcontent.com/pod-product-compliance
Ingram Content Group UK Ltd.
Pitfield, Milton Keynes, MK11 3LW, UK
UKHW021958180926
475701UK00003B/86
9780415821698